MILTON AND THE
RENAISSANCE HERO

MILTON AND THE RENAISSANCE HERO

BY

JOHN M. STEADMAN

OXFORD
AT THE CLARENDON PRESS
1967

Oxford University Press, Ely House, London W. 1

GLASGOW NEW YORK TORONTO MELBOURNE WELLINGTON
CAPE TOWN SALISBURY IBADAN NAIROBI LUSAKA ADDIS ABABA
BOMBAY CALCUTTA MADRAS KARACHI LAHORE DACCA
KUALA LUMPUR HONG KONG TOKYO

© *Oxford University Press 1967*

PRINTED IN GREAT BRITAIN

Foreword

Milton's 'Copernican Revolution'

THE uniqueness of *Paradise Lost* is implicit in the first enunciation of its theme—'Mans First Disobedience'. Unlike the usual heroic poem, it does not propose a victory, but a defeat. Its action is not some illustrious 'act of benefit', but a crime. Its hero is not a paragon of heroic virtue, but the archetypal sinner. The results of this conflict are not glory but shame, not dominion or deliverance, but servitude and death. Instead of celebrating his merit, the poem chastises his vice. Its argument is in reality an 'argument of human weakness rather than of strength'.

Its singularity does not consist simply in choosing a Biblical subject or in rejecting the conventional epic theme of *tristia bella*—'Warrs, hitherto the onely Argument Heroic deem'd'. It lies rather in the startling ethical contrast which Milton's hero and his exploits present to those of classical and Renaissance epic tradition. *Paradise Lost*, as Dryden well perceived, flagrantly violates the orthodox pattern of the heroic poem: '. . . and Milton [would have had a better plea for the title of heroic poet] . . . if the giant had not foiled the knight, and driven him out of his strong hold, to wander through the world with his lady errant. . . .'[1] The theme of Milton's masterpiece is poetically heterodox. The argument is an epic heresy.

Though personal tastes undoubtedly influenced this apparent breach with poetic tradition (Milton was 'Not sedulous by Nature to indite Warrs', and the experience of civil conflicts at home surely strengthened his bias against a military subject) a major factor in his radical departure from the conventional epic theme was the unresolved tension within

[1] Edmond Malone (ed.), *The Critical and Miscellaneous Prose Works of John Dryden* (London, 1800), iii. 442.

the heroic tradition itself—a conflict between the ethical and religious ends the poet was ideally committed to observe, and the type of heroic *ethos* usually celebrated in classical and Renaissance epic. Theoretically poetics was subordinate to ethics, politics, and theology; it derived its end, or final cause, from these disciplines; it accepted their standards and imitated their values. Yet it was equally committed to the artistic standards set by the ancients, to the imitation of classical models. The Renaissance epic poet thus found himself torn by contrary loyalties, by the conflicting demands of two distinct types of imitation—the literary imitation of the ancients and the ethical imitation of Christian norms. The hero as Christian philosophy defined him was essentially incompatible with the hero of epic tradition. Faced by an internal contradiction in the heroic tradition itself—a cleavage between poetic and philosophical conceptions of heroism—the poet had little choice. He must either gloss over (and minimize) their fundamental divergence, or else essay a drastic reorientation of the heroic tradition.

Confronted with this dilemma, most poets and theorists preferred to compromise. They continued to follow classical models in their choice of hero and subject, but idealized them in several ways—by stressing the protagonist's piety over and above his valour, depicting him as a champion of Christian orthodoxy in 'holy warfare' against infidels or heretics; by choosing Old Testament military heroes or Christian warrior-saints as their 'epic persons'; or by insisting on an ethical, allegorical significance behind the clash of arms, transforming physical combat into spiritual struggle, converting the battlefield into a *psychomachia*, a conflict of souls. Milton's solution is at once more sweeping and more radical. Frankly rejecting the classical conception of the hero, he explores the theological preconditions and limitations of heroic virtue. His innovation on the heroic tradition is not so much the substitution of a Christian exemplar for the older classical and pagan prototypes (other poets had anticipated him in this) as the central position he gives to the theme of human frailty. For the Christian moralist, the problem of human virtue was inextricably interwoven with the effects of Adam's fall. For the Christian poet, therefore, the issue of heroic virtue must be reconsidered in the light of man's fallen condition. Milton reconstructs the heroic poem in terms of the polarity of human depravity and divine mercy—'supernal Grace contending With sinfulness of Men' —and achieves thereby a 'Copernican revolution' in poetics no less radical than Kant's in philosophy. The German philosopher discovered a new basis for ethical and metaphysical inquiry in the limitations of the human mind. The English poet found new scope for the heroic poem in the limitations of human virtue. Both men diverted the conventional currents of thought or verse from their time-worn, traditional courses into fresher channels—toward newer fields, where they might nourish more substantial, though perhaps less colourful, fruit.

This volume is concerned primarily with one aspect of Milton's poetic 'revolution'—his 'critique' (to extend the Kantian metaphor) of the conventional heroic patterns established in epic tradition. Though the latter scarcely confronted him with a 'hero with a thousand faces', it did present him with a variety of heroic 'masks', a wide range of moral formulae for the epic *persona*. As the term 'epic formula' will occur frequently in the following pages, it is only fair to call attention to its ambiguity. In Homeric criticism and allied researches in the field of 'primary epic', it usually refers to purely *verbal* patterns—to the stereotyped phrases and epithets associated with the technique of 'oral composition'. Other critics, however, often employ the term in a broader sense to denote *ethical* patterns (e.g. fortitude, wisdom, temperance, or the composite *fortitudo et sapientia* formula). In the following chapters I have used this term exclusively in the latter sense.[1]

---

[1] To the studies cited in the footnotes, I should like to add the following references: C. A. Patrides, *Milton and the Christian Tradition* (Oxford, 1966); Roland Mushat Frye, *God, Man, and Satan* (Princeton, 1960); George Williamson, 'The Education of Adam', *Modern Philology*, lxi (1963), pp. 96–109; my 'Achilles and Renaissance Epic' in *Lebende Antike, Symposion für Rudolf Sühnel*, ed. H. Meller and H.-J. Zimmerman (Berlin, 1967); and the studies on heroic tradition and history of ideas collected in my forthcoming *Milton's Epic Characters: Image and Idea*.

Acknowledgements

THIS study reflects a long-standing debt to the staffs of the Bodleian Library, the Taylorian Institute, the British Museum, and the Huntington Library. In publishing it, I should like to thank the scholars who have broadened my understanding of Milton—Professor Thomas H. English of Emory University, Professors Robert R. Cawley and Maurice Kelley of Princeton University, and Miss K. M. Lea of Lady Margaret Hall, Oxford. For valuable criticism of the original manuscript, I am grateful to Professor Kelley and Dr. A. L. Rowse.

The Huntington Library
San Marino, California

Contents

Introduction

F O R the Christian poet the familiar heroic spectrum was no longer adequate, and Milton subjected it to searching criticism. His innovations on epic tradition appear most clearly in his revision of conventional formulae. What use does he make of these? To what extent does he retain the traditional heroic *ethos*? In raising these questions one is really asking how closely he approached the ends of the epic genre as Renaissance critics conceived them. If its chief purpose was to extol heroic virtue, then one must necessarily investigate his definition of the hero. In the following pages I shall consider three aspects of this problem: (1) his treatment of the heroic formulae commonly accepted as ethical and literary norms, (2) his distinction between their valid and invalid modes, and (3) his revaluation of epic tradition in terms of this dichotomy.[1]

Aristotle's definition of *virtus heroica* as an 'excess of virtue'[2]

[1] See, *inter alia*, the following studies on Milton's presentation of the heroic ideal and his relationship to the epic tradition: G. A. Wilkes, '*Paradise Regained* and the Conventions of the Sacred Epic', *English Studies*, xliv (1963), pp. 35–38; Ernest S. Gohn, 'The Christian Ethic of *Paradise Lost* and *Samson Agonistes*', *Studia Neophilologica*, xxxiv (1963), pp. 243–68; John Eugene Seaman, 'The Epic Art of *Paradise Lost*: A Study of Milton's Use of Epic Conventions', Stanford dissertation (1962); Davis P. Harding, *The Club of Hercules: Studies in the Classical Background of* Paradise Lost, *Illinois Studies in Language and Literature*, 1 (Urbana, 1962); C. M. Bowra, *From Virgil to Milton* (London, 1948); Burton O. Kurth, *Milton and Christian Heroism: Biblical Epic Themes and Forms in Seventeenth-Century England*, Univ. *of California Publications, English Studies*, xx (Berkeley and Los Angeles, 1959); Frank Kermode, 'Milton's Hero', *Review of English Studies*, iv (1953), pp. 317–30; Thomas Greene, *The Descent from Heaven: A Study in Epic Continuity* (New Haven, 1963); Milton Miller, '*Paradise Lost*: The Double Standard', Univ. *of Toronto Quarterly*, xx (1951), pp. 183–99; E. M. W. Tillyard, *The English Epic and Its Background* (New York, 1954); *The Miltonic Setting, Past and Present* (Cambridge, 1938); F. Buff, *Miltons* Paradise Lost *in seinem Verhältnis zur Aeneide, Ilias und Odyssee* (Munich, 1904); E. Pommerich, *Miltons Verhältnis zur Torquato Tasso* (Halle, 1902); F. T. Prince, *The Italian Element in Milton's Verse* (Oxford, 1954).

[2] See my 'Heroic Virtue and the Divine Image in *Paradise Lost*', *Journal of the Warburg and Courtauld Institutes*, xxii (1959), pp. 88–105. Cf. *Of Education* on

had fostered a conception of the hero based largely on degree rather than on quality. As heroic virtue differed from ordinary virtues not in kind, but in proportion, critics and moralists alike defined it in superlatives—'eminence', 'excellence', 'perfection', 'highest worth'. It was 'superhuman', 'extraordinary', 'unequalled', 'incomparable'. For many theorists, the merit of the heroic poem itself hinged on that of its hero; in Beni's view, this was the criterion that elevated Virgil above Homer, and Tasso above both. That Milton's epics reflect this emphasis is hardly surprising. Both poems stress heroic eminence and excess; both draw implicit or explicit analogies between different heroic types; both compare and revalue the worthies of classical and Biblical tradition. In *Paradise Lost* this preoccupation with superlatives underlies his comparison of the three most prominent 'heroes' (Adam, Christ, Satan) and their principal actions— the exploits of obedience or disobedience, the 'gests' inspired by 'exceeding' love or hate, the *magnalia* of war or peace, the heroic enterprises of destruction or creation or salvation. In *Paradise Regain'd* it influences the ascending scale of values which the tempter proposes to the hero. In *Samson Agonistes* it results in the recurrent emphasis on the protagonist's 'extraordinary' virtue. As the Archfiend himself recognizes, the hero characteristically 'aim[s] at the highest'.

Second—and more significantly—Aristotle had defined the hero as the 'godlike man', the *seios [theios] aner*. His source was the *Iliad*'s description of Hector; but Homer had, in fact, applied this and similar epithets to many of his warriors, Trojan and Greek alike. His imitators echoed him in describing the hero and heroic virtue as 'godlike' and 'divine'. Milton, almost alone among heroic poets, specifically related this definition to the image of God originally bestowed on man, subsequently obscured by sin, and finally restored by divine grace. Adam's fall had radically altered man's capacity for heroism, and in their concern with the loss and restoration of the divine image, both epics present

the role of 'true vertue' and 'faith' in recovery of godlikeness and 'highest perfection' (Yale Prose, ii, p. 367); *Of Reformation* on 'likeness to God' (ibid. i, p. 571).

the theological foundations of heroic virtue. In both poems the central parallel between Adam and Christ is based on the definition of heroic virtue as 'godlikeness'. As its essence is 'divine resemblance', then its perfect archetype must, *a fortiori*, be the 'perfect image of the Father', the Son of God himself. In mankind, heroism belongs, therefore, exclusively to the regenerate. By centring his epics on the image of God and its primary characteristics—truth, wisdom, holiness, freedom—Milton made a unique and radical contribution to the heroic tradition. He reoriented the heroic poem towards the essence of heroic virtue as the Christian poet should logically conceive it.

Third, in defining heroic virtue, Aristotle had identified its contrary—brutishness—as an 'excess of vice'. If heroic virtue was 'godlike' and 'divine', its antithesis must be 'diabolical' and 'infernal'. As a logician, Milton well knew the value of defining a concept by its opposite, and this method underlay his treatment of Satan and the conquerors idolized by the world. In both instances, their apparent heroism springs not from an 'excess of virtue' but from an 'excess of vice'—an 'eminence' in evil—and in both cases he ultimately exposes it as brutishness. The warriors are murderers and robbers, excelling in 'brutish vices'. Satan appropriately exemplifies the 'diabolical' contrary of 'divine' virtue; his final metamorphosis into a serpent exposes his 'godlike' pretensions as false and his apparent heroism as brutishness.

The conscious absurdity of a 'godlike' devil underlies Milton's deliberate delineation of Satan in seemingly heroic terms. The basic irony of this portrait consists in the contrast between two antithetical senses of 'godlike', between the external appearance (the devil's superficial and blasphemous efforts to imitate God) and the internal reality (the moral deformation of the divine image). Satan aspires to be 'like God'—and as a direct result he loses his 'divine resemblance'. The same paradox underlies the sin of Eve, whose desire to 'be as gods' results ironically in defacing God's image in man. The great difference between the two cases is that fallen man may regain the divine image through regeneration, whereas the fallen angel—forever unregenerate—can never retrieve it. Adam and his progeny may recover the capacity for heroic virtue; Satan and his angels neither can nor will.

Fourth, in embodying the heroic norm in the Messiah, Milton lays primary stress on the ideal of the Suffering Servant,[1] as manifested in Christ's ministry of redemption. Both epics give poetic expression to the theological imperative of the 'imitation of Christ'. As the true believer must 'conform' to the example set by the Messiah in his humiliation and exaltation, these provide the perfect exemplar of Christian heroic virtue and its reward. In epic and tragedy alike, the norm of the Suffering Servant underlies Milton's consistent emphasis on the virtues of obedience and patience.

This pattern merges, in turn, with the ideals of martyrdom and sanctity. As 'servants of God', Abdiel[2] and Christ are literally martyrs—'witnesses' who suffer for their testimony to divine truth—and it is from Christ's example that Adam learns the nature of heroic martyrdom, that 'suffering for truth's sake is fortitude to highest victory'. In *Paradise Regain'd* the hero not only rejects all ends or means that seem incompatible with his ordained role as Suffering Servant; he also redefines the heroic *ethos* and heroic poetry specifically in terms of sanctity. The poems of Greek bards, who 'sing The vices of thir Deities, and thir own', are 'unworthy to compare with *Sion*'s songs',

> Where God is prais'd aright, and Godlike men,
> The Holiest of Holies, and his Saints. . . .

The phrase 'Godlike men' reflects the Aristotelian and Homeric definitions of the hero, and the appositive thus identifies the true hero with the saint. It is holiness—the principal characteristic of the image of God—that renders a man 'godlike' and thus truly heroic. Where sanctity is lacking, true heroism is also wanting, and this defect makes 'void of virtue' the specious heroism of Milton's fallen archangel and of most

[1] See my 'The "Suffering Servant" and Milton's Heroic Norm', *Harvard Theological Review*, liv (1961), pp. 29–43.

[2] Though Abdiel is primarily an exemplar of zeal (and therefore of *pietas*), he embodies other conventional epic formulae—wisdom, fortitude, *amor*, and the like.

classical worthies. Thus the heroic tradition merges with the hagiographical and martyrological; the hero becomes the martyr and the saint.[1] This fusion is clearly evident in Spenser's St. George. Literally, the Redcrosse Knight is the *cavaliere errante* of medieval and Renaissance romance, as well as the patron saint of England; allegorically, he personifies Holiness—the essence of the divine image—and hence unites the ideals of hero and saint. Similarly, Giles Fletcher fuses the two concepts in extolling 'those heroicall Saincts, Moses, Deborah, Ieremie, Mary, Simeon, David, Salomon . . .'.[2]

As true heroism depends on sanctification, it lies potentially within the grasp of all the regenerate[3]—of every true believer. Nevertheless, like most authors of Christian epic, Milton preferred to stress *exceptional* sanctity. His heroes are, for the most part, God's 'extraordinary ministers',[4] men like Samson, the 'just men' of Old Testament history, and (in a more eminent degree) the Messiah himself.

Fifth, Miltons' conception of the false-heroic—the pseudo-heroism of Satan, Harapha, and the secular conquerors—derives from both classical and Scriptural tradition.[5] Though

---

[1] The conception of the saint as the true hero is rooted in the tradition stemming from St. Paul and St. Augustine and amplified by Christian moral theology. It reaches its fullest doctrinal development in Benedict XIV's treatise *De servorum Dei beatificatione et beatorum canonizatione*, which makes *heroicitas*—a heroic excess of virtue—an essential characteristic of sanctity and a prerequisite for canonization. See Merritt Y. Hughes, 'The Christ of *Paradise Regain'd* and the Renaissance Heroic Tradition', *Studies in Philology*, xxxv (1938), pp. 254–77.

[2] Giles Fletcher, *Christ's Victory and Triumph in Heaven and Earth, Over and After Death and Other Poems of the Seventeenth Century*, ed. William T. Brooke (London, 1888), p. 23. Vauquelin de la Fresnaye exhorts the Christian poet to celebrate the exploits of Christ and his saints and martyrs; see Joel Elias Spingarn, *A History of Literary Criticism in the Renaissance* (New York, 1899). Cf. St. Augustine, *The City of God*, trans. Marcus Dods (New York, 1950), pp. 326, 831.

[3] See Milton's *De Doctrina Christiana*, Book I, Chapter 18. For the relationship between the theological doctrines of Milton's treatise and *Paradise Lost*, see Maurice Kelley, *This Great Argument: A Study of Milton's De Doctrina Christiana as a Gloss upon Paradise Lost* (Princeton, 1941).

[4] See Milton's *De Doctrina*, Book I, Chapter 29; cf. Chapter 18 on the double sense of sanctification as (1) regeneration and (2) election or separation of an individual to some special mission or office.

[5] See my 'Image and Idol: Satan and the Element of Illusion in *Paradise*

there are Hellenic prototypes in the 'destroying wrath' of Achilles and the conquests of Alexander, there are also Biblical precedents in the giants of Genesis—the 'men of renown', who glory in their own might, and tyrannical conquerors like Nimrod,[1] who trust in their own strength and rebel against God and right reason. Like Satan's, their apparent heroism is actually folly or impiety. The Biblical refutation of this pattern provides the foundation for Milton's condemnation of the false-heroic.

In Satan the poet carefully builds up—and eventually shatters—a meticulously constructed portrait of spurious sovereignty and specious heroism, the 'Idol of Majestie Divine' and the 'counterfeit resemblance' of heroic virtue. Both epics involve a conscious antithesis between true and illusory patterns of hero or king, and the interplay between these contradictory norms underlies the ethical and poetic structures of both poems. It serves as a basis for Milton's reassessment of the conventional epic formulae.[2]

The heroic spectrum is a wide one, and in a single volume one cannot hope to cover the entire range of heroic virtues or their complex interrelationships with epic and romance, ethics, and history. I have, accordingly, limited this study to five of the more familiar epic formulae. All of them recur frequently in Renaissance criticism of heroic poetry; all occupy prominent positions in Milton's epics and tragedy; all exhibit a conventional ambiguity which enables Milton to adapt them to his critique of heroic virtue. For he pursues the moral ends of heroic poetry by emphasizing the equivocal senses of heroism and playing one meaning against another.

Lost', *Journal of English and Germanic Philology*, lix (1960), pp. 640–54; 'Milton's "Giant Angels": An Additional Parallel', *Modern Language Notes*, lxxv (1960), pp. 551–3; 'Men of Renown: Heroic Virtue and the Giants of Genesis 6:4', *Philological Quarterly*, xl (1961), pp. 580–6; 'Milton's Harapha and Goliath', *Journal of English and Germanic Philology*, lx (1961), pp. 786–95. Cf. Augustine, pp. 514, 524.

[1] For discussion of the parallel between Satan and Nimrod, see Merritt Y. Hughes, 'Satan and the "Myth" of the Tyrant', in *Essays in English Literature from the Renaissance to the Victorian Age Presented to A. S. P. Woodhouse*, ed. Millar Maclure and F. W. Watt (Toronto, 1964), pp. 125 ff.

[2] For comparison of Milton's Satan with the heroes and anti-heroes of epic tradition, see Lawrence A. Sasek, 'Satan and the Epic Hero: Classical and Christian Tradition' (Harvard dissertation, 1953).

By this ethical and poetic counterpoint he sharpens the distinction between heroic image and *eidolon*.

Fundamental to *Paradise Lost* and *Paradise Regain'd* is the poet's recognition of the ambivalence of the term 'heroic', and the same insight is implicit, though less obvious, in *Samson Agonistes*. All three works provide, in varying degrees, both an analysis and critique of heroic virtue and a reassessment of the heroic tradition. Juxtaposing Christian and secular ideals of the hero, discriminating between true and false conceptions of heroism, Milton reaches a definition of true heroic virtue by systematically divesting it of most of its conventional attributes and deliberately contrasting it with its opposites. He arrives at its essence by separating it from its accidents. By progressively distinguishing reality from appearance and truth from opinion, he isolates its 'form', its idea.

Though the heroic tradition was as multiform and elusive as Proteus, two of its aspects assumed particular significance for Milton—the philosophic and the poetic. Classical and Christian ethics had presented heroic virtue rationally and abstractly, as a general idea. Epic poetry had depicted it sensuously and concretely, in images of particular heroes. Milton inherited both approaches to the hero. On the one hand, the heroic tradition involved moral philosophy. On the other hand, it comprised the corpus of heroic poetry and poetic theory, a tradition embracing not only classical and romantic epic, but also the allied genres of tragedy and encomium.[1]

Poetic and ethical traditions alike showed a perplexing variety. Neither was entirely consistent in defining or delineating the heroic ideal. The most striking inconsistency, however, lay in the discrepancy between the two traditions themselves. Not only did the poetic conception of heroism fall notably short of the ethical norm; for the most part, it contradicted the latter entirely. Milton's sensitivity to this contradiction and his bold attempt to resolve it by basing the

[1] For discussion of heroic virtue in the seventeenth-century encomium, see Ruth Nevo, *The Dial of Virtue: A Study of Poems on Affairs of State in the Seventeenth Century* (Princeton, 1963).

heroic poem on 'the vanity of human merits' appear in all three of his major poems. To reorient the epic toward the norm of Christian heroism meant re-establishing it solidly on a moral paradox—the antithesis between mortal sin and supernal grace. To be worthy of his name and office, the heroic poet must reject the conventional foundations of the epic tradition and base his poem on the cornerstone of man's depravity. To paint a true image of heroic virtue, he must first cover his canvas with a likeness of moral deformity, the image of original sin. The result is a heroic poem unlike all that had preceded it.

Paradise Lost is to the tradition of heroic poetry what the 'anti-novel' is to the conventional novel. It is the fruit and symbol of a literary *renversement* that overthrows and displaces its predecessors. Undermining the established epic tradition by destroying its ethical foundations, *Paradise Lost* is at once both epic and counter-epic. If it imitates the established models of heroic poetry, it also refutes them. In its own way it achieves an intellectual revolution no less extraordinary than those of Copernicus and Kant.

I

'The Pattern of a Christian Hero': Epic Formulae and the Ends of Heroic Poetry

ALL revolutions are cruel, if not unjust, towards the *ancien régime*. Milton's is no exception. His indictment of his predecessors is sound, but overstated. The charge that they had regarded war as the sole heroic subject is true only in general outlines. As he well knew, there were notable exceptions. Not the least of these was Vida's *Christiad*,[1] an epic to which he himself had alluded in his early poem on 'The Passion'. Nor was military prowess the only ideal conventionally equated with heroic virtue. There were others—prudence, temperance, and piety.

In his own way Milton is as ruthless as Robespierre in disposing of his forerunners. At his hands the aristocrats of the old régime—heroes of classical and Renaissance poetry—meet a severer nemesis than the guillotine. He transforms them to devils, consigns them to hell, overwhelms them with ridicule. The grotesque penalty inflicted on the rebel angels in Book X does not merely punish Satan's particular crime; it also represents Milton's condemnation of virtually the entire epic tradition, the final humiliation of the conventional heroic ideal.

I

Milton's originality appears even more forcefully, however, in the profound contrast between the argument of *Paradise Lost* and the type of subject he had favoured earlier. The gulf between Adam's fall and the exploits of some British 'King or

---

[1] See Note A, p. 20.

Knight before the Conquest'[1] exposes the hidden fault line beneath the very foundations of the heroic tradition, the cleavage between Christian doctrine and the conventional poetic ethos. Adam's spiritual defeat was, as the poet realized, of far greater consequence for the 'pattern of a Christian hero' than the victories of any secular prince or warrior. By breaking with his predecessors in choice of subject, Milton approached, far more closely than they, the end of heroic poetry as Renaissance theory conceived it.[2] His innovation reveals his maturer insight into the relationship between the subject of epic poetry and its moral purpose, the relationship of material to final cause.

Reduced to its essentials, the function of heroic poetry was threefold—to instruct, delight, and move. Wonder[3] was the characteristic effect of this genre, for by arousing marvel at heroic deeds, the epic poet moved the will to virtuous action. His 'office' was to create images vivid enough to teach the nature of heroic virtue and sufficiently powerful to incite the reader, through admiration or *maraviglia*, to emulate the heroic exemplar. In Sidney's words, the 'Heroicall' poet 'doth not only teach and move to a truth, but teacheth and mooveth to the most high and excellent truth; [he] maketh magnanimity and justice shine throughout all misty feare-

---

[1] *The Reason of Church Government, Complete Prose Works of John Milton*, vol. i, 813–14, ed. Don M. Wolfe (New Haven, 1953), cited hereafter as Yale Prose. For discussion see James Holly Hanford, *A Milton Handbook*, Fourth Edition (New York, 1946), pp. 373–7; Ida Langdon, *Milton's Theory of Poetry and Fine Art* (New Haven, 1924), pp. 127–8, 249.

[2] For Renaissance epic theory, see Bernard Weinberg, *A History of Literary Criticism in the Renaissance* (New York, 1961); Marvin T. Herrick, *The Fusion of Horatian and Aristotelian Literary Criticism* (Urbana, 1946); Allan H. Gilbert, *Literary Criticism: Plato to Dryden* (New York, 1940); Vernon Hall, Jr., *Renaissance Literary Criticism: A Study of Its Social Content* (New York, 1945); J. W. H. Atkins, *English Literary Criticism: The Renascence* (London, 1947); Donald Leman Clark, *Rhetoric and Poetry in the Renaissance* (New York, 1922); H. T. Swedenberg, Jr., *The Theory of the Epic in England, 1650–1800* (Berkeley, California, 1944); Leah Jonas, *The Divine Science: The Aesthetic of Some Representative Seventeenth-Century English Poets* (New York, 1940); Joseph Cottaz, *Le Tasse et la conception épique* (Paris, 1942); Ralph C. Williams, *The Theory of the Heroic Epic in Italian Criticism of the Sixteenth-Century* (Baltimore, 1917); Berthé de Besaucèle, *J. B. Giraldi: Étude sur l'évolution des théories littéraires en Italie au XVIᵉ siècle* (Paris, 1920).

[3] See my 'Miracle and the Epic Marvellous in *Paradise Lost*', *Archiv f. d. Studium d. neueren Sprachen u. Literaturen*, cxcviii (1962), pp. 289–303.

fulness and foggy desires. . . . For as the image of each action styrreth and instructeth the mind, so the loftie image of such Worthies most inflameth the mind with desire to be worthy, and informs with counsel how to be worthy.'[1]

Such a view put an astonishingly high premium on the role of the poetic image. It was precisely through his power to fashion clear and compelling images of the virtues and vices that the poet taught the intellect and moved the emotions and the will. By portraying the essential beauty of virtue and the innate deformity of vice and by describing their merited rewards and punishments he not only imparted a positive knowledge of good and evil, but also—the more important task—inclined his audience to desire and pursue the one and to loathe and shun the other. Through such 'notable images of vertues [and] vices' he could teach more effectively than the moral philosopher:[2]

. . . for whatsoever the Philosopher sayth shoulde be doone, hee giveth a perfect picture of it in some one, by whom he pre-supposeth it was doone. So as hee coupleth the generall notion with the particular example. A perfect picture I say, for hee yeeldeth to the powers of the minde an image of that whereof the philosopher bestoweth but a woordish description: which dooth neyther strike, pierce, nor possesse the sight of the soule so much as that other dooth.[3]

The moral framework within which the epic poet must execute his designs was, indeed, extremely simple. Like other poets, he must weave his composition upon a loom whose warp and woof were the principle of poetic justice and the Aristotelian doctrine that poetry must imitate the Idea. The chief ethical difference between the heroic poet and other writers lay essentially in the nature, quality, and degree of the virtues he must imitate.

As Tasso saw it, the purpose of the heroic poem was to celebrate heroic virtue and 'praise it to the skies'.[4] As this

---

[1] *Elizabethan Critical Essays*, ed. G. Gregory Smith (Oxford, 1904), i. 179; cf. p. 171.
[2] Cf. ibid., p. 160, and my 'Milton, Valvasone, and the Schoolmen', *Philological Quarterly*, xxxvii (1958), pp. 502-4.
[3] Smith, *Elizabethan* . . ., p. 164.
[4] *Le prose diverse di Torquato Tasso*, ed. Cesare Guasti (Firenze, 1875), i. 165.

genre required 'the highest pitch of virtue', its persons should be 'heroic like the virtue' they exhibit.[1] By imprinting the images of the various virtues on the mind,[2] the epic poet spurred his audience to heroic exploits. Davenant declared that the heroic poem ought to 'exhibit a venerable and amiable Image of Heroic vertue';[3] and, in Dryden's opinion, 'The shining quality of an epic hero, his magnanimity, his constancy, his patience, his piety, or whatever characteristical virtue his poet gives him, raises first our admiration; we are naturally prone to imitate what we admire; and frequent acts produce a habit.'[4]

Ambitious though it was, this conception of the heroic image seemed to other critics altogether too modest. For Paolo Beni, nothing less than absolute perfection should be expected of an epic hero. The poet should not merely depict a 'loftie image' of a particular virtue; he should portray the 'height' of *all* the virtues required of a 'supreme commander in peace and war' and thereby 'express the idea of a most perfect captain and hero'.[5]

In establishing this conception of the epic hero, Beni raised two questions. First, would not the example of a *perfect* prince or captain defeat the end of the heroic poem by discouraging other 'princes and captains' from trying to emulate him? Would it not be preferable, therefore, to invest him with merely an *average* degree of virtue, which would be less difficult to imitate? To this argument, Beni replied that both the nature of the hero and the characteristic epic effect demanded that the poet portray the very *highest* degree of virtue. As only the most extraordinary achievements could arouse the 'high marvel' proper to the heroic poem, heroic virtue exhibited the 'excellence and flower of the moral virtues', and 'especially of the most illustrious and most noble'.

Except when otherwise specified, all translations from French or Italian are my own. In the case of the *Gerusalemme Liberata*, I have usually followed the Fairfax translation.

[1] Ibid., p. 115.   [2] Ibid., p. 71.

[3] J. E. Spingarn (ed.), *Critical Essays of the Seventeenth Century* (Oxford, 1908), ii. 60.

[4] Dryden, *Prose Works*, ed. Malone, iii. 433.

[5] Paolo Beni, *Comparazione di Omero, Virgilio, e Torquato*, in *Opere di Torquato Tasso*, vi (Firenze, 1724), p. 453.

Second, must the poet necessarily ascribe all the virtues to a single hero? May he not, like Homer, embody them in several distinct persons? Thus 'Nestor is the exemplar of prudence, Achilles of fortitude, Diomedes of endurance, and other heroes of other virtues'. In Beni's opinion, however, the Homeric technique violated the laws of the heroic poem. A hero who personifies only one of many virtues must inevitably fall short of the moral perfection demanded of him. The 'various heroic virtues should not be dispersed among various persons' as this would be contrary to the laws and nature of heroic poetry. The epic 'ought to form a perfect hero', so that other princes and leaders could admire and imitate his example.[1]

Spenser's heroic poem achieved a compromise between these two alternatives. In each book he portrayed a single dominant virtue in a different hero. To Arthur, however, he ascribed the complete and perfect virtue—the sum of all the moral virtues:

. . . I labour to pourtraict in Arthure, before he was king, the image of a brave knight, perfected in the twelve private morall vertues, as Aristotle hath devised, the which is the purpose of these first twelve bookes: which if I finde to be well accepted I may be perhaps encoraged, to frame the other part of polliticke vertues in his person, after that hee came to be king. . . . So in the person of Prince Arthure I sette forth magnificence in particular, which vertue for that (according to Aristotle and the rest) it is the perfection of all the rest, and conteineth in it them all, therefore in the whole course I mention the deedes of Arthure applyable to that vertue, which I write of in that booke. But of the xii. other vertues, I make xii. other knights the patrones, for the more variety of the history. . . .[2]

II

The high value that Renaissance theory placed on the poetic image made the choice of epic formulae a problem of compelling urgency. At the same time it also heightened the importance of a related issue—the selection of an appropriate

[1] Ibid., pp. 453–5.
[2] *The Works of Edmund Spenser*, A Variorum Edition, vol. i, ed. F. M. Padelford (Baltimore, 1932), pp. 167–8.

hero in whom the correct formula might be convincingly portrayed. The power of the image to instruct and move the reader made it imperative that the poet really aim at the ethical and religious ends of his art, that he actually derive 'all the instances of example' from the 'book of sanctity and virtue' and not from the libels of impiety and vice. Milton himself inveighed against the 'libidinous and ignorant Poetasters, who, having scars ever heard of that which is the main consistence of a true poem, the choys of such persons as they ought to introduce, and what is morall and decent to each one, doe for the most part lap up vitious principles in sweet pils to be swallow'd down, and make the tast of vertuous documents harsh and sowr'.[1]

The problem of the heroic ethos was, however, as complex as it was crucial. Tradition offered the epic poet a wide range of alternative ideals—sometimes complementary, but often incompatible. The most notable of these were the formulae of military fortitude, prudence, leadership, love, piety, and magnanimity. Singly or in conjunction, most of these had classical prototypes in the poetry of Homer or Virgil, and all six had long been standard patterns in Renaissance epic and romance.

The question of the appropriate epic formula was actually inseparable from the problem of the end and intent of the heroic poem. On one point Renaissance critics were agreed—that the epic achieved its moral purpose by presenting an exemplary pattern of heroic virtue. But on another crucial issue—the nature and attributes of heroic virtue—Renaissance ethics and poetics were in serious conflict.

Epic tradition had placed emphasis on military valour. Ethical and theological traditions, on the other hand, had usually condemned this ideal as either inadequate or vicious and had sought the essence of heroism in a loftier concept— a superhuman excellence inseparable from reason, justice, and piety. In place of the warrior-hero, they had identified the hero with the just man, the *honnête homme*, and the saint.

---

[1] Milton, Yale Prose, i. 818; cf. Ascham's condemnation of the *Morte Arthure* (Smith, i. 4): '. . . the whole pleasure of which booke standeth in two speciall poyntes, in open mans slaughter and bold bawdrye: In which booke those be counted the noblest Knightes that do kill most men without any quarell, and commit fowlest aduoulteres by sutlest shiftes. . . .'

Since the first moral criticism of Homer's epics in classical Greece, there had been an unresolved tension between poetic and philosophical conceptions of heroism. The literary theory of the sixteenth and seventeenth centuries sharpened this distinction. Jacopo Mazzoni found the two ideals so different as to be virtually irreconcilable. In the philosophical sense, he declared, heroic virtue consists in a purification of soul comparable to that of Scipio in the *Somnium Scipionis*. It requires a perfection so lofty that a soul still confined to the body cannot achieve it. In the poetic sense, however, it consists entirely in military *fortezza* (strength or courage) and the noble deeds of valiant soldiers. Imprudent, irrational, it frequently harms instead of benefiting mankind.[1]

To the same tradition belonged Le Bossu's attempt to trace the distinction between poetic and ethical conceptions of the hero back to Aristotle. According to the *Traité du Poëme Épique*, the *Poetics* and the *Nicomachean Ethics* treat altogether different species of heroism. Not only do these two species have 'nothing in common', they are often flatly contradictory, diametrically opposed:

Aristotle declares that a heroic and divine virtue is a superhuman virtue and that consequently heroes are divine men, whom their natural excellence raises above our condition. But he states this in his *Ethics*. In his *Poetics*, on the contrary, he teaches that the chief person of a poem, whom we call the hero, should be neither good nor bad, but between these two extremes. He should neither be above the common ranks of men through his virtue and righteousness nor below them through his crimes and wickedness. Thus there is nothing in common between the two species of hero. The one should be raised above other men through his virtue; the other should not even be in the rank of the most perfect men.

Indeed, Aristotle must have regarded a 'poetic hero' like Achilles as an exemplar of brutishness, 'directly opposed to the hero of his *Ethics*'.[2]

Confronted with this discrepancy between poetic and

---

[1] Jacopo Mazzoni, *Della Difesa della Comedia di Dante* (Cesena, 1688), pp. 280–5.

[2] René Le Bossu, *Traité du Poëme Épique* (Paris, 1675), pp. 41, 43.

philosophical conceptions of heroic virtue, critics felt com-
pelled to reassess the conventional warrior-hero. Thus Le
Moyne, in his *Traité du Poëme Héroïque*, denounced the theme
of the *Iliad* as shameful. Was Achilles' fatal wrath a matter to
celebrate or to detest? Did Homer propose it as a laudable
example or as an object for 'horror' and public execration?[1]
With Horace, Le Bossu contrasted the *Iliad* and the *Odyssey*
as negative and positive examples. The one exhibited vices to
be shunned; the other depicted a virtuous exemplar. As its
protagonist the epic may, with equal regularity, take the
most cowardly and criminal of men, or the most valiant and
laudable. It is not necessary that the hero of the poem be
a good and virtuous man, and there is no irregularity in
making him 'as perfidious as Ixion, as unnatural as Medea,
and as brutal as Achilles'.[2]

The problem of the vicious hero also engaged English
critics. Davenant accused the ancients of 'representing the
Gods in evil proportion and their *Heroes* with as unequal
Characters' and thus bringing 'Vices into fashion by inter-
mixing them with the vertues of great Persons'. The 'sanctity'
of the 'Ethnicks' was merely 'Honor, and their Honor onely
an impudent courage or dexterity in destroying'. Hobbes
acknowledged that ambition is 'a fault', but believed that it
'has somewhat Heroick in it, and therefore must have place
in an Heroick Poem'.[3] Citing Le Bossu as his authority for
the principle that 'a poet is not obliged to make his hero a
virtuous man', Dryden observed that Homer had portrayed
both Achilles and Agamemnon as morally vicious. Achilles'
vices served the moral function of the epic chiefly by pro-
viding an evil example to be shunned: 'If the hero's chief
quality be vicious, as, for example, the choler and obstinate
desire of vengeance in Achilles, yet the moral is instructive:
and, besides we are informed in the very proposition of the
ILIADS, that this anger was pernicious. . . . The courage of
Achilles is proposed for imitation, not his pride and dis-

[1] Pierre Le Moyne, *Traité du Poëme Héroïque*, in *Saint Louys ou la Sainte
Couronne Reconquise* (Paris, 1658).
[2] Le Bossu, pp. 45–46.
[3] Spingarn, *Critical Essays*, ii. 10, 51, 61.

obedience to his General, nor his brutal cruelty to his dead enemy, nor the selling of his body to his father.'[1]

Both assailants and apologists of the *fortezza* formula based their arguments on the character of Achilles. Only a minority of critics maintained that Homer had deliberately portrayed the hero's vices as a negative example. The majority accepted him as a prototype of perfect fortitude. Echoing St. Basil's opinion, Thomas Wilson asserted that 'in the Iliades are described strength and valiauntnesse of the bodie: In the Odissea is set forthe a lively paterne of the minde.'[2] According to Pigna, Achilles 'is formed as the image of perfect valor', while Ulysses 'is the example of perfect prudence'.[3] Sidney bids his readers to 'See whether wisdom and temperance in *Ulisses* and *Diomedes*, valure in *Achilles*, friendship in *Nisus* and *Eurialus*, even to an ignoraunt man carry not an apparent shyning. . . .'[4] In Tasso's judgement: 'In Aeneas one finds the excellence of piety, of military fortitude in Achilles, and of prudence in Ulysses.'[5]

III

One solution to the conflict between poetic and philosophical patterns of heroic virtue was to retain the Achilles-type hero, either as the protagonist (the 'epic person') or as a subordinate character, but to acknowledge his moral inadequacy—the insufficiency of 'mere fortitude', divorced from prudence and piety. An alternative solution was to emphasize loftier virtues—prudence, temperance, justice, patience, and sanctity—and present these either in isolation from military valor or in close conjunction with it.

Like martial fortitude, these alternative and higher modes of heroism had classical prototypes in the epics of Homer and Virgil. Just as Achilles and Turnus exemplified the norm of courage and strength (*fortezza*), so Ulysses provided a pattern of heroic prudence and wisdom, Agamemnon embodied

---

[1] Dryden, *Prose Works*, iii. 433–4.
[2] *Wilson's Arte of Rhetorique 1560*, ed. G. H. Mair (Oxford, 1909), p. 195.
[3] Camillo Guerrieri Crocetti, *G. B. Giraldi ed il pensiero critico del sec. XVI* (Milano, 1932), pp. 238–9.
[4] Smith, i. 165.   [5] Tasso, i. 115.

the qualities of heroic leader and governor, and Aeneas represented the fusion of valour with both prudence and piety.
Moreover, in their sufferings and labours, these classical
heroes exhibited, albeit imperfectly, a nobler type of *fortezza*
—the inner fortitude of patience. An even more notable
exemplar occurred in Biblical epic, in the book of Job.

As an exemplar of the *prudentia-sapientia* formula, Ulysses
displayed much the same moral ambiguity as Achilles, the
classical representative of *fortezza*. For some critics he embodied the perfection of the intellectual virtues—heroic
prudence and wisdom—and the ideal pattern of the contemplative life. According to Horace,[1]

> . . . quid virtus et quid sapienta possit,
> Utile proposuit nobis exemplar Ulyssem. . . .

In Tasso's opinion, 'Dante's *Commedia* and the *Odyssey* are
figures of the life of the contemplative man'.[2]

Other commentators showed greater severity in their
verdicts. Beni believed that Homer had intended to portray
'a knight and hero of singular shrewdness and knowledge,
who could serve as a portrait of prudence and virtue for
great princes and captains'. Taking as its hero 'the sagest and
most prudent' of the Greek heroes, the epic depicts, 'as in a
fair theatre, the life and ethos of the sage and prudent man,
who remains constant and perfect in adverse fortune as in
prosperity'. Nevertheless, as in the *Iliad*, the poet failed to
achieve his end. Ulysses reveals his weakness in forsaking his
chaste wife 'for the insidious and shameless Circe'. He resorts
to 'tricks and lies' and vents such a multitude of groans and
tears that he forfeits the title of 'brave captain and hero'. He
is composed entirely of 'wiles, tears, and sleep'. His versa-
tility and guile are not heroic virtues, and his failure to save
his companions accentuates his inadequacy as an epic hero.[3]

IV

Closely associated with the *prudentia* formula was the ideal of
the *dux*, the leader on whose decisions the welfare of an entire
nation might depend. Theoretically the epic derived its

---

[1] Epistle i. 2.   [2] Tasso, i. 302.   [3] Beni, pp. 366, 369, 473.

argument from the exploits of kings and captains, delineated the moral or political virtues especially appropriate for their station, and aimed primarily at instructing persons of similar rank. Whatever private virtues the epic hero might possess— fortitude, prudence, or piety—must be oriented towards the public good. As the head of a state or army, he possessed responsibilities of leadership, obligations to his companions and subjects. He was, as a rule, a 'public person' rather than a private citizen, and his merits as epic hero depended largely on how effectively he fulfilled his public and political duties.

The ideal of the just prince or governor became, therefore, a commonplace of the Renaissance heroic tradition. Sidney saw precisely this pattern in Xenophon's *Cyropaedia*:[1] 'For *Xenophon*, who did imitate so excellently as to give us *effigiem iusti imperii*, the portraiture of a iust Empire under the name of *Cyrus* . . . made him therein an absolute heroicall Poem. . . .'

Spenser found the ideal of the heroic leader personified in Homer's Agamemnon, Virgil's Aeneas, Ariosto's Orlando, and Tasso's Godfrey:[2]

. . . Homer . . . in the Persons of Agamemnon and Ulysses hath ensampled a good governour and a vertuous man, the one in his Ilias, the other in his Odysseis; then Virgil, whose like intention was to doe in the person of Aeneas: after him Ariosto comprised them both in his Orlando: and lately Tasso dissevered them againe, and formed both parts in two persons, namely that part which they in Philosophy call Ethice, or vertues of a private man, coloured in his Rinaldo: The other named Politice in his Godfredo.

For all his defects, Agamemnon provided the epic prototype of the governor and leader, and in the dire results of Achilles' estrangement from him readers perceived the disastrous results of civil discord and disobedience. Later epics, modelled in part on the *Iliad*, took the famous quarrel-scene as a model for similar episodes illustrating this theme. The strife between Belisarius and Corsamonte in Trissino's *L'Italia Liberata*, the dissension between Arthur and Lancelot in Alamanni's *L'Avarchide*, the estrangement of Orlando and Charlemagne in Ariosto's epic, and the discord between Rinaldo and

---

[1] Smith, i. 160.   [2] Spenser, Variorum Edition, i. 167.

Godfrey in Tasso's *Gerusalemme Liberata* were all deliberately reminiscent of Homer's quarrel-scene. In all of these poems, the discord between the principal ruler or commander and his foremost warrior proves an insuperable obstacle to the campaign. Only when they have been reconciled can the enterprise succeed.

V

On the validity of love as a heroic formula, critics were divided. Its nature was ambivalent. Like the two Venuses of Platonic tradition, it could be either a virtue or a vice. It had long been a conventional theme in chivalric romance, and the epics of Boiardo, Ariosto, Tasso, and Spenser bore witness to its popularity in Renaissance heroic poetry. Scaliger heightened its prestige as an epic formula by praising Heliodorus' prose romance—the *Aethiopica*—as a model epic. Lexicographers traced the very name of *hero* to *eros*. Renaissance Platonism, in emphasizing the significance of the 'ladder of love' for the contemplative life, associated *amor* with both philosophy and piety. Theoretically, love could be an exemplary virtue for the perfect hero.

Thus for many critics love seemed a suitable subject for the heroic poem. Davenant defended the right of poets to be 'Admirers of Beauty, and Inventors or Provokers of . . . *Love*'.[1] In Hobbes' opinion, 'the work of an Heroique Poem is to raise admiration, principally, for three Vertues, Valour, Beauty, and Love'. He extolled *Gondibert* for containing 'nothing but setled Valor, cleane Honor, calm Counsel, learned diversion, and pure Love'.[2] Tasso defended the *amor*-formula at greater length. According to his *Discorsi del Poema Eroica*, 'love and friendship are most appropriate subjects for the heroic poem'. Homer's authority, he declared, has misled certain theorists into believing 'that love is not a fit matter for heroic poetry' and into blaming Virgil 'for feeling that Dido was enamored of Aeneas'. Even if one classifies love as a passion, it may still be an appropriate epic subject—like wrath—and indeed the *Iliad* presents notable examples of

---

[1] Spingarn, *Critical Essays*, ii. 50.   [2] Ibid., pp. 68, 61.

both passions. Although Agamemnon's love for Chryseis and
Achilles' passion for Briseis are no more than a 'base love of
servant-girls' and fall short of true nobility, the warriors' love
for Helen is 'most noble'. Indeed, as Isocrates believed, 'all
the grace and beauty of Homer's poems stem from Helen's
beauty'.

   If love were only a passion, Tasso argued, it would be
clearly inferior to wrath as an epic subject. But it may be considerably more than a passion. It may be a positive virtue,
and the exploits it prompts can be more heroic than deeds
inspired by other motives. Although poets may not wish to
describe the divinity of love exhibited by men who expose
their lives for Christ, they can nevertheless depict love as a
constant habit of the will.[1]

   For other theorists, however, love was a passion contrary
to reason and therefore highly unsuitable for an epic hero.

VI

In their quest for a nobler hero embodying the perfection of
all the moral virtues, Renaissance critics extolled the composite formula exemplified in Aeneas. Combining Achilles' valor,
Agamemnon's leadership, and Ulysses' prudence, he united
the virtues of the active and contemplative lives. As Tasso
pointed out, the *Aeneid* presented 'a mixture of action and
contemplation'.[2] And, as Beni observed, its hero combined
fortitude with prudence and thus provided a 'perfect example'
for a supreme commander in both peace and war. For the
two virtues are interdependent. Prudence is essential for
true fortitude, and without the latter prudence is impotent,
'unable to accomplish difficult enterprise'.[3]

   Above all, however, Aeneas displayed the higher virtue of
pietas. Scaliger praised him for combining 'piety and fortitude'.[4] Dryden defended Virgil for 'placing piety before valour,
and making that piety the chief character of his hero'.[5] Yet,
despite his manifold virtues, Aeneas inevitably fell short of the
highest excellence. Founded on a vain, superstitious religion,

his piety was not true piety. The perfect epic hero, Beni insisted, must necessarily be a Christian and should add the Christian virtues to those of the classical heroes. Hence, 'in his Godfrey, Torquato Tasso had depicted a much nobler and more perfect idea of a valiant captain and hero, than had Homer or Virgil'.[1]

VII

The heroic spectrum was indeed comprehensive. It embraced both the active and passive modes of fortitude—the patience of suffering Job as well as the valour of Achilles. It included the perfect virtue tempered by prudence and piety, but also the incomplete heroism vitiated by lust and ire. It comprised not only the active life, but also the contemplative and 'mixed' lives. Epic tradition offered the poet a strikingly varied palette for portraying the 'pattern of a . . . hero', and Milton made effective and subtle use of the variety it afforded him.

The insistence of many Renaissance critics on the hero's perfection—on a complete and perfect virtue as comprehensive as it was high—made it imperative for the poet to enlarge the range of epic formulae. As the intellectual and theological virtues excelled the moral virtues, they were even more essential for true heroism.

Among the moral virtues magnanimity assumed a particular significance through its close resemblance to heroic virtue. According to Tasso's Discorso della virtù eroica e della carità, they differed primarily in their objects. Whereas magnanimity aimed at honour as the only reward proportional to its merits, heroic virtue aimed at glory. 'Heroic virtue stands in the same relation to magnanimity, as glory to honor.'[2]

In view of this close relationship, one is hardly surprised to find Spenser treating magnanimity as a heroic virtue and indeed as his chief epic formula. In Prince Arthur, he declared, he had expressed the virtue of 'magnificence', which Aristotle and other philosophers regarded as the 'perfection

---

[1] Beni, p. 366.   [2] Tasso, ii. 193.

of all the rest' and which 'conteineth in it them all'. Arthur's quest of the Fairy Queen ('glory in my general intention') symbolized the relationship between this virtue and its proper end or reward.

As the highest virtues were theological, these were even more fitting for the hero than the moral and intellectual virtues. Besides the emphasis which many Renaissance critics placed on the formula of heroic piety, Tasso drew a detailed comparison between heroic virtue and charity. Both included many subordinate virtues. Both consisted in an excess rather than in the Aristotelian mean. Both lacked a 'determinate subject' and appeared in both prosperous and adverse fortune. Both sought a reward of glory—charity in the glory of Paradise, heroic virtue in worldly glory.

Because directed towards an imperfect object, the charity of the Hebrews and Gentiles was necessarily imperfect. The former served God primarily for temporal goods. The latter limited their charity to friends, country, and parents. Neither achieved more than a mere shadow or figure of Christian charity, which reached heroic perfection in Christ's voluntary death to redeem mankind.[1]

VIII

In his conception of the ends of heroic poetry, Milton differed little from his forerunners and contemporaries. He too believed that its final cause was beatitude and that it should teach, delight, and move by forming images of heroic virtue. Yet, unlike most of his predecessors, he recognized that the conventional subject-matter of heroic poetry was ill fitted to attain these ends, that the character of its hero was usually at variance with its ethical intent.

In comparison with the theological virtues, the conventional epic formulae appeared shamefully inadequate. To accentuate this contrast, Milton juxtaposed Christian and secular ideals of heroic virtue within the same narrative framework and thus brought out the distinctive qualities of both. The old heroic patterns serve as foils for the new. The

[1] Ibid., pp. 195–200.

new serve as a yardstick to measure—and castigate—the old.
The conflict between two different norms of heroism thus
becomes both a *psychomachia*, in which heroic virtue routs its
contrary vice, and an epistemological struggle, in which the
true heroism exposes the false. By a systematic critique of the
traditional formulae Milton sharpens the distinction between
heroic image and idol.

Critics have often oversimplified the moral design of
Paradise Lost. For many commentators, the dominant ethical
pattern is a clear-cut antithesis between two contrasting
formulae, classical and Christian. Yet this is only partially
true, and like all half-truths it is misleading. The classical
tradition comprehends a wide variety of heroic norms, and
for many of these the epithet 'classical' has only a limited
validity. Most of them recur in the more or less 'Christian'
epics of the Middle Ages and Renaissance. More fundamental is the antithesis between divine and human conceptions
of the hero. The heroisms of flesh and spirit are at variance.
The world's opinion of heroic virtue contradicts God's. In both
of Milton's epics the basic contrast is really the dichotomy of
piety and impiety—obedience and disobedience towards God
—rather than Christianity and Hellenism.

But even this antithesis is deceptively simple. Its bare scaf-
folding supports a complex variety of heroic norms—fortitude, wisdom, leadership, love, magnanimity. Milton subjects
all of these to intensive analysis, discriminating between their
valid and invalid modes. In reassessing the epic formulae, he
is faithful to their variety.

In presenting the true image of a 'Christian hero', he
usually prefers the composite formula favoured by Beni and
exemplified in Spenser's Arthur. In both epics he 'lays the
pattern' of a perfect and comprehensive virtue in a single
dominant figure, like the Messiah, instead of distributing the
various virtues among several different individuals. This
emphasis on *complete* virtue is especially marked in the Christ
of *Paradise Regain'd*. In his 'brief epic' Milton's primary intent
is not merely to portray the *highest* degree of heroic virtue,
but also to display it in its *total* perfection, to depict the complex of heroic virtues in its entirety.

His chief negative exemplar is likewise a composite hero, albeit a false one. As a heroic *eidolon*, Satan displays the vicious modes of the conventional formulae—a fortitude that is really rashness, a prudence that is folly and fraud, a leadership that misleads, a magnanimity that strives for unmerited honours, accomplishes acts of destruction instead of 'acts of benefit', and turns out to be vainglorious ambition and pride. Milton has invested his Archfiend with the ethos of the 'vicious hero'. Satan conforms to a type which, for many Renaissance critics, was well established in poetic tradition, but incompatible with 'philosophical' conceptions of heroic virtue.

In attributing to Satan these characteristics of the conventional 'poetic hero', Milton reduces them to a logical absurdity and thus exposes their falsity. By ascribing them to the devil himself, he demonstrates that they are not properly heroic in themselves, but should necessarily be contingent on piety. They are not the essence of heroic virtue, but merely its accidents. They are just as applicable to vice as to virtue, to impiety as to piety. In an evil cause they become diabolical.

As a critical weapon this technique was double-edged. It challenged not only the formulae themselves, but also the particular literary prototypes in which they had been portrayed. In condemning the apparent fortitude or prudence dissociated from piety, it indicted Homer and his imitators for investing their heroes with specious rather than substantial heroism, egregious vices rather than exemplary virtues. As a method for discrediting the false heroic, it stands midway between the uncritical imitation of Homeric ethos, on the one hand, and the method of parody, on the other. It is a mean between the heroic and the mock heroic.

This technique was not altogether original. By modelling Turnus on Achilles, Virgil had emphasized Aeneas' superiority to both. Their fierce but imprudent fortitude shows to distinct disadvantage in comparison with the Trojan's piety and rational valour. In the *Gerusalemme Liberata*, Tasso had obliquely censured the Homeric heroes by transferring their traits to inferiors and infidels.[1]

---

[1] According to Beni, p. 369, Tasso 'deliberately painted the two ambassadors of the Egyptian king—Alete and Argante—with the characteristics and

Like Milton, Virgil and Tasso had decked an 'Antagonist of Heav'n' in the trappings of Homeric heroes. In opposing Aeneas, Turnus had resisted the will of Jove. In resisting the Crusaders, Alete and Argante had opposed God's intent. Yet Milton carried his critique of these epic formulae much further than Tasso. Whereas his predecessor had merely applied them to pagan envoys, he ascribed them to the devil himself. This was a brilliant innovation on the heroic tradition, but it was nevertheless an innovation *within* the tradition. The technique by which he exposed the conventional heroic ethos as diabolical was partially rooted in the precedent set by his forebears.

In his destructive wrath, his implacability, his pride in his own strength, his sense of injured merit, his martial fortitude divorced from right reason and piety, Satan offers more than a fortuitous parallel to Achilles. In his eloquence and cunning, his 'tricks, frauds, and lies', his professed attempt to 'save his companions', he resembles Ulysses. Like the wily Greek, he penetrates an enemy citadel in disguise and overthrows it by a simple ruse.

Though the influence of Homeric prototypes on Milton's heroic *eidolon* is considerable, one must not exaggerate it. Besides his marked affinities with Achilles and Ulysses, Satan also shows occasional resemblances to other classical or romantic heroes—the Argonauts, Aeneas, Capaneus, Turnus, Rodomonte, and others. The peculiar importance of the Homeric parellels lies in their unique position at the fountain-head of the European epic tradition. They are, in large part, the prototypes of Aeneas, just as Aeneas is the prototype of Tasso's Godfrey.

Milton's exploitation of classical parallels is much too complex to be epitomized as simply a technique of rejection. In

colors of Ulysses and Achilles, in order to show . . . that those colors and distinctive marks were not those of a wise and true hero, but rather of an astute messenger or proud champion'. The former is a 'flatterer' and a 'liar', an eloquent 'fabricator of calumnies', and a man of 'flexible manners and various mind, prompt to feign and skilled at deception'; as such he is 'almost entirely modelled on Ulysses'. His companion, in turn, is 'practically a living image of Achilles'—'impatient, inexorable, fierce, indefatigable and unvanquished in arms, a despiser of every God, a man who takes his sword as his law and his reason'.

Satan, he presents the Ulysses-myth in a pejorative light; in Samson, he gives it a more favourable treatment. If the devil exhibits certain affinities with Achilles, so—on at least one occasion—does the Son. These analogies with classical prototypes generally serve more than one purpose. Usually they reinforce 'epic decorum' and strengthen the continuity of the heroic tradition. When linked with piety, they heighten the superiority of Milton's heroes to the worthies celebrated by his predecessors. Conversely, when associated with impiety, they implicitly condemn both the conventional epic heroes and the poets who had sung their praises, 'The vices of thir Deities, and of thir own'.

Finally, despite the influence of epic tradition on Milton's heroic idol, the primary basis of this characterization is Biblical. This is true in the case of Harapha, the Philistine giant, and it is even more pronounced in Satan's instance. The essential outlines of his character and role had been determined by Scripture itself. These, and the theological and poetic traditions associated with them, were inevitably Milton's starting-point, the germ of Satan's characterization and action.

The Biblical sources contained the seeds of the traditional epic formulae. Satan's war in Heaven had involved force, his temptation of man had entailed fraud. Holy writ had characterized him as the proud rebel and the 'liar from the beginning'. These were the basic features of the Satanic ethos, according to Scripture; and they recalled familiar heroic types. As disguised deceiver, he resembled Ulysses, the chief exemplar of the *prudentia-sapientia* formula. As the proud warrior, sensitive to a real or imaginary affront to his honour, he was like Achilles, the most notable prototype of the *fortezza* pattern. Similarly, the formula of the *dux* was implicit in the Biblical conception of Satan as the leader and monarch of the devils. In the motives of Lucifer's rebellion— ambition and pride—there appeared the outlines of a false magnanimity.

In converting the Satan of Scripture into an epic figure, Milton advisedly sought support from the epic tradition itself. Accepting the Biblical sketch of Satan's character for his basic outline, he completed his portrait with details derived from classical and romantic exemplars.

Thus the 'True Image of the Father' and the 'Idol of Majestie divine' serve as antithetical archetypes of true and false heroism, essential and specious 'godlikeness'. By heightening the opposition between 'poetic' and 'philosophical' concepts of heroic virtue and 'laying their patterns' in Satan and Messiah, Milton resolves much of the moral ambiguity inherent in the conventional epic formulae. Through its contrast with the false, the true heroic image acquires sharper focus and greater capacity to 'teach, delight, and move'.

NOTE A

For an adequate survey of the critical and poetic tradition that Milton inherited and helped to reshape, one cannot limit one's inquiry to possible influences. Besides writers who probably *did* influence him (such as Tasso and Ariosto) and writers he *might* have read (such as Alamanni and Trissino), one must also consider several significant works which appeared in print altogether too late to influence him, yet throw considerable light on seventeenth-century controversy. Le Bossu's treatise and Dryden's 'Dedication' to the *Aeneid* belong to this category.

Most of the works cited in this chapter have been included for their bearing on the problem of the appropriate ethical 'formula' for an epic hero. They range in date from, roughly, the fifteenth to the seventeenth century. For the reader's convenience, I have added a brief alphabetical table, giving their relative dates, as well as the chronology of works mentioned in the later chapters.

Luigi Alamanni's *L'Avarchide* was published in 1570, nearly fifteen years after his death. Ludovico Ariosto's *Orlando Furioso* (a continuation of Boiardo's romance on Orlando) was begun around 1504 and first published in 1516; the first complete edition appeared in 1532. Sir John Harington's English translation appeared in 1591, along with his *Brief Apology* and his 'Allegory' of the poem.

Paolo Beni's *Comparazione di Homero, Virgilio e Torquato* was published in 1607. The first two books of Boiardo's *Orlando Innamorato* appeared in 1483; the third book of his incomplete poem was not published until about 1495 (a year after his death). Francesco Berni's 'modification' or *rifacimento* of this romance appeared in 1541. John Bunyan's *The Holy War* was published in 1682.

Luis de Camoens's *Os Lusiadas* was published in 1572, and Richard Fanshawe's English translation in 1655. Cervantes's *Don Quixote* appeared early in 1605. Jean Chapelain's *La Pucelle* was published in 1656. Abraham Cowley's unfinished *Davideis* appeared in his *Poems* in 1656; the date of composition is still subject to controversy, estimates ranging between 1638 and 1650–4.

The first four books of Samuel Daniel's *Civile Wars* were published in 1595; later editions in 1599 and 1601 increased the number to five and seven respectively. Davenant's 'Preface' to *Gondibert* and Hobbes's 'Answer' both appeared in 1650 in the first edition of his epic. Jason De Nores's *Poetica* was published in 1588. Michael Drayton's *Mortimeriados* appeared in 1596; his *Barrons Wars* (a much altered recension of this work) in 1603. Dryden's 'Dedication' of his translation of the *Aeneid* appeared in 1697; it quotes extensively from Segrais's preface to the French translation of this epic, published in 1668. Du Bartas's short epic *Judit* was published in *La Muse chrétienne* in 1574. Thomas Hudson's English translation appeared in 1584 and Sylvester's (entitled *Bethulians Rescue*) in 1614. Du Bartas's *La Sepmaine, ou Création du Monde* was published in 1578, and his *Seconde Sepmaine* in 1584–1608. Sylvester's translation appeared in 1605 as *Bartas his Divine Weekes and Workes*, though portions had been published earlier; the translator added the *Third Day* and *Fourth Day* in 1608. Du Bellay's *Monomachie de David et de Goliath* was published in 1560.

Erasmus's *Enchiridion militis Christiani* was written *c.* 1501 and published at Antwerp in 1504.

The first twenty-six cantos of Giovambattista Giraldi Cintio's epic *Ercole* were published in 1557. His *Discorsi intorno al comporre de i Romanzi* appeared in 1554. Girolamo Graziani's *Conquisto di Granata* was published in 1650.

Antoine de Harsy's dedication to the *Œuvres Poëtiques* of Mellin de Saint-Gelais was printed in 1574.

René Le Bossu's *Traité du Poëme Épique* was published in 1675. The 1658 edition of Pierre Le Moyne's epic *Saint Louys* included his *Traité du Poëme Héroïque*; a shorter version of the poem had already appeared in 1653, together with a *Dissertation du Poëme Héroïque*. Justus Lipsius's *De Constantia* was published in 1584 and Sir John Stradling's translation in 1595.

Giambattista Marino's *L'Adone* was published in 1623; his *La Strage degli Innocenti* in 1632. Part I of Jacopo Mazzoni's *Della Difesa della Commedia di Dante* appeared in 1587; the complete work was not published until 1688.

Giovanni Battista Pigna's *I Romanzi* appeared in 1554.

Ronsard's incomplete *Franciade* was published in 1572.

Julius Caesar Scaliger's *Poetices* appeared in 1561. Sidney's *Apologie for Poetrie* was composed around 1583 and published posthumously in 1595. Spenser's letter to Sir Walter Raleigh 'expounding his whole intention in the course of his worke' is dated '23. January. 1589' and first published in 1590.

Bernardo Tasso's *Amadigi* was published in 1560. His *Floridante*, an amplification of an episode in this work, was completed and published in 1587 by his more famous son. Torquato Tasso's *Rinaldo* appeared in 1562 and his *Aminta* in 1573. His *Gerusalemme Liberata* was begun about 1563 and completed in 1575. After a pirated edition of fourteen cantos had been published in 1580 under the title of *Il Goffredo*, the complete poem was published in 1581. His *Gerusalemme Conquistata*—a radical recension of the earlier work—appeared in 1593. Tasso's *Discorsi dell' Arte Poetica* were composed around 1564 and published in 1587; his *Discorsi del poema eroico* appeared in 1594, and his *Discorso della Virtù Eroica e della Carità* in 1582. His 'Allegoria' of the *Gerusalemme Liberata* was written in 1576 and included in the 1581 editions of the poem. His epic on the creation of the world—*Il Mondo Creato*—was written in the last years of his life (Antonio Belloni dates it in 1594); the sections on the 'first two days' were published in 1600 and all 'seven days' in 1607. Edward Fairfax's English translation of the *Gerusalemme Liberata* appeared in 1600.

Alessandro Tassoni's *La Secchia Rapita* was begun around 1614 and published in 1622. Giovanni Giorgio Trissino's *Italia Liberata da i Goti* was published in 1547.

Odorico Valmarana's *Daemonomachia* appeared in 1623 and, in a revised and enlarged edition, in 1627. Erasmo da Valvasone's *Angeleida* was published in 1590. Benedetto Varchi's *Lezzioni . . . sopra diverse Materie, Poetiche e Filosofiche* were published in 1590. Marco Girolamo Vida's *Christiad* appeared in 1535.

II

The Critique of Fortitude

IN the epic tradition fortitude[1] had long been the conventional heroic norm. Most Renaissance poets and critics accepted it as the heroic virtue *par excellence*. As Giraldi explained, the romance derived its very name from the Greek *romē* ('*fortezza*' or strength). Like the classical epic, it concerned the exploits of 'mighty knights' (*cavalieri forti*).[2]

Fortezza (strength of mind or body) served as the normal standard for evaluating or comparing heroes of different ages, nations, or religions. In the opening lines of the *Lusiads*, Camoens exalted Vasco da Gama's valour over that of classical heroes.[3] Milton likewise accepted the valour of classical worthies as a basis for comparison; in sheer might, the fallen angels surpassed the most famous heroes of epic and romance:

> For never since created man,
> Met such imbodied force, as nam'd with these
> Could merit more than that small infantry
> Warr'd on by Cranes. . . . Thus far these beyond
> Compare of mortal prowess. . . .

[1] For discussions of Milton's treatment of fortitude, see William C. Harris, 'Despair and "Patience as the Truest Fortitude" in *Samson Agonistes*', *ELH*, xxx (1963), pp. 107–20; Paul R. Baumgartner, 'Milton and Patience', *Studies in Philology*, lx (1963), pp. 203–13; A. B. Chambers, 'Wisdom and Fortitude in *Samson Agonistes*', *PMLA*, lxxviii (1963), pp. 315–20; W. W. Robson, 'The Better Fortitude', in *The Living Milton*, ed. Frank Kermode (London, 1960), pp. 124–37. In the *De Doctrina* (Book II, Chapter 1) Milton classifies fortitude and patience among virtues 'connected with the duty of man towards himself' and 'exercised in the resistance to, or the endurance of evil'. Fortitude appears chiefly 'in repelling evil, or in regarding its approach with equanimity'. Its opposites are 'timidity' and temerity (a 'rashness, which consists in exposing ourselves to danger unnecessarily'). The similarities with Aristotle's definitions are hardly surprising; Milton regarded him (Yale Prose, iii. 204) as 'one of the best interpreters of nature and morality'.

[2] *Scritti estetici di G. B. Giraldi Cintio*, Part I, ed. Giulio Antimaco (Milano, 1864), pp. 6–7.

[3] Luis de Camoens, *The Lusiad*, tr. Richard Fanshawe, ed. Jeremiah D. M. Ford (Cambridge, Mass., 1940), p. 30.

Similarly, in his hazardous voyage through Chaos, Satan faced more formidable dangers and graver labours than either Ulysses or the Argonauts.

In such passages as these Milton consciously evoked the standard epic formula for heroic virtue. But this apparent fidelity to epic decorum was really subversive. Line by line, stroke by stroke, he was painting—on glass—a portrait, far larger than life, of the conventional hero. When it was complete, he would shatter it. With it he would discredit not merely Satan's heroic pretensions, but the *fortezza* formula itself and the epic repertory of 'mighty knights'. (Writing *Eikonoklastes* had given him experience in smashing idols.) By the standard of 'mere fortitude', the Satan of *Paradise Lost* was a greater hero than either Achilles or Orlando, the worthies who 'fought at *Theb's* and *Ilium'*, or 'Jousted in *Aspramont* or *Montalban'*. In making him so, Milton sought to discredit this formula by a *reductio ad absurdum*. By the criterion of fortitude the devil himself could be a more heroic figure than the most celebrated warriors of epic tradition.

I

In substance and argument, Milton's critique of the *fortezza*-formula contains little that is truly original. For the most part it echoes commonplaces of Renaissance ethical or poetic doctrine. The novelty resides chiefly in the skill with which he marshals the conventional arguments against it.

In the first place, he makes effective rhetorical use of its ambiguity. Of several meanings, he singles out the lowest and most vulnerable for direct attack. Though fortitude properly denotes moral courage as well as physical strength, he frequently dissociates the two, reducing the conventional formula to little more than brute force. By stressing the etymological sense of *fortitudo*, he tends to equate it with fleshly might. Then he further debases this formula by contrasting it unfavourably with its passive mode, the 'better fortitude of Patience and Heroic Martyrdom'. Military valour is thus exposed as an inferior mode of fortitude; it falls short of heroic excellence.

Second, like other Renaissance poets and critics, Milton stresses the destructive character of military valour, its frequent dissociation from reason and virtue, and the transitory nature of its rewards. His condemnation of the Biblical 'men of renown'—'Giants of mightie Bone, and bould emprise'—is double-edged; it applies not only to the antediluvian giants, but also to most of the warriors celebrated by Greece and Rome. It represents, in effect a sentence of judgement on the whole heroic age and the most popular of classical formulae:

> For in those dayes Might onely shall be admir'd,
> And Valour and Heroic Vertu call'd;
> To overcome in Battel, and subdue
> Nations, and bring home spoils with infinite
> Man-slaughter, shall be held the highest pitch
> Of human Glorie, and for Glorie done
> Of triumph, to be styl'd great Conquerours,
> Patrons of Mankind, Gods, and Sons of Gods,
> Destroyers rightlier call'd and Plagues of men,
> Thus Fame shall be achiev'd, renown on Earth,
> And what most merits fame in silence hid.

These 'acts of prowess eminent And great exploits' are actually 'void' of 'true vertu'. Far from leaving any lasting achievement, they merely produce 'much waste Subduing Nations'. Instead of an enduring reward, they merely earn 'Fame in the World, high titles, and rich prey'.

Abdiel carries the critique of fortitude a step further. Might without right may seem invulnerable, but its apparent strength is weakness. If it lacks *virtue* (which bears the double sense of 'strength' and 'moral excellence') it cannot be truly strong. It may, therefore, be defeated by true virtue —by valour armed with reason and faith. For Raphael, too, the fortitude alienated from justice and truth is vicious and shameful.[1]

[1]   'For strength from Truth divided and from Just,
       Illaudable, naught merits but dispraise
       And ignominie, yet to glorie aspires
       Vain glorious, and through infamie seeks fame. . .

Messiah also censures the narrowness of the *fortezza* ideal. The rebel angels (he charges) cling to an inferior pattern of heroic eminence, ignoring the nobler virtues:

> ... by strength
> They measure all, of other excellence
> Not emulous, nor care who them excells. ...

Paradise Regain'd and *Samson Agonistes* advance the same conventional arguments against the ideal of military valour. In his later epic, as in *Paradise Lost*, Milton introduces the *fortezza* pattern with a visual pageant of armed might, and heightens the effect of this display by comparison with the powerful heroes of epic and romance. The forces of the Parthians surpass in might those of the armies celebrated in Boiardo's *Orlando Innamorato*, Ariosto's *Orlando Furioso*, and the romances of 'mighty knights':

> Such forces met not, nor so wide a camp,
> When *Agrican* with all his Northern powers
> Besieg'd *Albracca*, as Romances tell;
> The City of *Gallaphrone*, from thence to win
> The fairest of her Sex *Angelica*
> His daughter, sought by many Prowest Knights,
> Both *Paynim*, and the Peers of *Charlemane*.
> Such and so numerous was thir Chivalrie.

But the moral reality behind this display of might is—paradoxically—frailty. It is a 'vain' ostentation of 'fleshly arm, and fragile arms', and it is 'soon to nothing brought'. The 'cumbersome Luggage of war' is actually an 'argument of human weakness rather than of strength'.

The allusions to Renaissance epic and romance in this passage are not fortuitous. In Christ's rejection of the Parthian armies the poet is passing judgement on the epic tradition itself and its glorification of military prowess. Here, as in *Paradise Lost*, he stresses the vicious character of the *fortezza* ideal, its destructive effects, its inferiority to deeds of peace, and its inability to merit a valid reward:

> They err who count it glorious to subdue
> By Conquest far and wide, to over-run
> Large Countries, and in field great Battels win,

> Great Cities by assault: . . . Conquerours, who leave behind
> Nothing but ruin wheresoe're they rove,
> And all the flourishing works of peace destroy. . . .

To this vicious fortitude and its false, unmerited glory Milton opposes the fortitude of the martyr and saint—Job's 'Saintly patience' and the example of Socrates, 'For truths sake suffering death unjust . . .'.

In *Samson Agonistes* the dramatic situation is itself a powerful, though implicit, indictment of the *fortezza* ideal. The blind and captive strong-man and the crestfallen giant are telling arguments against the criterion of human strength. But the explicit criticism is, if not more forceful, at least more extensive and more detailed. The opening lines of the poem find Samson brooding upon the dissociation of reason and might. Lamenting his 'impotence of mind in body strong' he recognizes at last the necessary subordination of strength to wisdom:

> But what is strength without a double share
> Of wisdom, vast, unwieldy, burdensom,
> Proudly secure, yet liable to fall
> By weakest subtleties, not made to rule,
> But to subserve where wisdom bears command.
> God, when he gave me strength, to shew withal
> How slight the gift was, hung it in my Hair.

He has been, he perceives, heroically strong, but not heroically wise. Might he has possessed in heroic 'excess' or 'eminence', but he has not been endowed with a corresponding degree of wisdom. In the language of Renaissance criticism, his heroic fortitude has not been paired with heroic prudence.

Like his epics, Milton's drama accentuates the intrinsic weakness of this ideal. Ironically, Samson has exposed his inner frailty in the very act of revealing the secret of his physical strength:

> Who this high gift of strength committed to me . . .
> . . . weakly to a woman must reveal it,
> O'recome with importunity and tears.

Harapha's discomfiture, in turn, exposes the *fortezza*

formula to public ridicule, as the giant departs, a 'baffl'd coward', with the Hebrew's taunt 'bulk without spirit vast' still ringing in his ears. But it is misleading to regard him as merely a comic character.[1] On the contrary, he is cast in a recognizably heroic mould. His 'stock renown'd As *Og* or *Anak*' links him with a breed notable for exploits of a conventional, though false, heroism—with those Biblical 'men of renown', whose 'Might' had been miscalled 'Valour and Heroic Vertu,' and those 'Sons of *Anac*', whose feats of prowess Samson had excelled by 'acts indeed heroic'. His desire for the 'glory of Prowess' and his admiration for 'glorious arms Which greatest Heroes have in battel worn' are thoroughly characteristic not only of the Biblical giants but also of the classical heroes; they associate him not only with Goliath, but also with Achilles and Aeneas.

A third technique for demonstrating the fallacy of this pattern was to apply it to the patently vicious. When Milton invests the devil and his works with the conventional trappings of epic heroism, he exposes its illusory character. The fortitude Satan displays in undertaking the journey through Chaos does indeed involve contempt of danger, but his moral intent is categorically evil. He pursues his enterprise with courage, but in direct opposition to the divine will. His heroic endeavour is an act of disobedience—a deliberate sin. In thus dissociating valour from piety and ascribing fortitude to the author of all evil, Milton consciously presents a negative *exemplum* that discredits the pseudo-heroic pattern of epic tradition.

The vicious mode of fortitude appears most clearly in Moloch, 'the strongest and the fiercest Spirit That fought in Heav'n'. His strength and fierceness are qualities reminiscent of Achilles; they are traditional virtues of the epic hero. Yet Milton represents them here unambiguously as pure vice.

In Satan the idol of fortitude is less brutal and more complex. There is the conventional heroic ethos,

[1] For a study of Harapha and the *miles gloriosus* tradition, see Daniel C. Boughner, 'Milton's Harapha and Renaissance Comedy', *ELH*, xi (1944), pp. 297–306.

> . . . the unconquerable Will,
> And study of revenge, immortal hate,
> And courage never to submit or yield. . . .

There are the familiar pride in strength and the contempt of weakness:

> . . . by Fate the strength of Gods
> And this Empyreal substance cannot fail. . . .

> . . . to be weak is miserable
> Doing or Suffering. . . .

There is the traditional heroic enterprise—the siege, conquest, and destruction of the enemy's citadel:

> For onely in destroying I finde ease
> To my relentless thoughts. . . .
> To mee shall be the glorie sole among
> The infernal Powers, in one day to have marr'd
> What he *Almightie* styl'd, six Nights and Days
> Continu'd making. . . .

The pattern of heroic fortitude exhibited in Moloch and Satan is, of course, essentially ironic.[1] Its conscious purpose is to dramatize and discredit the *fortezza* formula by representing it as a diabolical ethos. Those critics who have regarded it as an unconscious lapse on Milton's part—the sign of an unintentional admiration for the fallen angel—have ignored his explicit and implicit critique of the conventional epic patterns of fortitude. They have also paid insufficient attention to the moral and literary traditions behind Milton's hell.

Most significant, however, is the fourth method whereby the poet reduces the *fortezza* ideal to its just dimensions. Since power is really the gift of God, bestowed on whom He wills, the creature has no just grounds for glorying in his own strength. He can only confess his own weakness and acknowledge his dependence on divine power. Trust in his own strength—or (in theological terms) 'carnal reliance'—

---

[1] Satan appears to hold the mean between Moloch's rashness and Belial's timidity and thus provide an exemplar of fortitude; this is, however, only the specious resemblance of true *fortezza*.

thus stands in direct opposition to trust in God. The ideal of heroic fortitude yields inevitably to that of heroic faith.[1]

We have seen Satan's heart 'hardning' as he reviews his battalions and glories in his military strength. We have also seen him prizing his personal might, as though it were his own, instead of a divine gift. Nevertheless, his companion has had a partial glimpse of the truth—that they possess their might not by their own merit and power, but only by divine permission.

The limitations of Satan's might are brought home to him even more forcefully at the conclusion of Book IV, when the providential sign in heaven reveals its weakness:

> *Satan,* I know thy strength, and thou knowst mine,
> Neither our own but giv'n; what follie then
> To boast what Arms can doe, since thine no more
> Then Heav'n permits, nor mine, though doubld now
> To trample thee as mire: for proof look up,
> And read thy Lot in yon celestial Sign
> Where thou art weigh'd, & shown how light, how weak,
> If thou resist.

Earlier, he had made a similar vaunt of self-sufficiency, and it had been similarly exploded. In plotting rebellion, he had boasted that his 'puissance' was his 'own', a force independent of the divine will. But in actual battle the Son shatters this claim. The divine lightnings of the Chariot of Paternal Deitie

> . . . witherd all their strength,
> And of thir wonted vigour left them draind,
> Exhausted, spiritless, afflicted, fall'n.

In Milton's tragedy, the moral opposition between *fiducia carnalis* and *fiducia in Deo*[2] finds its fullest dramatic

---

[1] The proof-texts whereby Milton substantiates his definition of fortitude (*De Doctrina,* Book II, Chapter 10) often associate it with faith: 'God is our refuge and strength . . . therefore will we not fear'; 'in God have I put my trust; I will not be afraid what man can do . . .'. The 'great pattern' of fortitude is Jesus Christ 'throughout the whole pattern of his life, and in his death'.

[2] In the *De Doctrina* (Book II, Chapter 3) Milton includes *fiducia* or trust among 'devout affections towards God' as a virtue 'belonging to the worship of God'. It is 'an effect of love' and 'a part of internal worship, whereby we wholly repose on him'. Its opposites are 'distrust of God', 'overweening presumption', 'carnal reliance', and 'trust in idols'.

expression in Samson's confrontation with Harapha. But the critique of 'carnal reliance' is to be found throughout the drama. Samson acknowledges his over-confidence in his own might:

> Fearless of danger, like a petty God
> I walk'd about admir'd of all and dreaded
> . . . swoll'n with pride. . . .

And Manoa confesses how 'ever failing' is 'trust in mortal strength'.

A fifth method of reducing the *fortezza* ideal to due proportions was to emphasize the preponderance of divine might over that of the creature. Just as the devils exceed mankind in strength, so the power of the Almighty immeasurably surpasses that of the rebels. The force which finally brings the angelic battles to an end is entirely the Father's, for the might exercised by the Son is actually an 'infused' virtue imparted directly by the Father himself. In the final episode of Book VI, as in the *peripeteia* of *Samson Agonistes*, Milton exploits the conventional theological distinction between those virtues which have been directly infused by God and those which have been acquired by training and exercise. The former are in reality divine virtues, the latter merely human. As the perfect Image of the Father's might, the Son presents the ideal pattern of fortitude. Not only does he embody the formula of strength subordinated to piety, but he also exemplifies the divine strength itself—*fortezza* as a celestial archetype and a divine virtue. 'Image of [his Father] in all things', the Son is 'Mightiest in [his] Fathers might'.

> Into thee such Vertue and Grace
> Immense I have transfus'd, that all may know
> In Heav'n and Hell thy Power above compare. . . .

Unlike Messiah, Samson is not the 'perfect image' of the Father, but he is none the less a true and valid 'Image of [God's] strength, and mighty minister'. The epithet 'miracle of men' is well chosen, for his power derives not from the order of nature, but from God himself. His strength is 'Heav'n-gifted', his exploits are of 'divine instinct', and the might with which he is armed is 'celestial vigour'.

Again, it is by an 'infused' virtue—a 'Godlike force' miraculously imparted by the Father—that the Christ of *Paradise Regain'd* succeeds in standing on the temple's highest pinnacle, and thus demonstrates his divinity.

In all three instances, the 'transfus'd' might of the Father produces a miracle and thus manifests its true origin and nature. It is, moreover, precisely this miraculous quality—the exploitation of the 'Christian marvellous'—that reconciles the conflicting demands of wonder and probability and thus enables Milton to achieve the characteristic epic effect —admiration—without forfeiting verisimilitude.[1] By emphasizing his hero's single-handed victory over forces more numerous and apparently more powerful, he brings out more clearly its miraculous character; Christ and Samson alike overcome their enemies not by their own intrinsic strength but by the power deputed to them by the Father.

II

With these vicious types of fortitude Milton contrasts its virtuous modes. To the formula of 'mere strength' (*mera fortezza*) he opposes two alternative ideals, (1) the active fortitude tempered by reason and piety and (2) the passive and 'better fortitude' of patience. Both of these norms were traditional heroic virtues, and heroic poetry had celebrated them as such. The first, exemplified in '*pius*' Aeneas, had long been a standard pattern for the heroes of Renaissance epic. Tasso's Godfrey, warring against the infidel, and the various champions of *The Faerie Queene*, fighting against personified vices, were notable examples. But there were also numerous less eminent parallels. Trissino's epic delineates a struggle between orthodoxy and heresy; Belisarius wars to deliver Italy from the yoke of the Arian Goths. Graziani's *Conquest of Granada* portrays a Christian victory over the Moors. The *Lusiads* celebrates a triumph of Catholic Europe over pagan Asia. The pattern of a holy war underlies most of the chivalric romances and even the romantic epics of Boiardo and Ariosto. Milton's projected epics on

[1] Cf. Tasso, i. 108–9.

Arthur and Alfred would probably have presented a similar pattern of 'a Christian hero'—the formula of valour conjoined with piety in a crusade against the pagan invader, whether Saxon or Dane.

The ideal of patience, in turn, was by no means a stranger to classical and Renaissance epic. The *Odyssey*, the *Aeneid*, and the *Gerusalemme Liberata* stressed the sufferings, as well as the actions, of their heroes. Primarily, however, this ideal had been personified by the hero of the 'divine' epic composed by no less a bard than the Holy Spirit—the Book of Job.[1] The two species of 'virtuous' fortitude, which Milton juxtaposes to the false and 'vicious' fortitude, were conventional epic formulae. Once again, his originality manifests itself not so much in the particular moral values he proposes to imitate, as in the techniques he utilizes in presenting them.

Both of these patterns, moreover, had been anticipated earlier in Milton's *Reason of Church Government*. The well-established formula of piety-plus-valour had been exemplified in 'the deeds and triumphs of just and pious nations doing valiantly through faith against the enemies of Christ'. The 'victorious agonies of martyrs and saints', on the other hand, represented the alternative formula—the pattern of heroic patience and the 'better fortitude' of suffering and martyrdom.[2] Both these patterns were appropriate for the

---

[1] Patience, as Milton defines it in the *De Doctrina* (Book II, Chapter 10) consists in 'the endurance of misfortunes and injuries'. Its opposites are 'impatience and an effeminate spirit', a 'hypocritical patience', and 'stoical apathy'. Milton cites the example of Job to demonstrate that 'sensibility to pain, and even lamentations, are not inconsistent with true patience . . .'. But patience is also one of the 'devout affections' pertaining to the worship of God (Book II, Chapter 3). In this sense Milton defines it as 'that whereby we acquiesce in the promises of God, through a confident reliance on his divine providence, power, and goodness, and bear inevitable evils with equanimity, as the dispensation of the supreme Father and sent for our good'. Its opposite is 'impatience under the divine decrees; a temptation to which the saints themselves are at times liable'.

[2] According to the *De Doctrina* (Book II, Chapter 6), the 'duty of making a consistent, and, when necessary, an open profession of [God's] true worship' becomes 'martyrdom' when 'it leads to death, or imprisonment, or torments, or disgrace'. The opposites of martyrdom are 'concealment of our religion', 'apostasy', and 'unseasonable profession'. Generally it is 'through the means of martyrdom that the gospel is more extensively promulgated', and it is one of 'the means by which the name of God is hallowed in word'.

heroic poem, a genre committed to 'Heroum laudes imitandaque gesta'.

Samson illustrates both modes of fortitude. For the greater part of the drama, his 'labours' (as the Chorus rightly points out) are those of the 'mind'. Until the final, valiant denouement of his tragedy, he conforms essentially to the type of the suffering hero. Though the play culminates in a 'tryal' of physical 'strength' and a physical victory over the Philistines, it primarily portrays a psychological ordeal—the trial of the hero's spiritual fortitude, patience, and faith—and his moral victory over the enemy within. The internal context precedes the external. Samson is a contender—an *agonistes*—in a dual sense, spiritual as well as physical. Indeed, he displays a nobler fortitude in his 'race of shame' than in his 'race of glory'.

In his final triumph, however, as in his exploits before his downfall, he exemplifies the alternative fortitude—the formula of pious valour defeating the enemies of the true faith. What chiefly distinguishes the virtuous fortitude from its vicious counterpart is the quality of piety. Samson's strength stands in striking contrast to that of the Biblical giants not merely in degree, but primarily in its subservience to the divine will and in its acknowledged dependence on God. By the formula of 'might' alone, his strength is greater (and hence, by definition, more 'heroic'); but its effectiveness is largely contingent on its moral and religious dedication, its consecration to the divine purpose. It is granted him only in his capacity as God's agent and 'minister', and when he forgets its origin and purpose it fails him. The passages in the drama which extol his superlative force also emphasize the more essential fact that he owes his strength entirely to God. His is a *'celestial* vigour'.

Paradise Lost sometimes unites the two modes of *fortezza* in the same person, sometimes presents them separately. Though the formula of active valour underlies the Son's military victory over the angelic rebels, his ministry of redemption exemplifies the alternative fortitude of patience; from his example Adam learns that 'suffering for Truths sake Is fortitude to highest victory'. These are, however, two distinct patterns of fortitude, and Milton takes pains to emphasize their difference.

The same moral antithesis appears in the angelic hymn which contrasts Messiah's military victory over the giant angels with his ministry of redemption:

> . . . thou that day
> Thy Fathers dreadful Thunder didst not spare. . . .
> Back from pursuit thy Powers with loud acclaime
> Thee only extold, Son of thy Fathers might,
> To execute fierce vengeance on his foes,
> Not so on Man. . . .
> He to appease thy wrauth, . . . offerd himself to die
> For mans offence.

The Son's 'works of peace' surpass his military exploits, and Milton takes pains to emphasize this dichotomy in both *Paradise Lost* and *Paradise Regain'd*. Messiah's voluntary sacrifice for mankind involves a nobler fortitude than his victorious warfare in Heaven, just as his creation of the world constitutes a greater achievement than his triumph in battle. Even in extolling the formula of pious valour, the poet carefully points out its limitations, and in the angelic hymn celebrating the creation he criticizes destructive valour as as an inferior ideal:

> Great are thy works, *Jehovah*, infinite
> Thy power . . .; greater now in thy return
> Then from the Giant Angels; thee that day
> Thy Thunders magnifi'd; but to create
> Is greater then created to destroy.

Messiah's victory over the rebels had exhibited the violent, destructive aspect of divine power. His act of creation reveals the same divine 'might' and 'Omnipotence' in its constructive phase:

> Who seekes
> To lessen thee, against his purpose serves
> To manifest the more thy might; his evil
> Thou usest, and from thence creat'st more good.
> Witness this new-made World, another Heav'n. . . .

By stressing the contrasts between works of peace and

exploits of war, between creative power and destructive
violence, Milton further 'degrades' the type of fortitude
traditional in epic poetry.

III

The paradox of strength in apparent weakness was one of
Milton's most deeply cherished convictions. It was a recurrent theme in his prose and poetry throughout his life, and it
held for him both personal and political implications. The
Pauline text ('God hath chosen the weak things of the world
to confound the things which are mighty') underlies his
views on the relationship between secular and spiritual
power. It is the basis for his assertion, in the *De Doctrina*,
that 'the pre-eminent excellency of Christ's kingdom over
all others' is manifested in the fact that 'he governs not the
bodies of men alone, . . . but their minds and consciences,
and that not by force and fleshly weapons, but by what the
world esteems the weakest of all instruments'.[1] It is by
'weakness' that the hero of his later epic 'shall o'recome
Satanic strength'. This is the formula he embodies in
Abdiel, in Enoch and Noah, in the Christian saints, and in
Christ himself.

How deeply and intensely he believed it is most evident
in its application to his own personal disabilities. In the
paradox of spiritual strength in physical weakness he finds
the inner meaning of his own predicament. In his blindness,
he takes the Pauline text ('My strength is made perfect in
weakness') as a personal motto and inscribes the Greek
words ἐν ἀσθενείᾳ τελειοῦμαι in two different autograph
albums in 1651 and 1656.[2] The full significance of this motto
is evident only in the fuller context of the Biblical passage:
'And he said unto me, My grace is sufficient for thee; for my
strength is made perfect in weakness. Most gladly therefore
will I rather glory in my infirmities, that the power of Christ
may rest upon me. Therefore I take pleasure in infirmities,

[1] Cf. *De Doctrina*, Book I, Chapter 15; cf. Yale Prose, i. 525, and Columbia
Edition, vi. 22.
[2] Columbia Edition, xviii. 271.

in reproaches, in necessities, in persecutions, in distresses for Christ's sake: for when I am weak, then I am strong.' In the *Second Defence* the same text underlies his treatment of the paradox between his physical weakness and the 'solace and the strength which have been infused into [him] from above'.[1]

The resolution of the paradox of strength in weakness lies in the distinction between acquired and infused virtues and in the decisive role of divine grace ('My grace is sufficient for thee'). The martyr's frailty is buttressed by divine power; his weakness is sustained by a strength infused by God.[2] All that is demanded of him is the acknowledgement of his frailty and a complete trust in providence. Like the fortitude of active valour, the better fortitude of patience hinges upon an exemplary faith. A heroism of trust (*fiducia*) underlies action and suffering alike, and both formulae are in reality the dual modes of a heroic piety.

Both modes of fortitude, however, have their false counterparts or idols. As, by definition, virtue cannot be dissociated from prudence, an irrational valour or patience is not true fortitude, but a counterfeit resemblance—an apparent virtue, perhaps, but in actuality a vice. The idol of the active fortitude is a brute violence divorced from reason and piety. The passive fortitude has likewise its spurious and specious counterpart—an illusory patience. True patience, as Milton defines it, is either 'the endurance of misfortunes and injuries', or else 'that whereby we acquiesce in the promise of God, through a confident reliance on his divine providence, power, and goodness, and bear inevitable evils with equanimity, as the dispensation of the supreme Father, and sent for our good'.[3] One would scarcely expect to find this pattern in the angelic rebels, and indeed Milton goes out of his way to emphasize their failure to achieve it. A fortitude incapable of enduring pain is a self-contradiction, even in Aristotelian terms, and Milton underlines the contradiction by attributing it to the powerful Nisroc:

[1] Ibid. viii. 73.
[2] Cf. *Paradise Lost*, xi. 138, 'strength added from above'
[3] Cf. *De Doctrina*, Book II, Chapters 3, 10.

> . . . for what availes
> Valour or strength, though matchless, quelld with pain
> Which all subdues, and makes remiss the hands
> Of Mightiest. . . . [P]ain is perfect miserie, the worst
> Of evils, and excessive, overturnes
> All patience.

Yet pain is the inescapable fact the rebel legions must face after their expulsion. Confronted with the necessity of adapting themselves to the conditions of their new environment, Satan and his companions meet the torments and ignominy of Hell with apparent fortitude, but not with true patience. Though their suffering is the merited reward of sin, it does not—cannot—induce repentance. The shame which ultimately proves the bitterest penalty of their transgression is altogether different in kind from the reproach which the martyr endures. The one is merited ignominy, shame in the eyes of God. The martyr's ignominy, on the other hand, is shameful only in the eyes of the world. Though he incurs the world's contempt and scorn, the persecuted witness to truth is rewarded with Heaven's praise.

Satan's opening speech presents what appears to be an admirable display of heroic fortitude. It seems to portray a strength of will triumphant over external force and all adversity, a strength of mind unmoved by outward violence:

> . . . so much the stronger provd
> He with his Thunder: and till then who knew
> The force of those dire Arms? yet not for those
> Nor what the Potent Victor in his rage
> Can else inflict do I repent or change,
> Though chang'd in outward lustre; that fixt mind
> And high disdain, from sence of injur'd merit,
> That with the mightiest rais'd me to contend. . . .

The moral reality behind this heroic vaunt, however, is not patient indifference to violence, but an obdurate refusal to acknowledge his guilt and repent. What appears to be firmness of mind is in actuality the obstinacy of the unregenerate sinner, the resolution of the hardened criminal. The martyr's patience is based on faith and hope; Satan's resolution is founded on the diametric opposite, on despair. The saint suffers in the cause of truth, the devil in upholding a lie.

Despair likewise underlies Beëlzebub's travesty of patient fortitude:

> But what if he our Conquerour . . .
> Have left us this our spirit and strength intire
> Strongly to suffer and support our pains,
> That we may so suffice his vengeful ire,
> Or do him mightier service as his thralls . . .?

Belial's concept of patience, on the other hand, involves hope—but a hope that is illusory and vain. He scoffs at the failure of the active fortitude to adapt itself to adversity:

> To suffer as to doe,
> Our strength is equal. . . .
> I laugh, when those who at the Spear are bold
> And vent'rous, if that fail them, shrink and fear
> What yet they know must follow, to endure
> Exile, or ignominy, or bonds, or pain,
> The sentence of thir Conquerour: This is now
> Our doom; which if we can sustain and bear,
> Our Supream Foe in time may much remit
> His anger. . . .

This appeal for patient fortitude—by the personification of *luxuria*—is patently absurd. Nor do the consolations of philosophy produce true patience; they serve merely as an anodyne. The terms in which Milton describes the devil's philosophical reflections are reminiscent of that hardening of heart which characterizes the reprobate.

In *Paradise Regain'd* the basic pattern underlying the hero's intellectual ordeal is that of a steady progression—a rational and moral evolution—towards the norm of heroic patience. The chief heroic norm that the Messiah must exemplify in his ministry is that of the martyr 'suffering for Truths sake'—the image of the Suffering Servant—and in the course of his temptation he systematically rejects the means and objectives that would be inconsistent with this ideal. As this is an altogether different mode of fortitude from the active valour he had displayed in repulsing the rebel angels, it is hardly surprising that his true identity eludes his Antagonist:

> His first-begot we know, and sore have felt,
> When his fierce thunder drove us to the deep;
> Who this is we must learn, for man he seems
> In all his lineaments, though in his face
> The glimpses of his Fathers glory shine.

On the former occasion the Son had triumphed through incomparable might. This time he is to conquer through patience and apparent weakness.

The paradox of strength in weakness is so closely interwoven with the formula of patient fortitude as to be virtually inseparable. Its obverse is the paradox of weakness in strength, whereby—in both of his epics as well as in his tragedy—Milton degrades the *fortezza* pattern. Satan's might is providentially exposed as 'light' and 'weak'. Zephon asserts the actual frailty of the strength dedicated to evil:

> Thy fear . . .
> Will save us trial what the least can doe
> Single against thee wicked, and thence weak.

And Samson likewise acknowledges that 'All wickedness is weakness'.

The evil fortitude relies on its own strength and is therefore intrinsically weak. The patient fortitude, cognizant of its own frailty, relies on the power and providence of God, and is therefore strong. For it is the method of God's providence to accomplish his purpose by what appear to be the weakest of instruments:

> . . . by small
> Accomplishing great things, by things deemd weak
> Subverting worldly strong, and worldly wise
> By simply meek. . . .

This, among other reasons, is why the Christ of *Paradise Regain'd* rejects the strength and wisdom of the world. He does not need them. Through his complete dependence on providence and the divine will, his frailty is stronger than the Parthian armies and wiser than the philosophy of the Greeks.

IV

Of the conventional formulae, Milton explicitly singles out only one—military fortitude—as the traditional heroic standard. 'Might' has been mislabelled 'Valor' and 'Heroic Vertue', and the truly heroic modes of fortitude have been neglected. Nevertheless, this accusation is an overstatement. For all its prominence, *fortezza* was not the only ideal his predecessors had celebrated heroically. There were, as we have seen, many others—prudence, love, temperance, and the 'politic virtues' of the leader. In thus overstressing the importance of the *fortezza* formula in previous epics, Milton was obviously unjust to such poets as Virgil, Tasso, Vida, and Spenser; but for his own poem this over-simplification possessed several distinct advantages. By emphasizing the weakest point in the epic tradition, it made his moral condemnation of his predecessors all the more forceful. It accentuated the novelty of his own epic subject and the greater excellence of the ideal of the Suffering Servant as a heroic norm. It provided him with a fulcrum for displacing the conventional epic subject—the argument of wars—and substituting an argument centred upon the crisis of moral choice. It gave rational justification for his breach with epic theory and practice in discarding physical combat for the theme of moral struggle—the 'temptation-motif'. In these respects, his oversimplification was a useful rhetorical aid. It exalted his own heroic poem over those of his precursors by demonstrating that *Paradise Lost* came closer than the *Iliad*, the *Odyssey*, the *Aeneid*, and other examples of its genre, to meeting the end of the epic—the delineation of heroic virtue.

But it also reflected his strong opposition to the use of force in ecclesiastical causes. The conventional argument of Christian epic was a holy war against the heretic or the infidel, and its characteristic formula was that of piety-plus-valour. Milton himself had extolled the poet's abilities to celebrate 'the deeds and triumphs of just and pious nations doing valiantly through faith against the enemies of Christ'. But essentially the ideal mode of Christian warfare is not physical, but spiritual, and in *A Treatise of Civil Power* he insists that Christ's 'spiritual kingdom' is 'able without worldly force to subdue all the powers and kingdoms of this world, which are upheld by outward force only'. Quoting the Pauline text, 'we do not warre after the flesh: for the weapons of our warfare are not carnal; but mightie through God to the pulling down of strong holds', Milton interprets it as evidence of 'how allsufficient [Christ's spiritual power] is, how powerful to reach the conscience and the inward man with whom it chiefly deals and whom no power els can deal with. In comparison of which as it is here thus magnificently describ'd, how uneffectual and weak is outward force with all her boistrous tooles. . . .' And he condemns the proponents of 'fleshlie force . . .: who think the gospel, which both began and spread over the whole world for above three hundred years under heathen and persecuting emperors, cannot stand or continue, supported by the same divine presence and protection to the worlds end . . .'.[1] Similarly, in *Of Reformation*, he censures those who believe that the church 'cannot subsist without clasping about the Elme of worldly strength and felicity, as if the heavenly City could not support it selfe without the props and buttresses of secular Authoritie'.[2] These arguments—primarily directed against the use of temporal power to enforce spiritual authority within the Christian commonwealth—are also valid for the 'holy war'. The gospel is propagated primarily by 'witnesses' to the truth, rather than by arms. For the growth and welfare of the church, the spiritual struggle of truth against falsehood is more significant than the physical combat between Christian warriors and the armies of infidels or heretics. Milton's attack on the *fortezza* formula is rooted in its actual irrelevance to the pattern of Christian warfare. The deeds of peace are more beneficial, more excellent—and hence more truly heroic—than those of military valour. The martyr's 'unresistible *might* of *Weaknesse*' can 'shak[e] the *Powers* of *Darknesse*'.

[1] Columbia Edition, vi. 23.   [2] Ibid. iii. 23.

III

The Critique of Sapience

MILTON did not limit his indictment to fortitude. Though this was, indeed, his primary target—the only formula he *explicitly* attacked as falsely heroic—he implicitly condemned other conventional norms. As in the case of *fortezza*, he contrasted the specious prudence with the real, the vain wisdom with the valid, the false love with the true, the evil leadership with the good, the hubristic magnanimity with the virtuous, and the apparent constancy of the reprobate with the true steadfastness of the saint.

In criticizing these patterns, he utilized the same techniques as in revaluing the ideal of fortitude. He exposed their fallacies by dissociating them from piety and associating them with evil persons or acts. He discriminated between specious appearance and moral reality, virtuous and vicious modes. He reduced them to their proper dimensions by weighing the merits of the creature against those of the Creator and contrasting their human or angelic prototypes with their divine archetypes.

I

The formula of 'heroic wisdom' (or 'heroic prudence')[1] occupies a central position in all three of the major poems.[2]

[1] Cf. Aristotle, *Ethica Nicomachaea*, tr. W. D. Ross, in *The Basic Works of Aristotle*, ed. Richard McKeon (New York, 1941), pp. 1022–9, for the distinction between prudence and wisdom in terms of practice or theory; the one is concerned with variable or temporal objects, the other with invariable or eternal. According to Milton's *De Doctrina* (Book II, Chapter 2), *prudentia* is 'that virtue by which we discern what is proper to be done under the various circumstances of time and place'. By *sapientia* 'we earnestly search after the will of God, learn it with all diligence, and govern all our actions according to its rule'. In his poetry Milton frequently blurs the distinction between these two intellectual virtues and sometimes employs the term 'wisdom' for both.

Notes 1 and 2 continued overleaf

The plot of *Paradise Lost* hinges on the Tree of Knowledge and its epistemological and moral implications for man's reason and will. In *Paradise Regain'd* the hero vanquishes his antagonist's 'hellish wiles' by 'wisdom'. In *Samson Agonistes* the Biblical Hercules outstrips his classical predecessor through the more arduous labours of the mind. Wrestling with his own tormenting thoughts and countering the doubts and persuasions of friend and foe alike, he achieves a true understanding of his own nature and a clearer insight into the essential nature of misery and servitude, blindness and deliverance.

In presenting this ideal, Milton placed primary emphasis on the disproportion between divine and human sapience, the contrast between the Father's Providence and the foresight (*providentia*) of men and angels. But he also stressed other distinctions—the antithesis between right reason and folly, sound logic and specious sophistry, truth and falsehood, prudence and guile, knowledge and opinion, the fallibility of human reason in comparison with revelation and faith. In short, he reduced the *sapientia* formula to the opposition between the 'wisdom of God' and the 'wisdom of the world'.

Ulysses' moral ambiguity made him the leading classical exemplar of this pattern in both good and evil aspects. Though he was commonly regarded as the ideal prototype of heroic wisdom and prudence, several critics denied his claim to these intellectual virtues. Dante consigned him to Hell as a type of fraud, and in Beni's opinion he exemplified subtlety and guile instead of true sapience. Milton

---

In this study it seems preferable to avoid drawing too sharp a distinction between them. Cf. *Of Education* on the 'end' of learning—'to repair the ruins of our first parents by regaining to know God aright, and out of that knowledge to love him, to imitate him, to be like him', etc. See also Tasso's *Discorsi del Poema Eroico* for a discussion of 'eroica prudenza'.

[2] For Renaissance conceptions of *sapientia* and other intellectual virtues, see Eugene F. Rice, Jr., *The Renaissance Idea of Wisdom* (Cambridge, Mass., 1958); Howard Schultz, *Milton and Forbidden Knowledge* (New York, 1955); Paul Oskar Kristeller, *Renaissance Thought: The Classic, Scholastic, and Humanist Strains* (New York, 1961); Ernst Cassirer, *The Individual and the Cosmos in Renaissance Philosophy*, tr. Mario Domandi (New York, 1964); Hiram Haydn, *The Counter-Renaissance* (New York, 1950). For Milton's use of the *sapientia* formula, see Arnold Stein, *Heroic Knowledge: An Interpretation of 'Paradise Regained' and 'Samson Agonistes'* (Minneapolis, 1957).

follows both schools and treats the Ulysses-myth as an *exemplum* of both right reason and fraud; he exploits the pejorative interpretation for his presentation of Satan,[1] but draws on more favourable conceptions of Odysseus for the Dalila episode in *Samson Agonistes*.

As in the case of *fortezza*, he makes piety his touchstone in distinguishing between true heroic virtue and its counterfeit resemblance. Dissociated from true religion and the will of God, the intellectual virtues, like the moral, become mere shadows of themselves. Milton accentuates their delusive character by ascribing them to demons.

The philosophical discussions of the fallen angels exhibit the appearance rather than the reality of speculative wisdom. Their arguments on the common themes of metaphysics and ethics lead nowhere, and the 'wandering mazes' in which they lose themselves are emblematic of the intellectual effects of the fall. Darkened by sin, reason can no longer attain a clear vision of the truth; like the 'darkness visible' of Hell itself, it merely illuminates their spiritual death. Their theorizing is, in fact, the infernal archetype of the spurious 'wisdom of the world', and as such it is merely 'Vain wisdom . . . and false Philosophie'. The problems they consider—Providence, fate, good and evil, happiness and misery—would subsequently engage the Gentile philosophers with similar results. Such questions exceed the capacity of the fallen intellect, human and angelic alike; their true solution lies less in philosophy than in theology. The demons' hopeless attempt to solve these problems is at once the effect and symptom of their fallen condition.

Hell likewise establishes the archetype of false prudence. In the angelic war and in his enterprise against man Satan displays, like Ulysses, a practical wisdom that turns out to be little more than cunning. As the ends at which he aims are contrary both to piety and to right reason, his claims to 'heroic prudence', like his pretence to 'heroic fortitude', are illusory. He may seem an exemplar of prudence, but he is merely the 'artificer of fraud'.

[1] See my 'Satan's Metamorphoses and the Heroic Convention of the Ignoble Disguise', *Modern Language Review*, lii (1957), pp. 81–85.

Cleverness and guile, as both Milton and Aristotle were aware, may resemble prudence, but the likeness is purely deceptive—sometimes deliberately deceptive. Thus, according to Milton's *Eikonoklastes*, Charles I had disguised his fraud as prudence.[1]

> *What providence deny'd to force*, he thought *it might grant* to fraud, which he stiles *Prudence*: But Providence was not couzen'd with disguises, neither outward nor inward.

Aristotle had drawn a similar distinction between prudence and mere cleverness. The one is a true virtue, but the other is merely an apparent virtue and may even be a vice:[2] 'There is a faculty which is called cleverness; and this is such as to be able to do the things that tend towards the mark we have set before ourselves, and to hit it. Now if the mark be noble, the cleverness is laudable, but if the mark be bad, the cleverness is mere smartness; hence we call even men of practical wisdom [prudence] clever or smart. . . .'

Milton applies the epithet 'prudent' to Satan once only (ii. 468), and the context is revealing. The Archfiend adjourns the conclave before any of his fellows can volunteer to accompany him on his expedition and thus deprive him of exclusive glory. By a series of ingenious disguises, admirably adapted to the circumstances of time and place, he obtains not only the additional information essential for his purpose, but also the means for accomplishing it.

The idol of true prudence, he is also the archetype of fraud, and the opening books of the epic fix his real character both by description and by explicit statement. In his first address to his troops, he openly states his preference for a strategy of guile:

> our better part remains
> To work in close design, by fraud or guile
> What force affected not. . . .

Subsequently, in promulgating his 'bold design' through his mouthpiece Beëlzebub, he proposes to overcome man either

---

[1] Yale Prose, iii. 545.   [2] *Basic Works*, p. 1035.

by 'force' or by 'suttlety'. His encounter with Sin and Death demonstrates his ability to tack with the wind and adapt his tone and policy to the situation. Learning his blood-relationship with his jailers, the 'suttle Fiend' instantly masters 'his lore' and promptly alters his manner from harsh hostility to a 'milder' and 'smoother' tone. Having just denounced them as a 'Sight . . . detestable', he now greets them as his 'Dear Daughter' and 'fair Son, . . . the dear pledge of dalliance', and bribes them to release him by offering 'ease' and 'prey' on earth.

It is Satan's parliamentary manœuvre to enhance his own reputation that Milton describes as 'Prudent'—not his proposed enterprise against God and man. His strategy of revenge, even though successful, cannot attain any true good and can only incur deeper damnation and harsher penalties. In evolving it and bringing it to a seemingly victorious conclusion, he relies primarily on subtlety and guile—not on 'true prudence'.

He is equally subtle as parliamentarian, as diplomatist and as spy. The infernal council demonstrates his skill in political manipulation; he phrases the terms of debate in such a way that his followers eventually welcome the very different scheme he had already planned in advance. His journey through Chaos proves his skill in forming strategic alliances with potential friends or enemies—with Sin and Death and the rulers of the Abyss—and in enlisting their aid in his designs. By winning over the custodians of Hell-gate with promises of spoil and dominion, he escapes his infernal prison. By offering to restore Chaos's empire, he wins the Anarch's favour and learns the route to the newly created world.

To elicit further information from Uriel, he chooses the disguise and the pretext most appropriate to the occasion—the mask of a 'stripling Cherube' inspired with an 'Unspeakable desire to see, and know' God's 'wondrous works'. By thus counterfeiting religion as a cloak for his intelligence-activities, he becomes the first exemplar of 'Hypocrisie, the only evil that walks Invisible', and entrenches himself all the more deeply in his role of 'false dissembler' and 'fraudulent

Impostor'. The same traits appear in his attempt to conceal the violent passions which expose his disguise.

In choosing the serpent as the fittest instrument for his design, he gives additional proof of his ability to adapt his disguise to the occasion. At the same time he demonstrates how deeply he has identified himself with the ethos of the fraudulent dissembler. The very qualities that make the 'suttlest Beast of the Field' the 'fittest Imp of fraud' and the 'Most opportune' tool to 'serve his Wiles' are the traits which have become most characteristic of Satan himself. There is a moral affinity between the 'wilie Snake' and the 'Diabolic power' which possesses it; the serpent not only serves as Satan's instrument, but also provides a concrete symbol of his character. He chooses it because its 'native suttletie' resembles his own, and in the end it becomes the spiritual form or hieroglyph of his own guile.

In the war in Heaven Satan pursues a strategy of violence; nevertheless he also resorts to guile in plotting his rebellion, in seducing his followers, and in deploying his artillery. Withdrawing his troops under a pretended 'command' to 'prepare Fit entertainment to receive our King The great *Messiah*', he persuades them to active revolt by means of specious arguments and the 'calumnious Art of counterfeted truth'—and thus draws a third part of the heavenly host 'into fraud'. In bringing his cannons into play he conceals the 'devilish Enginrie' with 'shaddowing Squadrons Deep, To hide the fraud'. A 'liar from the beginning', he demonstrates even in Heaven the qualities of subtlety and guile that subsequently dominate his actions in Hell and on earth.

The same ethos governs his strategy in *Paradise Regain'd* where he attempts to overcome his adversary not by 'force', but by 'well couch't fraud, well woven snares'. 'Girded with snaky wiles', he tempts the Messiah with 'all guile', with 'utmost subtilty', and with 'great cunning'. 'Compos'd of lyes', the author of 'Delusions' displays his 'craft' in 'mixing somewhat true to vent more lyes'.

II

To some critics, Satan's techniques of deception have seemed an arbitrary 'degradation' of his character.[1] In their opinion the ruses and disguises he employs in executing his enterprise contradict the heroic image Milton had presented in the first two books. Yet, in fact, this alleged inconsistency between the heroic Satan and the fraudulent impostor is largely imaginary. From start to finish the poet consistently represents the Adversary in terms of the false-heroic, and this heroic *eidolon* is finally shattered only by the sudden intrusion of divine judgement in Book X. Up to this point there is nothing in his characterization that violates the pseudo-heroic pattern; in the intervening books he embodies essentially the same epic formulae as in Books I and II.

The devil's decision to direct his hostilities against man rather than risk another battle against God actually occurs as early as the first book. In his first formal address to his army he indicates his preference for 'close design' and 'fraud'. At the conclusion of the infernal council he has definitely committed himself to a policy of attacking earth's frail inhabitants rather than the stronger forces in Heaven. Though he has not yet fully decided whether to destroy the world by 'force' or seduce its rulers by 'suttlety', he makes this decision very soon after entering the garden of Eden and overhearing the special conditions of man's tenure:

> One fatal Tree there stands of Knowledge call'd,
> Forbidden them to taste. . . . Hence I will excite their minds
> With more desire to know, and to reject
> Envious commands, invented with designe
> To keep them low whom knowledge might exalt
> Equal with Gods. . . .

His choice of fraud[2] over force on this occasion is hardly a

---

[1] Cf. A. J. A. Waldock, *Paradise Lost and Its Critics* (Cambridge, 1947), p. 65; John Peter, *A Critique of Paradise Lost* (New York, 1960), p. 46.

[2] Satan could not, of course, have destroyed Adam by force, as the Biblical account depicts man's ruin through fraud. Milton must, however, make the events of the narrative—derived from Scripture—seem both 'probable' and 'consistent' with the character of the principal figures in the fall: Satan, Adam,

symptom of degradation; it is simply the more rational of the two alternatives he has already defined in the infernal conclave. He prefers to operate by subtlety rather than by violence because the former offers him the most expedient means of success. His tactics of fraud are the corollary of decisions already made in Books I and II; and all of his subsequent lies, ruses, and disguises follow logically and almost inevitably from these tactics. They are quite consistent with the character established in the earlier books. The subtlety and guile he exhibits in the temptation of man are the same traits he had displayed in Pandaemonium, at Hellgate, in his journey through the Abyss, and his interview with Uriel.

Just as there is no fundamental ethical inconsistency between the Satan of the early books and the Satan of the middle and final sections of *Paradise Lost*, neither is there any inherent contradiction in Milton's delineation of the false-heroic. How closely Satan's character resembles that of Ulysses is evident in the traditional application of the same adjective—'*callidus*' or 'subtle'—to both the Ithacan hero and the serpent of Genesis iii. Their ethical similarity, in turn, gives additional point to the similarities between their exploits. Superficially at least, the techniques of deception Milton's pseudo-hero employs in fulfilling his designs resemble those of the wily Greek. Both are masters of the art of dissembling, virtuosos of the *ars mentiendi*. Like Ulysses, he skilfully adapts his speech, tone, and arguments to the demands of each particular occasion. Like Ulysses, he resorts to tactical disguises—sometimes ignominious disguises —in order to acquire military intelligence and to accomplish his enterprise. His voyage through space invites comparison with the Ithacan's voyages. Like Ulysses, he takes the enemy's citadel by fraud. Both in character and in action he conforms to a conventional heroic formula, and—far from finding his tactics unheroic—he boasts about them: 'Him [man] by fraud I have seduc't From his Creator, and the more to increase Your wonder, with an Apple.'

Eve. Only in this way could he meet the demands of Renaissance epic theory. He must make Satan *choose* the tactics of fraud rather than force, and he must motivate this choice in terms of Satan's character.

In actuality, the same fundamental ambiguity underlay Satan's tactics of fraud and his tactics of force. Both were consistent with the norm of the warrior, but in a purely ethical context both seemed inherently evil. Both were conventional methods of prosecuting a military campaign, and epic tradition had celebrated them as such. But, once divorced from piety and deployed against the divine will, both became vicious. A Gentile poet might acclaim Ulysses' wiles and Achilles' violence; for a Christian, they did not merit praise, but shame. The 'virtues' of the Homeric heroes could serve equally well as the vices of the criminal—or the devil.

Milton maintains this basic ambiguity consistently throughout the poem. Sustaining the heroic pretence from the opening scene until the triumphant return to Pandaemonium, he invests his devil with a variant of the *prudentia* formula that *looks* like heroic prudence, but is actually diabolical fraud. Not until divine Providence intervenes and transforms Satan and his companions into serpents—the conventional symbol of guile—does the poet finally expose the heroic idol as bestial vice. He dispels the shadow in the light of moral reality, the illusion by divine truth.

For Satan's guile is only one pole of Milton's poetic axis; it derives its full significance only from contrast with its opposite. As the false image of *prudentia*, it must be brought face to face with its contraries—with right reason in unfallen man and angel, with the faith of the regenerate, and with the wisdom of divine Providence. At the very moment of rebellion the sophist encounters right reason in Abdiel, whose testimony to the truth rebuts his fallacies. In first tempting Eve, he finds his lies and excuses refuted by the angelic guard. In *Paradise Regain'd* his 'wiles' and sophistries meet their match in his antagonist's superior wisdom—right reason, the Scriptures' divine testimony, and the higher 'knowledge' which 'God reveals'.

III

Underlying the structure of both epics is a clearcut epistemological struggle between Truth and Error, a spiritual war prosecuted on the one side by divine revelation, on the other by infernal sophistry and lies. God reveals, Satan beguiles. God instructs, Satan deceives. Dramatically, this dichotomy finds fullest expression in the antithesis between Messiah, the 'wisdom of God' and the perfect image of the Father, and his Antagonist, the 'Idol of Majestie Divine'. But this epistemological conflict also appears in the devil's encounters with lesser angels and in the divine 'machinery' itself. Abdiel denounces his heresy. Uriel penetrates his disguise. Zephon and Ithuriel frustrate his first assault on Eve. Gabriel exposes his lies and intrinsic weakness and puts him to flight. Raphael counters his temptation with divine instruction. Even after Satan has succeeded in seducing mankind, Michael counters the effects of sin and death by opening Adam's eyes to the future history of the world and the essential principles of the Christian faith.

By thus presenting truth and error as contrasting strategies in an angelic war, Milton gave dramatic force to the logical axiom that truth and falsehood appear more clearly through their opposition. But he was also following a precedent set by other epic poets. Like the moral opposition of contrary virtues and vices, this intellectual antithesis had notable prototypes in the heroic tradition. One of the most common methods of portraying error was to personify it in the figure of an evil enchanter—Ismeno, Sacripant, Hydraort, Armida, Circe, Archimago—who attempts to thwart the heroic enterprise by magical illusions. In Christian epic, such figures are usually infidels—enemies of the true faith who invoke infernal aid to prevent its inevitable victory over their own superstitions. An allied method was to depict demonic inspiration, temptation by an evil spirit or a hostile god. Thus in the *Iliad* Zeus brings disaster to the Greek hosts by sending Agamemnon a lying dream. In the *Aeneid* a Fury possesses Amata, the Latian queen, and thus precipitates the war against the Trojans. In Milton's 'In Quintum Novembris', Satan, disguised as St. Francis, instigates the Gunpowder Plot. In Tasso's *Gerusalemme Liberata* demonic forces inspire and assist the infidels in resisting the First Crusade.

In depicting Satan's techniques of deception, Milton

exploits both of these methods. In *Paradise Lost* the devil assaults Eve's imagination with evil dreams and 'possesses' the serpent's 'brutal sense' to inspire it 'With act intelligential'. These are familiar aspects of demonic inspiration. In *Paradise Regain'd* he utilizes the techniques of Renaissance sorcerers—the magical banquet of elemental spirits, the portents and terrors of the night, and the supernatural vision of the world's kingdoms.

IV

Another method of presenting the conflict of Truth and Error was to embody true and false values in similar, but antithetical figures. For this opposition between reality and its counterfeit resemblance, the Renaissance poet could draw on an extensive literary tradition. The matter of Troy provided both a true and a counterfeit Helen; the woman who precipitated the Trojan war was merely an *eidolon* of the true. If, as the Neo-Platonists maintained, Helen herself symbolized absolute beauty, the false Helen was no more than a spurious imitation of *to kalon*. In *The Tablet of Cebes*, False Education misleads the pilgrim before he eventually encounters True Education. Arthurian romance discriminated between the true Guinevere and a false and magical likeness. In Niccolo d'Agostino's continuation of the *Orlando Furioso* there is a similar antithesis between the true Angelica and the false. Spenser's *Faerie Queene* contrasts the true and false Florimels, and expresses the familiar Protestant dichotomy between the True Church and the False in the rivalry of Una and Fidessa (Duessa).

Paradise Lost exploits this convention in embodying the false and genuine modes of heroism in the two paramount figures, Satan and Christ. In this respect there is a subtle difference between the two epics. Though they portray essentially the same moral and intellectual antitheses, the later poem represents them primarily through a different medium—that of the debate. In *Paradise Regain'd*, Satan *proposes* the false norms and values; in the earlier epic he also *embodies* them.

In both epics the juxtaposition of false and true, of appearance and reality, confronts the principal figures with an intellectual dilemma. Psyche's task[1] of discriminating between good and evil, and distinguishing knowledge from opinion, devolves upon both faithful and unfaithful angels, upon the first man and the first woman, and upon the second Adam as upon the first.

Wisdom is, in fact, the pivotal concept on which both the infernal and the celestial tactics hinge. Satan tempts Eve with a knowledge essentially godlike in quality, a wisdom that seems heroic in its divinity, its excellence, and its daring. God will 'praise [her] dauntless vertue' for risking death in pursuit of 'happier life'. From his first entry into Paradise Satan's plan is to 'excite their minds with more desire to know'. The divine counter-strategy, in turn, centres upon knowledge of a different order. Raphael's revelation warns Adam against his infernal enemy; Michael's revelation gives him the spiritual knowledge essential for ultimate victory. The plot resolves itself into a clearcut struggle between demonic illusion and divine instruction.

This quest for knowledge is skilfully counterpointed in Satan's quest for military intelligence and in the devils' philosophical speculations. Both represent the degradation of the angelic intelligence through sin and spiritual death. Through their alienation from truth and the supreme good, the fallen angels can no longer direct their thought towards its true end and are therefore confined to the labyrinth of their own speculations, the 'wandring mazes' of their fallen understanding. Having renounced perfect knowledge of the highest truth in the Beatific Vision, they can only wander in the murky, inconclusive realm of Opinion, a knowledge as vague and shadowy as the 'darkness visible' of their new abode. As in the case of fallen man, their wisdom is limited to the experience of evil, not to the apprehension of the good.

A similar distortion of the ends of wisdom appears in Satan's quest for military intelligence. From the persons he encounters on his journey—Sin, Chaos, Uriel, and finally

---

[1] Cf. *Areopagitica*, Yale Prose, ii. 514.

Adam and Eve—he seeks and learns only the practical information necessary for prosecuting his scheme of revenge. His interview with Uriel exposes the alienation of the angelic intellect from its true object. By feigning a 'desire to see, and know' God's 'wondrous works'—and 'chiefly Man'—he gains the information that will enable him to destroy mankind. But there is a double irony in this passage. If Satan praises God's creation with the sole design of destroying it, he also unwittingly emphasizes the extent of his own ruin. The abuse of knowledge is the measure of his own exile from the chief good.

Having renounced the knowledge of God—the true end of the creation and the ultimate object of natural history—Satan has automatically cut himself off from any valid knowledge of the world. Ideally, the contemplation of nature should quicken and enhance the love and worship of God;[1] Satan, on the contrary, utilizes it to serve his hatred. Detesting the Creator, but impotent to destroy Him, he directs his vengeance towards the divine image reflected in the creation and expressed most notably, most eminently in man.

Satan's attitude towards the creation is, in fact, marked by sharp contradictions. His first 'sudden view of all this World at once' fills him with 'wonder', but it also arouses 'envy'. While it increases his knowledge of the Creator, it also magnifies his hatred for God and all His works. In the sun he recognizes a hieroglyph of divine majesty, whose glory overshadows that of the angels just as the sun itself darkens the lesser lights. But this analogue of God's dominion merely entrenches him in his crime. Though it brings a fresh recognition of divine supremacy, it also arouses hatred and envy, wrath, and despair—the very passions that had prompted his original rebellion and that now impel him to augment (indeed, to recapitulate) his sin. The sun's divine resemblance hardens him in his revolt against supernal authority and in his refusal to submit. Although the contemplation of nature leads him—correctly—to meditate on God's glory and universal sovereignty, it also strengthens his resolution

[1] Cf. *Of Education*, Yale Prose, ii. 368–9.

to make a second desperate attempt against God the Father's dominion and glory:

> Evil be thou my Good; by thee at least
> Divided Empire with Heav'ns King I hold
> By thee, and more then half perhaps will reigne;
> As Man ere long, and this new World shall know.

In his next encounter with the divine image—this time in its fuller expression in Adam and Eve ('whom my thoughts pursue With wonder, and could love, so lively shines In them Divine resemblance')—Satan, who had once known the Beatific Vision, can still behold the image of God with wonder, and indeed almost with love. He can still contemplate the Creator in the creature. Nevertheless, he neither can nor will direct this recognition to its true end. Against God's image in created man he turns the same destructive intent he had earlier directed against God himself. Even the limited understanding that remains to him in his fallen state he distorts to serve his purpose of revenge.

V

Adam's mode of knowledge before his fall is in many respects diametrically opposite to Satan's. Despite the vast difference between the angel's 'intuitive' reason and man's 'discursive' thought and despite Satan's superiority in range of knowledge and experience, Adam's intellect has not yet suffered spiritual death. Moreover, it has the still greater advantage of orientation towards its proper ends—knowledge of his Creator, his own nature, his moral obligations to both, and his true beatitude. Virtually from the moment of creation he demonstrates his ability to reason from the visible to the invisible, from the creation to the Creator. Besides the knowledge acquired through right reason, he also possesses the higher wisdom of direct revelation.

His first act of consciousness is to recognize his own ignorance ('But who I was, or where, or from what cause, Knew not') and to seek from other creatures the knowledge of his origin, his Creator, and the proper modes of worship.

This early acknowledgement of his derivative nature stands in sharp contrast with Satan's boast of having been self-created, just as his insight into his true happiness contrasts with Satan's alienation from true felicity:

> . . . how came I thus, how here?
> Not of my self; by some great Maker then,
> In goodness and in power praeeminent;
> Tell me, how may I know him, how adore,
> From whom I have that thus I move and live,
> And feel that I am happier then I know.

Divine revelation gives him the essential knowledge that right reason cannot bestow, such as the danger of the tree of knowledge. He knows the nature of the various beasts:[1]

> I nam'd them, as they pass'd, and understood
> Thir Nature, with such knowledg God endu'd
> My sudden apprehension. . . .

In the course of his divine colloquy, face to face with God himself, he acquires, as in a Socratic dialogue, the self-knowledge essential for the discharge of his moral, domestic, and religious duties. He recognizes the metaphysical differences which set him apart from the beasts on the one hand and from God on the other. He realizes his incompleteness in his celibate state. He proves himself 'knowing not of Beasts alone, . . . but of [him]self . . .'.

Rightly used, the contemplation of nature is a means of worship; it heightens both the knowledge and the praise of God. In contrast to Satan, who perverts it from its true end and turns it against the divine glory, the morning prayer of Adam and Eve finds in the creation itself the shadow of divine attributes and a means of divine praise:

> These are thy glorious works Parent of good,
> Almightie, thine this universal Frame,
> Thus wondrous fair; thy self how wondrous then!
> Unspeakable, who sitst above these Heavens

---

[1] Cf. *De Doctrina*, Book I, Chapter 7: 'Certainly without extraordinary wisdom he [Adam] could not have given names to the whole animal creation with such sudden intelligence, Gen. ii. 20.'

To us invisible or dimly seen
In these thy lowest works, yet these declare
Thy goodness beyond thought, and Power Divine. . . .

In Adam's conversation with Raphael the epistemological method is more complex. For the knowledge surpassing his unaided reason, he depends on the divine revelations given him by the angel. Nevertheless, here too one finds a comparable progression from the visible to the invisible, from the particular to the universal, from the contemplation of nature to the principles of metaphysics, ethics, and theology. Here too natural history is directed *ad majorem Dei gloriam*, to the greater glory of God.

Thus it is the most elemental of material data—a rural repast—that provokes a more abstract discourse on angelology and the scale of nature. In inviting the angel to dinner, Adam poses the leading question ('unsavourie food perhaps To spiritual Natures') and contributes the only premiss his limited knowledge allows him ('only this I know, That one Celestial Father gives to all'). Raphael, endowed as he is with superior faculties and experience, then draws the logical conclusion:

Therefore what he gives
(Whose praise be ever sung) to man in part
Spiritual, may of purest Spirits be found
No ingrateful food . . .,

and proceeds to explain the nature of angels—'those pure Intelligential substances'—and their relation to man. When Adam returns to this topic, he again takes as his point of departure the immediate experience of the senses. Even though he is moved by the lofty desire 'to know Of things above his World, and of thir being Who dwell in Heav'n', he nevertheless bases his question on the simple datum of their rustic meal.

The angel's reply properly stresses the true end of *sapientia*. Outlining the progression of human knowledge through the study of nature to the contemplation of God, Raphael touches on metaphysical problems, such as the great chain of being, only to emphasize the limitations of the *condition humaine* and to direct the human reason higher towards a divine end and object. As his pupil recognizes, he has

> . . . taught the way that might direct
> Our knowledge, and the scale of Nature set
> From center to circumference, whereon
> In contemplation of created things
> By steps we may ascend to God.

Though Raphael's account of the angelic war describes events 'which human knowledge could not reach'—'Things above Earthly thought, which yet concerned Our knowing, as to highest wisdom seemd'—the 'Divine Historian' makes his excursion into prehistory largely on ethical grounds. Besides satisfying Adam's curiosity, the revelation contains a moral; the revolt and fall of the angels provides an *exemplum* of the nature and rewards of disobedience. As elsewhere in *Paradise Lost*, Milton places his primary emphasis on the ends and practical uses of wisdom rather than on wisdom for wisdom's sake.

Again, in seeking knowledge of the world's creation, Adam pursues the true end and object of such knowledge— the greater glory of God:

> . . . thou maist unfould
> What wee, not to explore the secrets aske
> Of his Eternal Empire, but the more
> To magnifie his works, the more we know,

and his angelic instructor acknowledges this end:

> Yet what thou canst attain, which best may serve
> To glorifie the Maker, and inferr
> Thee also happier, shall not be withheld. . . .

This scene is the virtuous counterpart of Satan's interview with Uriel. Unfallen man and fallen archangel ask essentially the same question concerning the creation and give substantially the same reasons for asking it. The essential difference lies in their intent. Though both claim to be seeking the glory of God, this is merely a pretext in Satan's case. For Adam, on the other hand, Raphael's discourse does not merely allay his 'thirst . . . of knowledge' and inspire him with 'wonder' and 'delight' at 'Things else by me unsearchable'; it also redounds to the 'glorie' of 'the high Creator'.

Similarly, when Adam inquires about the movements of the heavenly bodies, his interlocutor takes pains to point out the proper end of astronomy:

> . . . for Heav'n
> Is as the Book of God before thee set,
> Wherein to read his wondrous Works, and learne
> His Seasons, Hours, or Days, or Months, or Years. . . .

Science is not an end in itself. The study of nature, like nature itself, is designed to glorify its Creator or to serve man, for whom it had been created. For man, wisdom resolves itself primarily into self-knowledge and the knowledge of God—the practical knowledge which should enable him to know and obey God's will.

Moreover, sapience is relative to the scale of being and the intellectual disparity between the different created orders and the Creator. The limited understanding of Adam, Eve, and Satan emerges with greater clarity through their contrast with one another and with divine wisdom. Eve's sin and the serpent's argument both involve a specious wisdom which violates the scale of nature. She seeks the type of knowledge appropriate to the gods; and the false evidence which persuades her is the serpent's unnatural power of reason and speech, his miraculous exhibition of intellectual capacities proper to man:

> That ye should be as Gods, since I as Man,
> Internal Man, is but proportion meet,
> I of brute human, yee of human Gods.

The end the tempter invokes is paradoxically the goal of happiness, 'what might lead To happier life, knowledge of Good and Evil'. This was not only a familiar *topos* of classical rhetoric, but also a cornerstone of classical ethical theory. Aquinas placed man's highest happiness in contemplation, and, for Greek and Christian ethics alike, beatitude was the final object of virtuous activity. Hence Satan's suggestion that Eve's pursuit of knowledge would demonstrate her 'dauntless vertue' might well seem a valid argument, 'impregn'd With Reason, to her seeming, and with Truth'. Much of the irony of the temptation-scene lies in the incongruity of Eve's pretence to heroic virtue. Though heroic fortitude and heroic wisdom would be appropriate for Adam, formed as he is for 'contemplation' and 'valor', they do not fit the characteristic ethos of his wife, fashioned for 'softness' and 'sweet attractive grace'. These heroic formulae are as unsuitable for Eve as Mars' armour for Venus; they are a charming, but ridiculous breach of decorum.

VI

One of the simplest modes of discrediting the *sapientia* formula was to contrast the creature's limited knowledge with the Creator's omniscience. Eve's folly consists in doubting 'divine testimony' and trusting instead in the evidence of her own senses and the serpent's tale. She prefers the testimony of another creature to that of the Creator himself. Thereupon she heightens her folly by choosing as intellectual 'guides' the 'fallacious' tree and her own experience:

> Experience, next to thee I owe,
> Best guide; not following thee, I had remain
> In ignorance, thou op'nst Wisdoms way,
> And giv'st access, though secret she retire.

At the end of the poem, however, she has learned to rely on Providence as the 'better guide'.

Adam's interviews with the two angels—the 'Divine Historian' and the 'Seer blest'—bring into still sharper focus the finite scope of human wisdom. His supernatural tutors can inform him only of things 'not surpassing human measure'. The very technique of accommodation—adapting 'what surmounts the reach Of human sense' to the limitations of man's mind and 'lik'ning spiritual to corporal forms'—heightens the emphasis on his finite understanding and his need to rely on revelation. His mentors stress how much remains that he does not know and how much of the revelation already vouchsafed must elude his full comprehension. Raphael warns him to keep his 'desire For knowledge within bounds':

> . . . beyond abstain
> To ask, nor let thine own inventions hope
> Things not reveal'd which th' invisible King,
> Onely Omniscient hath supprest in Night,
> To none communicable in Earth or Heaven. . . .

Unless he heeds the natural boundaries of his own intellect ('to know In measure what the mind may well contain') he will fall short of true knowledge and embrace 'Folly', instead of 'Wisdom'.

The problem of celestial motion ('whether Heav'n move or Earth') is irrelevant, and God 'Did wisely to conceal, and not divulge His secrets to be scann'd by them who ought Rather admire . . .'. Man's astronomical disputes and speculations are merely 'quaint Opinions' which merit little more than laughter. Practical wisdom is far more significant for him than the knowledge of the stars and other worlds. The proper study of mankind is man:

> . . . Heav'n is for thee too high
> To know what passes there; be lowlie wise:
> Think onely what concerns thee and thy being;
> Dream not of other Worlds, what Creatures there
> Live, in what state, condition or degree,
> Contented that thus farr hath been reveal'd
> Not of Earth onely, but of highest Heav'n.

Ethical knowledge—practical wisdom—is much more valuable than speculative science, and Adam himself finally accepts the archangel's lesson:

> That not to know at large of things remote
> From use, obscure and suttle, but to know
> That which before us lies in daily life,
> Is the prime Wisdom, what is more, is fume,
> Or emptiness, or fond impertinence,
> And renders us in things that most concerne
> Unpractis'd, unprepar'd, and still to seek.

The revelation of the world's future course and the scheme of salvation leaves him satisfied with his 'fill Of knowledge, what this vessel can containe; Beyond which was my folly to aspire'.

The limitations of human reason even in the state of innocence and the further limitations resulting from the Fall thus reduce the *sapientia* formula to the necessary tenets of faith. They leave little room for theoretical knowledge and restrict the scope of philosophy to practical wisdom. So wide is the gulf between human and divine wisdom that only revelation can bridge it. Man can achieve true wisdom only by submitting his own reason to the guidance of providence and subordinating the intellectual virtues to such moral or theological virtues as patience, obedience, and faith.

Self-knowledge—the insight into one's own nature, its essence, its capacities, its weaknesses, and its obligations—provides the foundation, therefore, both of intellectual humility and of magnanimity. To perform his proper function and offices and to observe his proper end, the rational creature must recognize his peculiar position in the scale of being and the distinctive properties which differentiate him from other creatures—both higher and lower than himself—and from God.

VII

Although Milton's major emphasis falls on the limits of human wisdom, he also stresses the finite knowledge of higher orders. God's secret counsels exceed the comprehension of the angels, and they greet the prophecy of the incarnation with wonder 'what this might mean, & whither tend'. Indeed, they even betray ignorance of details already known to man. Adam's 'Storie' is new and fresh to Raphael, who was 'absent' at the time of man's creation. Moreover, like human reason, the angelic intelligence is fallible. Satan's lies deceive a third part of the heavenly host, and even Uriel fails at first to penetrate his disguise. The limited knowledge of even the highest of rational creatures stands in striking contrast to the infinite wisdom of God.

This antithesis between the creature's limited foresight and the Creator's Providence plays a major role in the structure of Milton's fable. In all three of his major poems, it is the precondition for the *peripeteia*, the 'reversal contrary to expectation'; and in *Paradise Lost* it appears primarily in the conflict between the infernal and celestial strategies. Satan boasts that the foresight acquired by the angelic battle will give him greater advantage in later campaigns:

> Since through experience of this great event
> In Arms not worse, in foresight much advanc't,
> We may with more successful hope resolve
> To wage by force or guile eternal Warr. . . .

His subsequent address to his troops amplifies this point. In the heavenly war they had not foreseen their defeat because they did not know the enemy's full strength. Now, however, they know by experience the relative power of their own forces and those of the foe:

> . . . what power of mind
> Foreseeing or presaging, from the Depth
> Of knowledge past or present, could have fear'd,
> How such united force of Gods, how such
> As stood like these, could ever know repulse?
> . . . But he who reigns
> Monarch of Heav'n . . . still his strength conceal'd,
> Which tempted our attempt and wrought our fall.
> Henceforth his might we know, and know our own. . . .

Unlike God, who beholds past, present, and future in 'one view', Satan can base his prediction of the future only on his knowledge of 'past or present'. His strategy of frustrating Providence 'by fraud or guile' is, therefore, a palpable absurdity doomed to inevitable failure. Attempting to outwit an infinite wisdom—to achieve 'the contrary of [God's] high will' and 'disturb His inmost counsels from their destind aim'—he pits his own subtlety in an impossible and unequal struggle against God's foresight:

> If then his Providence
> Out of our evil seek to bring forth good,
> Our labour must be to pervert that end,
> And out of good still to find means of evil. . . .

Though Belial perceives the futility of trying to deceive divine Providence, he fails to press this point to its logical conclusion. His argument against an assault on God himself ought also to invalidate the alternative scheme—to attack the Creator indirectly through destroying his creation:

> . . . for what can force or guile
> With him, or who deceive his mind, whose eye
> Views all things at one view? he from heav'ns highth
> All these our motions vain, sees and derides;
> Not more Almighty to resist our might
> Then wise to frustrate all our plots and wiles.

Thus Belial himself helps to expose the infernal prudence as an empty illusion.

In the celestial war Satan had denied divine omniscience. Arguing that the first day of battle had disproved God's omnipotence, he maintained that the concept of God's infinite wisdom must likewise be false:

> . . . then fallible, it seems,
> Of future we may deem him, though till now,
> Omniscient thought.

After his defeat the archangel no longer denies divine fore-knowledge, but he nevertheless argues that his own foresight can assure him success in his enterprise against man. Basing his policy on the experience acquired in his earlier warfare, he assumes that divine justice must inevitably destroy man. What he does not foresee is the role of divine mercy. He does not anticipate the covenant of grace. This alone— totally unforeseen by the infernal strategists—is sufficient to forestall the devil's revenge.

With the limited foresight derived from the experience of his own disobedience and its penalty, Satan expects God to punish man just as he had punished the rebellious angels. He foresees the role of divine justice, but does not realize that this will be supplemented by grace. The providential scheme for fallen man differs from that devised for the fallen angels. When God foresees and foretells man's fall, he also 'declares his purpose of grace towards him, in regard he fell not of his own malice, as did *Satan*, but by him seduc't':

The first sort by thir own suggestion fell,
Self-tempted, self-deprav'd: Man falls deceiv'd
By the other first: Man therefore shall find grace,
The other none: in Mercy and Justice both,
Through Heav'n and Earth, so shall my glorie excel,
But Mercy first and last shall brightest shine.

Thus, once again, the formula of heroic wisdom reduces itself essentially to faith. The wise man, recognizing the limitations of his own unaided reason, relies instead on the revealed wisdom of God. Armed with divine testimony, he champions the truth against a host of errors and in spite of violence, persecution, and shame. The *sapientia* formula finds its ideal exemplar in the teacher and the patient witness to truth—the hero of faith and the martyr.

VIII

This pattern appears primarily in the faithful angel Abdiel, in the 'just men' of Old Testament history, in Christ himself, and in the martyrs and teachers of the Christian church. The very paucity of their numbers enhances their heroic eminence. Supporting the truth single-handed against the third part of heaven's host, Abdiel provides an exemplar of heroic faith, constancy, and zeal. His verbal and physical encounter with Satan embodies the epistemological conflict between truth and error—a conflict given historical expression in the struggle between the wisdom of the world and the small sect of true believers armed with the wisdom of God, between the kingdoms of the world and the true church.[1] In the world's eyes the champion of truth seems a heretic and supporter of error. But, even though the world judges him 'perverse', the 'sight of God' affirms the righteousness of his cause. In Abdiel's case we find a dual witness to the truth —both the martyr's testimony to divine verity and God's

[1] Abdiel contrasts his own 'Sect' (which prefers 'Faith . . . and Pietie to God') with Satan's 'World erroneous' (in which the faithful man seems 'to dissent From all'). He foreshadows the role of the Nonconformist 'dissenter' in England as well as the Protestant position against the Church of Rome. His 'open profession' of 'true worship' (*De Doctrina*, Book II, Chapter 6) is consistent with his role as an exemplar of zeal and heroic martyrdom.

own testimony to his servant's fidelity. Abdiel's antagonist, on the other hand, errs without 'end', forever 'from the path of truth remote'.

Enoch likewise conforms to the pattern of heroic teacher and martyr, a solitary witness threatened with violence for his testimony. 'Eminent in wise deport', he is unique in his generation in preaching divine truth,

> The onely righteous in a World perverse,
> And therefore hated, therefore so beset
> With Foes for daring single to be just,
> And utter odious Truth, that God would come
> To judge them with his Saints.

Noah similarly encounters scorn and derision in his solitary testimony to truth in the midst of a perverted world:

> So all shall turn degenerate, all deprav'd,
> Justice and Temperance, Truth and Faith forgot;
> One Man except, the onely Son of light
> In a dark Age, against example good,
> Against allurement, custom, and a World
> Offended; fearless of reproach and scorn,
> Or violence, hee of thir wicked wayes
> Shall them admonish, and before them set
> The paths of righteousness, how much more safe,
> And full of peace, denouncing wrauth to come
> On thir impenitence; and shall returne
> Of them derided, but of God observd
> The one just Man alive. . . .

This pattern of the single just witness to truth reaches its perfection in the example of Jesus and his disciples, preaching the gospel, and in the small Protestant minority persecuted by the world for persevering in 'the worship . . . Of Spirit and Truth'.

IX

In both of Milton's epics the *prudentia–sapientia* formula has strong theological implications. It is one of the hallmarks of the divine image lost by Adam and restored by Christ. Before their transgression Adam and Eve are radiant with the 'image of thir glorious Maker'—'Truth, Wisdome, Sanctitude severe and pure, Severe, but in true filial freedom plac't'. Once they have lost this divine resemblance through sin, they never entirely regain it, although the final books portray its partial restoration in a regenerated Adam.

Adam's long dialogues with the archangels are more than a device inherited from classical epic for relating past and future events beyond the time-limits of the main action. They are also indices of the protagonist's spiritual condition. Much of the felicity of the paradisal state consisted, as theologians observed, in the contemplative life which the first man led before his fall. Milton modifies this tradition slightly by stressing the greater importance of *practical* over theoretical wisdom and by coupling Adam's intellectual activities with the easy labours of a genteel gardener. On the whole, however, Adam's eager inquiries and Raphael's extended explanations represent the author's conscious effort to portray the blessings of the contemplative life and man's intellectual capacities in the state of original innocence. Michael's revelation, on the other hand, is directed towards an intelligence fallen, but partly revivified by supernal grace. Just as Adam's discussion with Raphael exhibits the divine image in its pristine perfection, so the more formal instruction he receives from Michael—preceded by repentance and concluded by an act of faith—manifests, however dimly, the divine lineaments which his sin had effaced but which grace has partially restored. Through the dual agency of revelation and regeneration, he can once more perceive his highest good.

In *Paradise Regain'd* the intellectual dialogue so dominates the fable that the poem is less an 'imitation of an action' than a mimesis of thought. The ethos of both protagonist and antagonist reveals itself in the epistemological struggle between Truth and Error. Divine wisdom counters the apparent wisdom of the world. God's 'living Truth', incarnate in the Messiah, refutes the archliar's fallacies. Like the single 'just men' of the earlier epic, the hero of *Paradise Regain'd* is the teacher-martyr, suffering reproach and violence for his witness to divine truth. 'Serious to learn and know, and thence to do What might be publick good', he believes himself born 'to promote all truth, All righteous things', and he interprets his royal duties largely in terms of spiritual instruction:

> But to guide Nations in the way of truth
> By saving Doctrine, and from errour lead
> To know, and knowing worship God aright,
> Is yet more Kingly, this attracts the Soul,
> Governs the inner man, the nobler part. . . .

As the 'wisdom and power of God', he is, *a fortiori*, the perfect exemplar of *sapientia*.

As in *Paradise Lost*, the false resemblance (or idol) of this formula finds expression in Satan. Relying on 'subtilty' and 'guile' rather than true prudence or wisdom, he pits his own limited 'providence' against divine Providence and thus unintentionally hastens his own defeat. Unable to penetrate God's secret designs, his own foresight is little more than sophisticated ignorance, and, as in *Paradise Lost*, he becomes the unconscious instrument of the divine intent,

> But contrary unweeting he fulfill'd
> The purpos'd Counsel pre-ordain'd and fixt. . . .

The divine purpose behind the temptation escapes the tempter, but it also eludes Christ himself, his disciples, and his family. His followers are torn by doubt and anxiety, and he himself does not realize the full significance of his desert ordeal. His very ignorance, however, provides a test for faith; it makes him rely all the more strongly on the guidance of the Spirit and on divine revelation:

> And now by some strong motion I am led
> Into this wilderness, to what intent
> I learn not yet, perhaps I need not know;
> For what concerns my knowledge God reveals.

But one must not overstress the contemplative element in *Paradise Regain'd*. Though its *method* is contemplative, its orientation is essentially ethical. Christ's wisdom is directed towards the end of obedience. His trial is not entirely intellectual; it is also moral. It involves not only the rational discrimination between true and false goods, but also voluntary choice or rejection. It engages the will as well as the reason. It involves the values of the voluptuous and active lives as well as those of the contemplative life. The ultimate intent of Christ's intellectual trial is ethical decision, an act of moral choice.

In considering the apparent goods offered by these different modes of life, Milton's Christ is primarily concerned with their relationship to the conditions of his own ministry and to the goal of man's happiness and final good. In his correct knowledge of ends and means, he manifests the divine image which Adam had lost. As its perfect representative, he is the prototype of the 'new man renewed in knowledge after the image of him that created him', as well as the foil and antithesis of the 'old man' represented by fallen Adam and his evil seed.

Though recent criticism has correctly stressed the distinction between 'old' and 'new' types of heroes in Milton's poetry,[1] it has largely overlooked the theological presuppositions of this distinction. Milton is not merely contrasting the heroes of classical and Christian tradition; he is also stressing the vital distinction between the 'old man' and the 'new man' of the Pauline epistles. The whole scheme of redemption hinges on the antithesis between two archetypal images, that of the fallen Adam and that of the victorious Christ. Since regeneration involved a spiritual transformation from the 'old' pattern to the 'new'—'putting off' the 'old man' and his deeds and 'putting on' the 'new man, renewed in knowledge' and in the image of his Creator—heroic poetry ought to experience the same rebirth. Like the individual believer, putting off the moral pattern of the 'old Adam', a regenerated epic tradition should reject the old heroic formulae of a fallen humanity and conform itself instead to the divine exemplar embodied in Christ himself. This was what Milton attempted in *Paradise Lost* and *Paradise Regain'd*, and it made his approach to the problem of Christian epic markedly different from that of his predecessors.

[1] Cf. Kermode, *supra*.

Both of Milton's epics and, to a lesser extent, his single tragedy present the divine image as the true heroic norm and stress the inevitable tension between degenerate and regenerate conceptions of heroic virtue and the heroic enterprise. However glorified by classical epic and drama, the virtue of the Gentiles was marred by sin and could therefore seem heroic only in the eyes of a fallen world. In the light of the Spirit of Truth it must necessarily appear tarnished, if not altogether bestial. To emphasize this contrast, Milton does not merely reorient his poem towards the true heroism of the 'new man', the 'godlike' pattern exhibited in Christ and his saints; he also builds up, in fallen mankind and fallen angel alike, a detailed portrait of the 'old man' and his spurious heroism.

In the epic the course of regeneration is substantially the same as in the individual. The poet delineates the image of the secular hero, the 'earthy man', only to reject it and to validate in its stead the ideal of the spiritual hero, the 'heavenly man'. Though one must beware of pressing too far this analogy between the renovation of an individual soul and that of a literary species, one nevertheless finds the pattern of regeneration inherent in the very structure of Miltonic epic. Not only do the arguments of both epics hinge on the comparison and contrast between the merits of the first Adam and those of the second. Not only does this comparison receive explicit expression in the opening lines of both poems and at numerous other places in the text. Not only does it acquire additional force through parallels between Adam's temptation and Christ's. The process of 'putting off' the 'old man' and assuming the image of the new appears in the very course of the narrative. *Paradise Lost* begins with a vivid—and by no means unconventional—picture of the secular-type hero. It ends with a prophetic vision of the spiritual hero. The intervening sections of the poem amplify and refute the 'old' heroic norm through a variety of examples which emphasize its degenerate character.

This image of the unredeemed and unregenerate 'old man' is, moreover, a 'fallen' heroism in a dual sense. It is an ideal that appears heroic only to a fallen intelligence, and it finds

its expression in the vicious exploits of the fallen creature—
man and angel alike. When Milton first portrays this pattern
in the rebel angels, it is immediately after their fall from
Heaven. When he delineates it in the Biblical giants, it is as
evidence of the human depravity resulting from Adam's fall.
In both cases he 'puts off' this image of the old man by
showing its true nature, its origins, and its merited reward.
Essentially it reduces itself to sin, and its condign reward is
death, whether spiritual or physical.

Similarly in *Paradise Regain'd* the hero 'puts off' the old
man by rejecting the carnal and secular values Satan offers
him and thereby reveals his perfect likeness to his heavenly
father. The prominence of the 'contemplative element' in
this poem is due in large part to the poet's conscious attempt
to portray the renewed 'knowledge' and wisdom that characterize the divine image both in Christ himself and in the
regenerate who are conformed to his example. In *Paradise
Lost* we have seen the divine image in its unfallen condition,
its subsequent obscuration by sin, and its partial restoration
in Adam himself and the 'just men' of the final books. In
Paradise Regain'd we see it in its highest human perfection.
Finally, in *Samson Agonistes* we see it reasserting itself in the
signs of the hero's inner regeneration—his repentance, his
faith, and his insight into the true nature of good and evil.
These are the theological evidence of his inner recovery and
the restoration of divine resemblance.

In all three poems the same imbalance of human and
divine characterizes the *sapientia* formula as the *fortezza*
ideal. As the lowest of the intelligences, man falls so far
short of God's wisdom that any pride in his own intellect and
its achievements seems an empty boast. Paradoxically, he
shows himself wisest in recognizing the limits of his own
reason and in relying instead on faith, revelation, and Providence. To overestimate his natural capacities is the supreme
folly. In *Paradise Lost* Milton scoffs at the intellectual pretensions of the astronomers and the vain philosophy of the
fallen angels. In *Paradise Regain'd* the hero rejects the
learning of the Gentile philosophers as fallacies, 'dreams,
Conjectures, fancies, built on nothing firm'. In their

ignorance of their own nature, the origin of the world, the true God, and the fall of man, they possess only the 'false resemblance' of wisdom. This is a superfluous knowledge, for, as Milton's Christ observes, God's revelation is the only essential wisdom:

> . . . he who receives
> Light from above, from the fountain of light,
> No other doctrine needs. . . .

Milton's drama, in turn, emphasizes the basic contrast between the limited foresight of the human agents—the hero himself, his aged father, and his comforters—and the 'highest wisdom' of divine Providence, which accomplishes its design 'against expectation' and against obstacles that appear insuperable. Samson paradoxically displays his wisdom in recognizing his intellectual limits and his own past folly. Heroically strong rather than heroically wise, he buttresses his own fallible reason with his faith in God's wisdom and power. Acknowledging the comparative weakness of his own foresight and relying instead on divine Providence, he turns his very limitations into heroic virtues. If he is not, like Ulysses, primarily an exemplar of heroic wisdom, he is still, like Job, essentially a hero of faith.

X

Milton's critique of the *prudentia–sapientia* formula places primary emphasis on three aspects. First, there is the classical role of right reason as the governor of the passions and the prerequisite of all the virtues. This reaches its perfection in *Paradise Regain'd*, where Christ's victory over appetite counters Adam's defeat through passion. Nevertheless, the hero's very perfection makes the philosophical duel between Truth and Error fully as prominent as the moral combat between higher and lower faculties. He exercises his reason not only in curbing his appetites, but even more notably in countering his opponent's false arguments. The internal action stresses the logical disputation as heavily as the psychological struggle between reason and desire.

In *Paradise Lost*, appetite plays a more successful role in psychological warfare. Neither Satan nor Adam is the incarnate Logos, and in both characters passion gains a decisive victory over reason. Satan's enterprise against man gives the reins to his own emotions—ire, envy, despair, hatred, and the same fatal ambition to reign which has inspired his earlier revolt. In Adam's case, love dethrones reason. He transgresses 'not deceav'd, But fondly overcome with Femal charm'.

In *Samson Agonistes* the struggle is even more substantial. After surrendering to passion, he finally overcomes it by reason. Countering the 'swoonings of despair' and Dalila's erotic blandishments with right reason, he shows marked affinities with Ulysses, the classical prototype of heroic prudence. The imagery of the Dalila episode heightens this analogy by allusions to Ulysses' encounters with Circe and the Sirens.[1]

Secondly, there is the cardinal importance of divine testimony. In presenting the conflict of truth and error, Milton follows accepted logical procedure in juxtaposing these contraries and thus giving clearer definition to both. Again, by first delineating the infernal ethos in detail and afterwards proceeding to the character of unfallen man and angel in their original innocence, he observes the principle outlined in the *Areopagitica*—that in his fallen state man must learn good by the contemplation of evil, and truth by the study of

---

[1] In contrast to the pejorative treatment of the Ulysses-myth in his portrait of Satan, Milton places it in a favourable light in *Samson Agonistes* and several other works. Cf. *Comus*, line 636 ('wise *Ulysses*'), the *Second Defence* (Columbia Edition, viii. 85). In his Commonplace Book he quotes Berni's adaptation of Boiardo's *Orlando Innamorato*, which praises Ulysses as an example of 'prudentia' for dissimulating and concealing the truth (Columbia Edition, xviii. 142). Among his outlines for tragedies is one in which Alfred 'in disguise of a minstrel discovers the danes negligence' and slaughters them; and he observes that 'A Heroicall Poem may be founded somewhere in Alfreds reigne. especially at his issuing out of Edelingsey on the Danes. whose actions are wel like those of Ulysses.' See Columbia Edition, xviii. 243. For Renaissance allegorical interpretations of Ulysses and Circe, see Douglas Bush, *Mythology and the Renaissance Tradition in English Poetry* (Minneapolis, 1932). According to the *De Doctrina* (Book II, Chapter 8): 'Righteousness [*Iustitia*] towards ourselves consists in a proper method of self-government [and] the regulation of the affections.'

error. He proceeds logically from the false to the true, from the corrupt to the impure, from the evil to the good. But his most significant method in distinguishing truth and error is his poetic exploitation of divine testimony.[1]

In all three poems this plays a dual role in separating truth and error. It provides the crucial test of obedience and faith, and it constitutes the final verdict on the creature's merits and due reward.

In *Paradise Lost* error and falsehood first make their appearance in opposition to divine truth. Satan's heresies arise in direct contradiction to the decree elevating the Son to universal kingship. Justifying his rebellion by 'argument[s] blasphemous, false and proud', he propounds the heresies that the angels are 'self-begot, self-rais'd By our own quick'ning power', that they are Messiah's equals, and that they have been 'ordain'd to govern, not to serve'. Similarly, though Eve's chief sin is disobedience, she is also guilty of disbelief, ranking the serpent's testimony and the evidence of her own senses above divine testimony. Again, Adam's descendants compound their guilt by scorning God's word and His prophets.

In *Paradise Regain'd* the Scriptures themselves offer divine witness for the Messiah's predestined role as Suffering Servant. As in the previous epic, Satan's arguments test his opponent's faith as well as obedience. He seeks to persuade the hero that the power and wisdom of the world are more effective means of acquiring his kingdom than the way of humiliation set forth by the prophets. In *Samson Agonistes* the divine datum is the prophecy that Samson should deliver Israel. A theological paradox—God's apparent failure to fulfil this promise—precipitates a crisis of faith for Samson himself and his fellow countrymen.

But, if divine testimony provides the test that separates the obedient and faithful champion from the rebellious infidel or heretic, it also serves as an absolute standard for distinguishing truth from error and virtue from vice. God himself bears witness to Abdiel's faith, Christ's obedience, and the merits of Enoch, Noah, and other 'just men' of Biblical

---

[1] Cf. Milton's *Artis logicae plenior institutio*, Columbia Edition, xi. 278–83.

history. Conversely, divine judgement intervenes constantly in the course of Milton's fable to set its final condemnation on fallen angel and fallen man alike. In *Paradise Lost* the 'perfet Witnes of all judging *Jove*', discriminating truth and virtue from their counterfeit resemblances, introduces the divine standard of judgement at critical points in the narrative—through the Father's predictions in Book III, through the providential scales of Book IV, through the sentence of judgement passed on man and serpent in Book X, and through the fate of the world and of worldly men in Books XI and XII. In *Paradise Regain'd* the final miracle[1] on the temple's pinnacle, like the earlier descent of the dove at Jesus' baptism, constitutes divine testimony of his Sonship. In *Samson Agonistes* God's spirit finally returns to bear 'witness gloriously' to the hero's 'faithful Champion[ship]' and to punish the hitherto triumphant infidels.

Thirdly, there is the contrast between the creature's limited wisdom and the Creator's Providence. For man and angel alike the chief ends of sapience are moral and theological—knowledge of their own nature and of its end, the worship and service of God. Perverted from this end through disobedience, human and angelic intelligence inevitably lose themselves in error, in their own 'vain imaginations' and fallacious 'inventions'.[2] In all three poems this is a persistent theme. Not only does it receive explicit expression in Adam's dialogues with the angels, in Christ's denunciation

---

[1] Cf. *De Doctrina*, Book I, Chapter 8, on God's 'extraordinary providence', whereby he 'produces some effect out of the usual order of nature, or gives the power of producing the same effect to whomsoever he may appoint', i.e. 'a miracle'. The 'use of miracles is to manifest the divine power, and confirm our faith', as well as 'to increase the condemnation of unbelievers, by taking away all excuse for unbelief'.

[2] According to the *De Doctrina* (Book II, Chapter 2), *stultitia* consists (1) chiefly 'in an ignorance of the will of God', (2) 'in a false conceit of wisdom', (3) 'in a prying into hidden things, after the example of our first parents, who sought after the knowledge of good and evil contrary to the command of God', and (4) 'in human or carnal wisdom', such as 'the devices of the crafty'. The second and fourth of these are particularly marked in Milton's portrait of the fallen angels, the third in his account of the fall of Adam and Eve. The judgements of Hell reflect a false wisdom, but they also spring from 'an evil conscience', which 'judges erroneously or with a wrong bias, and not according to the light derived from nature or grace' (ibid., Book II, Chapter 2).

of Greek philosophy, and in the Chorus's warning against 'vain Reason' and the atheist's folly; it also enters into the very structure of the fable. In opposing God's providential designs the reprobate invite their own nemesis, and Satan's blind folly, like that of the Philistines, hastens his own destruction.

As Milton adapts it to the demands of Christian epic, the *sapientia* formula reduces itself to a 'false conceit of wisdom' as ludicrous as it is tragic, or else to a recognition of human ignorance and a corresponding dependence on revelation. The ideal of wisdom becomes inextricably involved with the norms of Christian fortitude, obedience, and faith. As in the case of the *fortezza* formula, its highest human exemplar is the patient martyr. The hero of wisdom is really a hero of faith. Acknowledging his limited powers, relying on Providence, he trusts divine testimony and obeys its laws even without fully understanding them; to the world's contumely and violence he opposes his faith in revealed truth.

IV

The 'Good Governor':
The Critique of Leadership

THE contemplative hero pursued wisdom in retirement.
The active hero moved among men. But, regardless of their
theatres of operation—the battlefield or the arena of the
mind—they were rarely 'private persons'. They were as a
rule 'public' figures, charged with the 'safety' of the commonwealth in peace and war. Their moral attributes could entail grave political consequences. As pursuit of public good
necessarily demanded fortitude and wisdom, these formulae
fused with the ideal of the *dux*, the leader or 'good governor'.

As the protagonists of Milton's epics are 'heads' of mankind, their private crises acquire public significance. The
'weal or woe' of '*all*' Adam's descendants hinges on his temptation. Christ's victorious ordeal in the desert achieves a
'recover'd Paradise' for '*all* mankind'. Though he is tempted
'in private' and returns 'private' to his mother's house, the
subject of his trial is his public ministry. The hero of Milton's
tragedy is likewise a 'public person':[1]

> ... no private but a person rais'd
> With strength sufficient and command from Heav'n
> To free [his] Countrey. ...

In all three poems Milton follows the Renaissance doctrine
that the chief figures of epic and tragedy should be men of

---

[1] For the opinion that the chief characters of epic and tragedy should be
'public persons' rather than 'private citizens' like those of comedy, see Tasso,
i. 19, 115; Mazzoni, *Difesa*, p. 310; idem, *Discorso . . . in difesa della 'Commedia'
del poeta Dante*, ed. Mario Rossi (Firenze, 1898), p. 105; H. B. Charlton,
Castelvetro's Theory of Poetry (Manchester, 1913), pp. 135–7; Spingarn, *Literary
Criticism*, pp. 64, 69–70; Hall, pp. 42, 48–49; Gilbert, p. 319. That Adam and
Christ were 'public persons' and hence involved all mankind in their respective
defeat and victory was a theological commonplace.

pre-eminent civil or military dignity—kings, princes, 'valiant captains', 'magnanimous heroes'. Samson is not only the most powerful warrior of his day; he is also a 'judge' in Israel, with a divine commission to liberate his people. Until his fall, Adam is monarch of the earth. Christ is God's vicegerent, and a 'universal king'. Satan is emperor of Hell, prince of the fallen world, sovereign of a third part of the angels and the greater part of mankind. The principal characters of all three poems are persons of elevated station, 'great-souled leaders and kings'.

I

In both epics the royal theme looms large. Emphasizing God's providential 'government' of men and angels, both depict Him consistently as an absolute king, with all the panoply of regality. The structure of the fable is based on the promulgation and execution of His decrees. In *Paradise Lost* His special edicts dominate the plot—crowning Messiah and thus precipitating Satan's rebellion; creating the world; countering Adam's fall with the decree of predestination.

A poem that sets out to justify 'eternal Providence' must inevitably lay heavy stress on God's role as universal governor —on that 'general government' of the universe, whereby He creates good out of evil and utilizes 'good' or 'evil' temptations to exercise the virtues of the elect or unmask the hypocrisy of the reprobate.[1] This providential strategy controls the actions of Satan and Adam and thus dominates the whole narrative structure of *Paradise Lost*. Scarcely less emphasis falls on a more particularized aspect of Providence—the 'special government' of men and angels.[2] The paradisal life in Eden involves the principal features of God's government *before* the fall, as outlined in the *Christian Doctrine*—the institutions of marriage and the Sabbath, and the injunction concerning the forbidden tree. The special government of man *after* the fall—a scheme that embraces his sin, his consequent misery, and his eventual restoration—receives

---

[1] Cf. *De Doctrina*, Book I, Chapter 8.
[2] Cf. ibid., Chapters 9–14.

its first expression in the opening lines of the poem and undergoes further elaboration in the celestial council (Book III),
the regeneration and judgement scenes (Book X), and
Michael's prophecies (Books XI and XII). The final lines
recapitulate this theme; Adam and Eve wander through
Eden with 'Providence thir guide'.

The converse of this emphasis on the Father's supreme
kingship is the subordinate—if not subservient—position of
His creatures. Good or evil, they are still servants, whose
proper office is to honour and obey their Creator. Even in
rebellion they involuntarily augment His glory and perform
His will. Like the faithful angels, the mutinous devils remain 'ministering spirits' in spite of themselves, and man's
disobedience leads ultimately to God's greater glory. The
very argument of the poem—disobedience to a divine command—heightens the prevailing emphasis on supernal
majesty. Divine sovereignty—the authority of an absolute
monarch who makes his own laws and is free to command or
forbid—is the central political datum of *Paradise Lost*; only
in relation to this universal kingship do the regal pretensions
of other characters—Satan, Adam, Christ, Chaos, Sin, and
Death—have real significance.

In both epics Satan's primary motive is lust for dominion.
Even in Heaven he counterfeits divine majesty, and in Hell
itself he is still motivated by greed for supreme power; it is
'Better to reign in Hell than serve in Heaven'. He founds an
infernal empire and establishes its capital. In his opening
address to his parliament he stresses the security of his
régime—'a safe, unenvied throne'. He presents his campaign
against man as a strategy of imperialism as well as revenge. In
justifying his attack on mankind, he urges 'public reason just,
Honour and Empire with revenge enlarg'd, By conquering
this new World'. In *Paradise Regain'd* the threat to his 'reign'
moves him to essay the temptation in the wilderness. Milton
consistently represents him as the arch-rebel—the ambitious
peer who revolts against his feudal lord for the sake of a
crown.

Even Sin and Death are Satan's 'vicegerents' appointed
to rule his conquered territory until Christ shall finally

dethrone them. Milton presents ethics and eschatology alike through the idiom of politics.

Central to both epics is the issue of just and unjust kingship. In De Nores's opinion, the heroic poem should treat the actions of 'good and legitimate princes, or of some other great personage'. Its characteristic effect—'marvel'—resulted from the recovery of a lost kingdom: 'Having lost his state and country or some other thing, whose loss severely diminishes his greatness and dignity (and usually leads to vile condition and despair), some good prince valiantly returns in time to recover it and to regain the same lofty station through divine favor and his own virtue.'[1] *Paradise Lost* presents this antithesis between the legitimate king and the usurper in the sequence of events initiated by Messiah's exaltation. Christ the true king, crowned by divine authority and expressing the true image of God, offers a striking contrast to Satan, the tyrannical 'Idol of Majestie Divine'. The parallels between the divine and infernal council accentuate this antithesis. The enthroned devil imitates God's royal state, and in the course of the session, his role parodies those of Father and Son.

The motif of the legitimate king, who has lost his kingdom and now returns to reclaim it, is explicit in the opening lines of *Paradise Lost*. A 'greater Man' will regain the 'seat' the first man has lost. The same pattern underlies the argument of *Paradise Regain'd*. The second Adam reclaims for mankind the native liberty, paradisal happiness, and inner sovereignty lost by the first. Christ, the legitimate heir, has come to 'expel a Tyrant' and regain his kingdom—though it is not Tiberius whom he must expel, nor the Roman empire that he must regain.

Samson Agonistes portrays the same pattern, but with marked variations. As the political context of the drama is republican, not monarchical, Samson is not a 'prince'. Nevertheless, much of the action and dialogue turns on the issue of his 'legitimate'—indeed, his divinely appointed—leadership, and the hero's descent into 'vile condition' and 'despair' is much more drastic than in *Paradise Lost*. In the tragedy, as

[1] Hall, p. 49. Translation mine.

in the narrative poems, the argument and fable exhibit the pattern of loss and recovery. The epics embody this scheme in 'One Man' representative of all mankind. The drama narrows it to a single champion, God's 'extraordinary minister', especially elected for the purpose of delivering his nation from foreign bondage. What Samson has lost has been more than eyesight and liberty; he has lost (he feels) his *raison d'être* and appointed function; he has lost himself. Yet the course of the action restores to him much that had seemed irrevocably lost. He regains his inner liberty and inner vision. He regains his identity as hero and man of battle. He regains his role of elected champion and 'extraordinary minister'. He regains his function as the saviour and deliverer of his people. In the end, 'Samson quit[s] himself Like *Samson*, and heroicly . . . finish[es] A life Heroic'.

In one respect Milton's choice of heroes breaks sharply with contemporary literary theory and practice. This particular point of divergence, however, is precisely what one might have expected from a poet of his republican principles. Neither his 'epic person' nor the 'tragic person' of his drama is a secular king or prince. Although Samson is a 'judge' in Israel, he is not of royal rank. Though Adam exercises dominion over the beasts, he has no human subjects. Though the Christ of *Paradise Regain'd* is lord of a spiritual kingdom, by secular standards he is merely a private person. In his distaste for secular monarchy, Milton avoids introducing it altogether, except as one of the effects of the fall in *Paradise Lost* and as a temptation which Christ specifically rejects in *Paradise Regain'd*. The kingdoms he portrays in both epics are spiritual realms—Christ's sovereignty over angels and men, Satan's empire of sin and death, Adam's inner dominion over his own soul. The political order in both poems is essentially psychological. Its polity is internal; its frontiers are mental rather than geographical.

In both epics the true and false modes of heroic leadership appear primarily in two antithetical figures—Messiah, the 'Head' of the faithful angels and of redeemed mankind, and Satan, the usurper and tyrant. Like the traditional epic hero, both are 'valiant captains', but the singular characteristic of Milton's Christ is that as the 'Captain of salvation' he is 'made perfect through suffering'. The pattern of the *dux* thus merges into that of the Suffering Servant. The leader exhibits his moral excellence in learning to 'suffer' and 'obey'. He performs his public mission by his private pain. In both poems it is by 'humiliation and strong sufferance' that the anointed king accomplishes his people's salvation and re-establishes his dominion in the human soul.

The ethical postulates of the Satanic kingdom are diametrically opposed to those of the Messianic reign, and Satan's character as leader is the direct contrary of Christ's. Where Christ achieves his kingdom by humility and patience, Satan founds his empire on ambition and pride. Though, like Messiah, he voluntarily humbles himself by assuming the body of an inferior being to achieve his ends, the motives behind these parallel incarnations are exactly opposite. Renouncing his celestial throne, the Son assumes human flesh to save man; Satan, on the other hand, enters the serpent's body in order to destroy mankind and to enlarge his own kingdom. The Son gladly offers to take man's flesh and its sins upon him; Satan is reluctant 'this essence to incarnate and imbrute'. The one is truly a 'faithful leader'; the other merely a counterfeit resemblance.

II

In depicting the antithetical polities of Heaven and Hell, Milton fuses two distinct, though closely related, epic traditions—warring nations and rival gods. Normally the first concerned human agents only, provided the epic argument, and dominated the fable. The second played a minor role, subordinate to the human struggle and limited to the 'machinery'. Yet both usually occurred in the same poem. Though the subject matter of the *Iliad* is the conflict between Greeks and Trojans, Homer extends this struggle to the immortals by engaging the sympathies of rival gods in the fortunes of particular warriors on both sides. On the human level, the *Aeneid* treats the war between Trojans and Latians and foreshadows the future conflict between Rome and

Carthage. On the divine level, the principal opposition is between Juno and Venus.

In substituting Christian machinery for the pagan gods, Renaissance poets placed greater emphasis on the moral and spiritual antithesis underlying the supernatural struggle. Instead of a single Olympus, torn by the mutual jealousies of its deities, they portrayed the clearcut polarity of Hell and Heaven.[1] Instead of classical divinities of virtually the same nature and rank, they depicted the spiritual conflict of angels and demons. Instead of rivalries within a single pantheon, they described the perpetual warfare between contrasting eschatological dominions, the realms of God and Satan.

An analogous development took place on the human plane. The struggle between rival states acquired the more hectic coloration of a spiritual war, a conflict between the true faith and rival creeds. The naïve dichotomy enunciated in *The Song of Roland* ('We Christians are right, those pagans are wrong')[2] is still implicit in Boiardo's *Orlando Innamorato* and Ariosto's *Orlando Furioso*. It underlies such epics of the crusades as Tasso's *Gerusalemme Liberata*, Bargaeus's *Syrias*, and Le Moyne's *Saint Louis*. The *Clovis* of Desmarets and Graziani's *Conquista di Granata* transfer this conflict to French and Spanish settings; Trissino's *Italia Liberata* transmutes it into the hostilities of orthodox Catholic and Arian heretic. Renaissance heroic poems based on the Old Testament—Du Bartas's *Judith* and the Davidic epics of Walther, Du Bellay, and Cowley—substitute the holy warfare of Hebrew and Gentile.[3]

These Christian epics sharpened the pattern of conflict by giving it moral and theological significance. On divine and human levels alike, the ethical contrasts between the contending states and armies became more pronounced, more

---

[1] Camoens's *Lusiads* is a notable exception. Retaining the Olympian council in what is nevertheless a Christian epic, it makes Bacchus the hero's chief supernatural adversary. In other Christian epics such a role is often assigned to the devil.

[2] 'Nos avons droit mais cist glotons ont tort.' Cf. Graham Hough, *A Preface to the Faerie Queene* (New York, 1962), p. 16.

[3] For other examples, see Antonio Belloni, *Storia dei generi letterari italiani: il poema epico e mitologico* (Milano, n.d.); R. A. Sayce, *The French Biblical Epic in the Seventeenth Century* (Oxford, 1955), pp. 78–79.

fundamental, than in classical poetry. In Greek and Roman epics, the deities hostile to the hero and his people were, for the most part, neither superior nor inferior in character to the gods who supported him. Neither Poseidon, who opposed Odysseus' homecoming, nor Juno, who harassed Aeneas on his voyages and after his arrival in Italy, was essentially an evil deity. Classical epic was relatively free from the ethical and theological issues that dominated the machinery of Christian heroic poetry. Its contending deities usually aligned themselves with different heroes or objectives according to personal sympathies or antipathies rather than moral or religious principles. Despite ethical variations among the rival gods, the question of a clear-cut division between good and evil divinities rarely entered the picture.

In Christian epic, however, such considerations were all but inevitable. If the poet substituted the 'machines' of his own religion for those of the ancients, he could hardly avoid introducing the dichotomies of divine truth and infernal illusion, celestial virtue and diabolical vice. In this way he invested both the supernatural machinery and the central action with ethical and religious contrasts usually minimized in classical epic.

On the human level likewise, the wars depicted in classical epic were largely devoid of spiritual significance. The issues were primarily national, and the two opposing armies differed little in moral excellence or depravity. The ethos of the principal antagonist might (as in Hector's case) be superior to that of the 'epic person'. Moral differences among the principal characters of classic epic tended, on the whole, to be individual rather than general. In the *Iliad* Paris was a philanderer and a coward, but these were his personal vices rather than the generic character of a Trojan. In Statius' *Thebaid*, Capaneus was an atheist and a blasphemer, but this too was rather an individual trait than a characteristic of the attacking forces; his ally, Amphiarus, was as eminent in piety as Capaneus in sacrilege. In the *Aeneid* the antithesis between Aeneas' piety and Mezentius' impiety was largely personal; it was not representative of any deep-seated contrast between the Trojan forces and their Italian opponents.

Christian heroic poetry sharpened the pattern of moral and spiritual opposition on both divine and human planes. Reducing the action to a conflict between Christian and infidel, it transformed the supernatural machinery into a struggle between God and devil. Though Ariosto and Boiardo might blur the ethical distinctions between the Christian warrior and his pagan adversary, they could still express the moral antithesis allegorically. In the epics of Tasso and Spenser such distinctions are clearly articulated on both literal and allegorical levels.

The use of Christian 'machines' heightened the importance of Providence in the plot. Just as classical poets had presented the epic enterprise as a decree of Fate or the will of Jove, Christian heroic poets often grounded it on the intent of God the Father. Thus the enterprise itself could serve as a moral or religious criterion to judge the contending parties. As the measure of obedience and disobedience, it divided the principal characters of the poem into two well-defined camps—supporters and opponents of God's will. In classical epic the persons who struggled against fate or the will of Zeus were not necessarily impious; to oppose Troy's destruction, Odysseus' homecoming, or Aeneas' settlement in Italy was not in itself a sacrilege. In the context of Christian epic, however, persons hostile to the hero and his enterprise easily acquired a sinister character; they seemed enemies of God. The epic conflict became a 'holy war' between His servants and His foes, a *psychomachia* between faith and infidelity, obedience and rebellion. Once God had declared His intent and dispatched His messengers to initiate the enterprise, the hero's opponents became, *a fortiori*, adversaries of Providence. Whatever their motives—patriotism, love, ambition, superstition—their action and strategy became tainted with impiety through their opposition to the divine will. The shift from a polytheistic religion to a monotheistic faith as the basis of the epic machinery inevitably gave a stronger ethical and theological coloration to the epic enterprise and to the conflict between the 'epic person' and his antagonists.

This exploitation of the Christian supernatural as epic

machinery also accentuated the parallelism between the divine and human councils. In classical epic, where deities favourable or hostile to the hero's enterprise might sit in the same council, the analogy was less elaborately developed. The conciliar pattern tended to become triangular; normally it involved at most a single conclave of gods and the councils of war held by the two opposing armies. Christian epic, however, usually replaced the hostile deities with devils, and the threefold pattern yielded to a fourfold design. An infernal conclave complemented the celestial council, paralleling the councils of Christian and pagan warriors. The *Gerusalemme Liberata* contains four distinct conclaves—the assemblies of Crusader and Saracen, God and devil.

This shift from the threefold scheme to the fourfold design not only increased the symmetry and balance of the councils; it also produced a tighter logical structure by bringing into sharper focus the two primary relationships existing among the four conclaves—cause and effect, and logical antithesis. The 'conciliar rectangle' reduced itself essentially to two sets of logical contraries. It presented the contrast between good and evil, virtue and vice, both in terms of divine or infernal causality and in terms of human effects. By exhibiting the same ethical and religious polarity on both natural and supernatural planes, it tended to reduce the human struggle to a mere shadow of the divine. The spiritual combat seemed the ultimate reality, the physical battle merely an extension of the war between Heaven and Hell. The eschatological pattern governed the psychological and historical. Underlying the temporal conflict of worldly societies was the eternal warfare between the kingdoms of God and Satan.

Milton's epics reduce the conciliar pattern to an even more radical simplicity. As his subject precludes the human council, it exaggerates the role of the supernatural conclaves. The burden of strategic planning falls primarily on the 'machines' at the expense of the human agents, simplifying the 'conciliar rectangle' of Christian epic tradition to the clear-cut polarity of two spiritual societies at war for the human soul. The politics normally associated with the human council are transferred to the supernatural sessions. In Milton's heroic poems the contrast between these councils not only mirrors the basic opposition between Providence and Satanic guile; it also exaggerates the antithesis between their warring governments, their conflicting strategies.

In the conventional epic, the argument was usually based on the hostilities of two rival societies. The *Iliad* portrayed the struggle between Greek and Trojan, the *Punica* the conflict between Carthage and Rome. In the *Aeneid* Juno's enmity towards Aeneas was prompted largely by her jealousy of Rome's imperial destiny at the expense of her beloved Carthage. The *Italia Liberata* depicted the war between Roman and Goth; the *Gerusalemme Liberata* and the *Conquista di Granata* the rivalry of Christendom and Islam.

Milton shifts this motif of rival polities from the human to the supernatural plane, from the 'epic person'[1] to the epic machinery. Just as he has utilized his 'machines' to exemplify contrasting conceptions of the heroic ideal, so he employs them now to portray antithetical and antagonistic dominions. Christ and Satan do not merely embody true and false norms of heroism; they also represent contrasting *imperia*. Instead of depicting a conflict between two national states, the poet portrays the rival polities of God and Satan, the antithesis between divine order and the corrupt dominion of the fallen creature. Like their warfare, these societies are spiritual rather than physical. Their battlefield is the human mind, and the immediate object of their conflict is the human soul.

For the usual epic argument Milton substitutes the psychological action of the morality play, elevating the rival angels and devils of the morality tradition to the level of epic 'machines'. Modified by the requirements of epic technique, the morality pattern takes on political significance; its actors become 'public' persons. The protagonist legally represents the entire human genus. The spirits who contend for his soul—the *Bonus angelus* and *Malus angelus* of the morality tradition—act as the official agents of rival kingdoms. In thus combining epic and morality conventions, Milton has altered both.

[1] This is true primarily of *Paradise Lost* rather than of Milton's later epic.

III

In spiritualizing the conventional argument of the epic, Milton also spiritualized its political structure. Having rejected the national conception of the epic, he also rejected the conventional conception of the epic struggle as a conflict of nations. In its place he substituted the pattern of ecclesiastical warfare—the struggle between the Church Militant and its demonic Adversary. Underlying the rival polities of *Paradise Lost* is the opposition—long familiar in Christian tradition—between the heavenly and earthly kingdoms.

In developing this opposition, he relies for the most part on the Biblical contrast between the kingdom of Heaven and the principality of Satan. Nevertheless, for the background of his rival dominions, he also drew on patristic, medieval, and Protestant elaborations of this dichotomy. Reducing the whole course of human history to an eschatological war between the realms of God and Satan, this interpretation provided a pattern comparable to the quasi-historic feuds of classical antiquity—the rivalry of Rome and Carthage or Europe and Asia. This concept had already received epic expression in Dante's *Commedia*, with its imagery of Babylon and Jerusalem and its structural antithesis between Lucifer's 'doloroso regno' and the kingdom of Heaven. Indeed, just as Dante's poem is the epic comedy of the Christian church, Milton's heroic poem is its epic tragedy. Exploiting the same antithesis as Dante, but in a different genre, he represents the conflict of the two kingdoms[1] not statically, like his Italian predecessor, but

[1] For Milton's exploitation of the opposition between the Augustinian 'cities' of the world and of God, see Schultz, pp. 222–36; C. A. Patrides, *The Phoenix and the Ladder: The Rise and Decline of the Christian View of History* (Berkeley, California, 1964), p. 62; Louis L. Martz, *The Paradise Within: Studies in Vaughan, Traherne, and Milton* (New Haven, 1964), pp. 110–16. Milton usually prefers the term 'kingdom' to 'city' in contrasting the polities of Heaven and Hell, the church and the world. Nevertheless he sometimes uses these terms interchangeably. In *Of Reformation* the 'Church' is 'the heavenly City' and can 'support it selfe without the props and buttresses of secular Authoritie' (Columbia Edition, iii. 22–23) and the author speaks of 'our eternall City in Heaven' (p. 53). Similarly, in *The Reason of Church-Government* (p. 262) the church is 'the houshold and City of God'. Cf. the contrast between '*Jerusalem*, The holy City' (*PR*, iv. 545–6) and the 'Cities of men' (*PR*, ii. 470; *PL*, xi. 636).

dynamically, through the contrary strategies—the open and covert warfare—of two opposing governments.

Between the infernal and secular empires there is a 'Toynbean' relationship of 'affiliation' and 'apparentage', and Milton's Pandaemonium is partly modelled on the kingdoms of the world. Spiritually, the earthly kingdoms imitate Hell; poetically Hell imitates the secular society. The strength and sagacity of Pandaemonium foreshadow the power and wisdom of the world. Its wealth and splendour anticipate the world's specious riches and vainglory. Its standards of value are the prototypes of the world's false criteria. It exhibits the distinctive traits that will subsequently characterize Satan's 'perverted World' and the Protestant's Babylon, the Church of Rome.

In describing the seat of the 'prince of this world' Milton employs the idiom which Hebrew and Christian writers had applied to the rivals of the true church—the empires of Egypt, Assyria, Persia, and Rome. He compares Pandaemonium specifically with Babylon and with the towns of Egypt, 'types' of the 'city of the world':

> And here let those
> Who boast in mortal things, and wond'ring tell
> Of *Babel*, and the works of *Memphian* Kings,
> Learn how thir greatest Monuments of Fame,
> And Strength and Art are easily outdone
> By Spirits reprobate. . . .
>   Not *Babylon*,
> Nor great *Alcairo* such magnificence
> Equall'd in all thir glories, to inshrine
> *Belus* or *Serapis* thir Gods, or seat
> Thir Kings, when *Egypt* with *Assyria* strove
> In wealth and luxury.

But the parallel goes deeper than this explicit allusion. Like the Assyrian and Egyptian Babylons,[1] Pandaemonium is both a seat of empire and a shrine of idolatry. Satan's followers both honour him as monarch and worship him as a god. The same duality of spiritual and temporal tyranny

---

[1] For Cairo as the Egyptian Babylon, see *The Columbia Lippincott Gazetteer of the World*, ed. Leon E. Seltzer (New York, 1952), s.v. Cairo.

appeared (as Puritans insisted) in the Roman Catholic church and the government of Charles I and Archbishop Laud.

Moreover, the founders of Babylon (the *locus* of the first monarchy) and Pandaemonium are cast in the same mould. Both are motivated by ambition and seek to 'dispossess Concord and law of Nature from the Earth'. Both found their 'Empire tyrannous' on rebellion against God and imitation of the divine majesty.[1] Both pursue glory and fame by evil means, and both find these pretensions frustrated by divine judgement. In their 'despite of Heav'n' Nimrod and Satan exhibit the same overweening *hubris*, and the rewards of their pretentious exploits are virtually the same. Pandaemonium and Babylon alike end in confusion and ridicule.

Milton's critique of leadership is fully intelligible only against this background of antithetical spiritual polities. His images of the true and counterfeit leader—embodied in Satan, Adam, and Messiah—presuppose the dualism of the infernal and celestial dominions. It is in terms of these societies that he presents the conventional political motifs of the epic—the foundation or deliverance of the commonweal and the pursuit of public good.

For Tasso, the most appropriate themes for heroic poetry were the establishment and preservation of kingdoms. He praised Virgil for choosing as his argument Aeneas' arrival in Italy—an event that ultimately gave rise to the Roman empire—and he commended Trissino for depicting Italy's liberation from the Goths. Enterprises on behalf of the Christian faith or for the exaltation of church and empire were suitable subjects for the epic 'illustrious'. The heroic poet ought to celebrate his nation's glory, the origin of cities and illustrious families, the beginnings of kingdoms and empires.[2]

Fundamental to both of Milton's epics is the antithesis

---

[1] For Nimrod as the founder of Babylon, see St. Augustine, *The City of God*, tr. Marcus Dods (New York, 1950), p. 527. This detail represents an additional link between the Biblical giants and the 'earthly city' of the world and flesh; cf. Augustine, pp. 441, 514, 524. For a comparison of Nimrod and Satan, see Hughes in *Essays . . . Presented to A. S. P. Woodhouse*, pp. 125 ff.

[2] Tasso, i. 121–4.

between the secular (or infernal) dominion, founded on the corruption of the intellect and will, and the spiritual (or divine) dominion, founded on their regeneration. Under the vicegerency of Sin and Death, the world has been annexed to Satan's empire; it can be restored to Heaven's sovereignty only by conquering Sin and Death. The kingdoms of the world belong to the devil, for he rules the hearts of their kings; and the institution of secular monarchy itself derives from the spiritual degeneration of mankind after the fall. The kingdom of God, on the other hand, establishes itself in and through the regeneration of the human soul. The two polities are founded on antithetical principles and extend their dominions by contrary means.

The later books of *Paradise Lost* trace the evolution of the secular *regnum* under the contagion of Sin and Death, but they also depict the inner regeneration that liberates man from this tyranny. After the fall Heaven and Hell continue to pursue the contrary strategies already outlined in the earlier books. The infernal and celestial polities incarnate themselves in the battle of flesh and spirit, world and church. Christ and his apostles are persecuted by the 'worldly strong' and despised by the 'worldly wise'. A corrupt and worldly church persecutes the minority who worship in spirit and in truth. The infernal *regnum* imposes its image not only on Nimrod's Babylon and on pagan Egypt, Persia, and Rome, but also on the Christian church itself.

In *Paradise Regain'd*, where the action primarily concerns Christ's rejection of the kingdoms of the world, the opposition between the heavenly and infernal societies is even more pertinent. The Messianic *regnum* is not to be established by means of the world's kingdoms; these are actually subject to the 'prince of this world' and administered by rulers dominated by Satan's vicegerents, Sin and Death. On the contrary, it is to be achieved by freeing the human heart itself from the tyranny of Sin and Death, and the Messiah demonstrates his own immunity to their tyranny by rejecting all that Satan's dominions can offer him. In developing the theme of the opposition of the church and the world, Milton emphasizes the contrast between the spiritual character of

Christ's kingdom and the carnal—and, therefore, corrupt—nature of secular dominion. Though the specific ends and means which Satan proposes may be appropriate for worldly kingdoms, they are fatal to the integrity of the church. In effect, Satan is urging Christ to rebuild Babylon, whereas his mission demands that he restore Jerusalem.

IV

As the 'heads' or 'captains' of two antithetical societies, Messiah and Satan embody mutually contradictory ideals of the leader. The one seeks, the other *pretends* to seek, the liberty and safety of his people. Their merit as champions and leaders depends largely upon the fidelity and success with which they pursue these aims. In the shorter epic, Satan plays the role of 'great Dictator' of the 'infernal Crew'. As ruler of the 'Powers of Air and this wide world', his immediate task is to preserve his kingdom and prevent the loss of 'all our power . . ., our freedom and our being In this fair Empire won of Earth and Air'. The issue involved in his spiritual duel with Christ is no less than the destinies of the infernal and Messianic kingdoms. To preserve his own realm, he must overcome the 'Enemy . . . who no less Threat'ns then our expulsion down to Hell' before the Messiah has achieved his dominion,

> E're in the head of Nations he appear
> Their King, their Leader, and Supream on Earth.

In *Paradise Lost* Satan's followers consistently hail him as 'leader', and he himself lays heavy stress on his right to this title. He devotes his speech from the throne largely to justifying his authority as 'Dictator':

> Mee though just right, and the fixt Laws of Heav'n
> Did first create your Leader, next, free choice,
> With what besides, in Counsel or in Fight,
> Hath bin achievd of merit, yet this loss
> Thus farr at least recover'd, hath much more
> Establisht in a safe unenvied Throne
> Yielded with full consent.

When detected by the angelic guard, he attempts to clear himself by pleading the responsibilities of a faithful leader to his people:

> [It] behooves . . .
> A faithful Leader, not to hazard all
> Through wayes of danger by himself untri'd.

This claim draws a sharp rebuttal from Gabriel. Exposing the apostate's pretensions to heroic leadership as false, the captain of the angelic guard argues that Satan is neither a true leader nor a faithful one. He is only the spurious image —the idol:

> To say and strait unsay, pretending first
> Wise to flie pain, professing next the Spie,
> Argues no Leader, but a lyar trac't. . . .
> Faithful to whom? to thy rebellious crew?
> Armie of Fiends, fit body to fit head. . . .

Milton offsets this portrait of infernal leadership[1] by stressing Messiah's captaincy.[2] Anointed 'Head' of the angels and 'Head of all mankind' in '*Adams* room', the Son unites men and angels in the single structure of the church militant. Under his headship the angelic hierarchies are 'imbodied all in one' in the heavenly war against the apostates, and the same pattern reappears subsequently in the spiritual battles of the church militant in the world. The heavenly war is, in fact, the archetype of the church's combats with her spiritual and temporal enemies on earth; Messiah's office as head and saviour of the angelic forces is the celestial paradigm of his role in human history as 'captain of our salvation'.

Christ's authority as leader rests on his divine unction, Satan's on his own ambition and his faction's consent. In both instances, however, the title and office depend largely on personal merit. A 'sence of injur'd merit' provokes Satan's revolt, and his own 'merit' exalts him to be the 'bad eminence' of Pandaemonium's throne. (This is the infernal counterpart of Messiah's exaltation, and Satan's pretence

---

[1] For Satan as 'prince' and 'leader' of the fallen angels, see *De Doctrina*, Book I, Chapter 9.

[2] For Christ's mediatorial office and kingdom, see ibid., Book I, Chapter 15.

to merit is the *eidolon* of the Son's genuine worth.) His
rebellion springs from a misconception of his own dignity
and from a false opinion of the angelic office. Regarding himself as Messiah's equal, he denies that the Son can 'in reason
. . . or right assume Monarchie over such as live by right
His equals . . .'. Ignoring the true nature of the angels—
'ministering spirits' who minister to the 'heirs of salvation'—
he misinterprets the 'Imperial Titles' of the hierarchies as
evidence of 'Our being ordain'd to govern, not to serve'.

Abdiel, who as 'Servant of God' fulfils the true function of
the angels, properly rebukes these claims. God has exalted
the angels by placing them under Messiah's captaincy—
'bent rather to exalt Our happie state under one Head
more neer united'. Even if it is 'unjust That equal over
equals Monarch Reigne', Satan is not 'Equal to him Be-
gotten Son, by whom As by his word the mighty Father
made All things . . .'. Satan's merits cannot equal the Son's,
and the 'Sovran voice' of God confirms Abdiel's thesis:
'*Messiah* . . . Reigns' over the angelic hosts 'by right of merit'.
Again, it is by his own merits that the Son shall achieve his
universal reign.

In *Paradise Regain'd* likewise, the Son's office as king and
leader is founded on his superlative worth. God exposes him
to temptation in order that men and angels may discern
'From what consummate vertue I have chose This perfect
Man, by merit call'd my Son, To earn Salvation for the
Sons of men'. And the Messiah himself argues that his
humiliation—the trial of patience and obedience 'in humble
state, and things adverse'—is the best preparation for his
exaltation and the best proof of merit:

> . . . that he may know
> What I can suffer, how obey? Who best
> Can suffer, best can do; best reign, who first
> Well hath obey'd; just tryal e're I merit
> My exaltation without change or end.

V

In their relationship to such political ideals as the 'public
good', 'general safety', and 'deliverance', the three chief

persons of *Paradise Lost* are sharply contrasted. These are a conventional end of the epic hero, and the merits of Adam, Christ, and Satan as heads of state depend largely on their abilities to achieve them. Ulysses and Aeneas had endeavoured to save their companions. Godfrey had striven to deliver Jerusalem and the Holy Sepulchre, Belisarius to liberate Italy, Judith to save Bethulia. The very titles of Renaissance epics—*Italia Liberata, Gerusalemme Liberata, Bethulians Rescue*—reflect the prominence of deliverance and salvation as heroic themes.

Posing as a defender of his people's good, Satan pleads 'public reason just' as his excuse for destroying man. He volunteers for the perilous expedition through chaos in the name of 'public moment'. But primarily he pretends to be a 'Patron of libertie', who strives, in Heaven as in Hell, to free his companions from bondage. By his rebellion he has

> . . . in one Night freed
> From servitude inglorious welnigh half
> Th' Angelic Name. . . .

He undertakes the voyage to earth in order to 'seek Deliverance for us all', 'to set free From out this dark and dismal house of pain, Both [Death] and [Sin], and all the heav'nly Host Of Spirits that . . . Fell with us from on high'. Upon the completion of his enterprise, Sin extols him as a liberator:

> Thou hast atchiev'd our libertie, confin'd
> Within Hell Gates till now. . . .

Satan's pretensions of seeking the welfare and liberty of his companions are as spurious as his claims to be a 'faithful Leader'—a title easily refuted by Gabriel. Having renounced the Supreme Good, he has renounced the true object of the state—the public good and happiness. Warring against God, he is contending against his own 'chiefest bliss' and that of his comrades. Far from saving them, he drags them with him into damnation. Instead of leading, he misleads.

Equally vain is his pretence of seeking their deliverance. The loss of inner freedom makes the pursuit of external liberty superficial and vain. In Satan's case, as in Adam's, the fall entails the destruction of 'Rational Libertie':

Since [his] original lapse, true Libertie
Is lost, which alwayes with right Reason dwells
Twinn'd, and from her hath no dividual being:
Reason in man obscur'd, or not obeyd,
Immediately inordinate desires
And upstart Passions catch the Government
From Reason, and to servitude reduce
Man till then free.

As inward freedom is the true and essential liberty, its loss leads, justly, to the destruction of the external, accidental freedom. As man 'permits Within himself unworthie Powers to reign Over free Reason', God's 'Judgement just' often 'Subjects him from without to violent Lords: Who oft as undeservedly enthrall His outward freedom . . .'. At other times, 'Justice, and some fatal curse' deprive nations 'of thir outward libertie, Thir inward lost'.

Like fallen man, the fallen angel is enslaved to his own passions. Having lost their inner freedom, the devils cannot achieve true deliverance even by escaping from Hell. Coloni- zing the earth and air, they can gain only the accidents of liberty, not the substance or the reality. And indeed, like Satan himself, they bring their own prison with them:

Which way I flie is Hell; my self am Hell;
And in the lowest deep a lower deep
Still threatning to devour me opens wide,
To which the Hell I suffer seems a Heav'n.

Satan does not really deliver his companions, any more than he achieves their safety and public good. Though he conquers a new kingdom, he has lost dominion over himself. His empire is merely apparent, for God continues to rule Hell with his iron sceptre, just as he governs Heaven with his golden. Satan has gained a world, but not his own soul. Though he overcomes the lord of Paradise, he is never able to enjoy the delights of Eden. Like the heavenly stairs he beholds on his journey through space, his conquest merely emphasizes his exclusion from beatitude.

In his apparent pursuit of the public good, the 'general safety', and his companions' liberty, Satan reflects the ideal of the 'good Governor'. But, in fact, he is merely the *eidolon* of the 'faithful Leader'. None of these ends lies within his capabilities, and he can pursue only their specious resemblance. Misleading and self-misled, he can only achieve public evil rather than public good, general damnation instead of general safety, his companions' self-enslavement in lieu of deliverance.

Adam's sin results from an abrogation of leadership. Besides permitting his wife to expose herself to great danger,[1] he allows her to set the example for him in crime. Though a 'public person', he shirks his obligations as 'head' of mankind and sets his private feelings above the interests of human society. Unlike Satan, he makes no pretence of seeking the public good, the general safety, or the pursuit of liberty and happiness. 'Not deceiv'd', but overcome by 'Femal charm', he enslaves himself and his posterity with open eyes. Although Raphael has warned him against letting 'Passion sway [his] Judgement' and has stressed his obligation to his posterity,

> . . . thine and of all thy Sons
> The weal or woe in thee is plac't . . .

he fails in his duties as 'head' and allows his private emotions to imperil the 'general safety' and fetter the liberties of the whole race. His personal passions destroy the public weal.

It is Milton's Christ, accordingly, who best exemplifies the ideal of the 'faithful Leader'. In both epics, he is the 'head' or 'captain' who achieves the public good and his people's salvation and deliverance. Regaining Paradise, he reclaims man's *summum bonum* and true happiness, the knowledge and love of God. Delivering his race from bondage to sin and death, he restores the will to its true freedom, to 'rational liberty'. Achieving the 'general safety', he accomplishes the salvation of the world.

From his childhood the Christ of *Paradise Regain'd* has been 'Serious to learn and know, and thence to do What

---

[1] Though it can be argued that Eve (like Milton in *Areopagitica*) has a right to trial, and that Adam cannot consistently forbid her to exercise this right, the fact remains that it is her duty to obey her husband instead of exposing herself to possible dangers against his wishes.

might be publick good'. A similar concern for the public
weal underlies his conception of kingship:

> For therein stands the office of a King,
> His Honour, Vertue, Merit, and chief Praise,
> That for the Publick all this weight he bears.

Though man's actual salvation and deliverance lie outside
the scope of the fable, the poem nevertheless places central
emphasis on Christ's role as Saviour and Deliverer. (Milton's
most common epithet for his hero is 'our Saviour'.) God has
chosen 'This perfect Man . . . To earn Salvation for the Sons
of men'. Satan has overheard the angelic hymn which 'sung
[him] Saviour born', and his first temptation cleverly
presents an ironic parody of the Messianic role. Christ has
come not to save himself, but to ransom others, and the
means of salvation he offers them are not carnal but spiritual.
Satan, by contrast, urges him not only to save *himself*, but
to relieve others with *physical* nourishment:

> So shalt thou save thy self and us relieve
> With Food, whereof we wretched seldom taste.

Christ's mission of salvation is the heroic enterprise for which
he is being prepared by his ordeal in the wilderness, and the
angelic chorus concludes by exhorting him to begin his
'glorious work as Saviour'.

The ideal of deliverance receives equal emphasis. As a
child the Messiah had dreamed of liberating his people from
Roman tyranny, but even in his childhood he had preferred
the inner, spiritual emancipation to the external freedom
achieved by external means:

>   . . . victorious deeds
> Flam'd in my heart, heroic acts, one while
> To rescue *Israel* from the *Roman* yoke,
> Thence to subdue and quell o're all the earth
> Brute violence and proud Tyrannick pow'r,
> Till truth were freed, and equity restor'd:
> Yet held it more humane, more heavenly first
> By winning words to conquer willing hearts,
> And make perswasion do the work of fear; . . .

To the ideal of the military liberator, he prefers a nobler alternative—the pattern of the martyr and teacher.

As the essential liberty is that of the soul, this is the object of his ministry and the target of his adversary's attack. Skilfully substituting carnal for spiritual deliverance, the tempter urges the Messiah to free his people—the end for which he was divinely ordained—but proposes the wrong sort of deliverance and the wrong sort of means. Without internal freedom, physical liberty is no more than an empty shell, and Satan in effect offers accident for substance, superficial liberty for essential freedom. He pleads the obligations of zeal and duty as incentives for liberating Israel from external bondage:

> If Kingdoms move thee not, let move thee Zeal,
> And Duty; Zeal and Duty are not slow; . . .
> Zeal of thy Fathers house, Duty to free
> Thy Country from her Heathen servitude. . . .

But Christ rejects as vain the ideal of outward liberty without the internal freedom bestowed by knowledge of the truth; he has come that men might know the truth, and that the truth might make them free. As the lost tribes can only be liberated spiritually by 'some wond'rous call' of God, the Messiah leaves them to God's 'due time and providence'.

In offering the empire of Rome, Satan presents the ideal of secular deliverance in a different guise. Urging Christ to expel Tiberius 'from his Throne', he exhorts him to assume Caesar's place and thus free a 'victor people . . . from servile yoke'. Once again, however, Christ counters Satan's offer with the argument that it is futile to attempt to free from external servitude a people who remain internal slaves:

> For him I was not sent, nor yet to free
> That people victor once, now vile and base,
> Deservedly made vassal. . . .
> What wise and valiant man would seek to free
> These thus degenerate, by themselves enslav'd,
> Or could of inward slaves make outward free?

He subjects this ideal to further criticism in denouncing the 'Conquerours' who seek glory by ruin and destruction and unjustly assume the title of 'Gods, Great Benefactors of mankind, [and] Deliverers'.

In *Paradise Lost* likewise, Christ embodies the ideals of the saviour and liberator in their perfection. In contrast to the carnal deliverance sought by the worldly hero, he achieves for his people the essential liberty, the inner freedom of the soul. The poet represents the norms of 'general safety' and deliverance in spiritual and psychological terms. In the crucial council of Book III the purport of the Father's decree is the salvation of man. Whoever accepts His free offer of grace and perseveres to the end shall 'safe arrive'. He calls for a volunteer to become mortal for man's sake and thus 'just th' unjust to save'. He spares the Son from His 'bosom and right hand' in order 'to save, By loosing [him] a while, the whole Race lost'. Messiah has quitted 'all to save A World from utter loss', and the essence of his mission is comprised in the title with which the angels extol him— 'Saviour of Men'.

The final books of *Paradise Lost* offset the pattern of salvation against the pattern of destruction. Alternating 'good with bad' and 'supernal grace' with 'sinfulness of man', Michael's survey of human history utilizes the principle of opposition to throw the concepts of 'general safety' and universal ruin into bolder relief. The ark contrasts with the flood; the salvation of the elect with the destruction of the reprobate. As a 'type' of the church, Noah's ark is designed to 'save [him] and [his] houshold from amidst a World devote to universal rack'; it prefigures the future redemption of the faithful in and through the church of Christ. In leading Israel through the wilderness to Canaan, Joshua foreshadows the 'Name and Office' of Jesus, who shall 'bring back Through the worlds wilderness long wanderd man Safe to eternal Paradise of rest'. Israel's subsequent rulers are also instruments of salvation; although the people's sins provoke God 'to raise them enemies', He nevertheless 'saves them penitent By Judges' and 'under Kings'. The salvation-motif reaches its climax, however, in the promise of the Messiah ('thy Saviour and thy Lord') and in the propagation of the gospel by his apostles:

> . . . to them [he] shall leave in charge
> To teach all nations what of him they learn'd
> And his Salvation . . .

Thus the ministry of Christ and his apostles fuses the ideal of the saviour with those of the martyr and teacher. At the same time it also elevates the saviour-ideal by raising its scope from the national to the universal. For the norm of the national leader Milton substitutes that of the universal redeemer, the saviour of 'all Nations'.

Like Milton's epics, his drama counterpoints the themes of public and private safety, and the tension between the two provides the foundation for much of the play's intrinsic irony. Though Samson has been divinely elected for the 'great work' of God's glory and the 'peoples safety', he now seems 'unequal match To save himself against a coward Arm'd At one spears length'. He has not only failed to achieve his nation's salvation; he has lost his own safety, and his amorous bondage to his wife has led to a grotesque parody of his ordained role as national saviour. Having betrayed to her the 'key of [his] strength and safety', the 'most sacred trust of secresie, [his] safety, and [his] life', he has recklessly thrown away the public safety with his own. Ironically, it is Dalila who has fulfilled the role of national saviour. To the Philistines she has proved a *salvatrix* comparable to Jael and Judith among the Hebrews—a public heroine, 'who to save Her countrey from a fierce destroyer, chose Above the faith of wedlock-bands'. Her situation is, therefore, diametrically opposite to Samson's; where he has sacrificed his nation's security for domestic peace, she has sacrificed her marriage for her country's safety.

But Milton rings further changes on the salvation-motif. In the end Samson secures his people's salvation by sacrificing his own life. Having wrongly placed his safety in Dalila's power, he finally accomplishes his mission by trusting in God alone. To Harapha's reliance on 'glorious arms', the 'ornament and safety' of 'greatest Heroes', Samson opposes his 'trust . . . in the living God'. The Lord is his salvation, and he achieves Israel's safety neither through carnal strength nor through carnal love, but through divine assistance.

Milton similarly counterpoints the theme of deliverance. Contrasting internal with external freedom, individual with national liberty, he accentuates the distinction between divine and human instruments of liberation. The central irony of the drama is the paradox of the enslaved deliverer; the central action is the resolution of this paradox. In the opening speech Samson gives definitive expression to this dilemma by stressing the apparently irreconcilable contradiction between his mission and his situation:

> Promise was that I
> Should *Israel* from *Philistian* yoke deliver;
> Ask for this great Deliverer now, and find him
> Eyeless in *Gaza* at the Mill with slaves,
> Himself in bonds under *Philistian* yoke. . . .

Both in his self-accusations and his self-justification his primary concern is his divinely appointed mission of liberation. In breaking Hebrew wedlock-customs by marrying the woman of Timna, his ulterior purpose was 'that by occasion hence I might begin *Israel*'s Deliverance, The work to which I was divinely call'd . . .'. That '*Israel* still serves with all his Sons' he blames neither on himself nor on God, but fixes the guilt on '*Israel*'s Governours, and Heads of Tribes', who have neglected God's 'Deliverance offerd' and have loved 'Bondage more then Liberty'. It is a symptom of national corruption

> . . . to despise, or envy, or suspect
> Whom God hath of his special favour rais'd
> As thir Deliverer. . . .

The antithesis between God's purpose of deliverance and the servility of the people, who reject the means of deliverance, recurs throughout the drama. The Chorus finds in Gideon and Jephtha similar examples of a 'great Deliverer contemn'd' by his people. Yet it also points out that God has 'never wanted means, Nor in respect of the enemy just cause To set his people free'. Against Harapha's taunts Samson pleads his divine 'command from Heav'n To free my Countrey' and castigates the 'servile mind' of his countrymen, who refused to receive 'Me thir Deliverer . . ., But to thir Masters gave me up for nought . . .'.

In his final act, as in his earlier exploits, Samson leaves his people a conditional freedom. God has put 'invincible might' into 'the hands of their deliverer', and the hero has fulfilled the 'work' of deliverance 'for which [he was] foretold'. He has achieved his nation's liberty:

> To *Israel*
> Honour hath left, and freedom, let but them
> Find courage to lay hold on this occasion. . . .

In sharp contrast to Samson's mission to free his country are his father's endeavours to deliver him from Philistine bondage. Manoa exercises 'a Fathers timely care To prosecute the means of [Samson's] deliverance By ransom or How else . . .'. By interviewing the Philistine Lords he acquires 'hope . . . With good success to work his liberty'. The Chorus finds these 'hopes . . . Of his delivery' plausible, and it is only the news of Samson's death that reveals the old man's hope for his son's 'Delivery' as a 'windy joy'.

The Philistine officer likewise raises hopes of Samson's deliverance by suggesting that his compliance in attending Dagon's feast may 'win the Lords . . . to set thee free'. Both Manoa's efforts and the officer's prophecy point towards Samson's freedom as a 'private person'. But in actuality the course of events which seems to move towards this end leads to public rather than private deliverance. Instead of winning his personal liberty, Samson's *agon* secures Israel's. The very act that frustrates Manoa's hope for Samson's liberation procures his people's freedom. Samson accomplishes his mission as public deliverer through his nemesis as a 'Private'. Paradoxically, it is in the role of a 'public servant' and the 'Slave' and 'Captive' of his enemies that he wins his country's deliverance.

Manoa's efforts to secure his son's freedom not only accentuate the contrast between public and private deliverance, but also emphasize the limitations of human foresight in comparison with divine Providence and the infinite disproportion between divine and human power. Where Manoa fails to free a single individual, the blind slave, under divine guidance, miraculously liberates an entire people. God accomplishes His 'propos'd deliverance' in His own time and in His own way. The means and the occasion He chooses seem contrary to probability and human expectation, but their very improbability emphasizes the gulf between man's strength and knowledge and the wisdom and power of God. The destruction of the Philistines is a divine miracle, and the 'admiration' belongs properly to God.

Another prominent motif in Milton's heroic tragedy is the antithesis between external and internal freedom. While the basic dramatic situation inevitably stresses the hero's physical blindness, physical captivity, and physical servitude, the action and dialogue emphasize their moral and spiritual counterparts. Samson's external predicament serves as a point of departure for defining the nature of spiritual blindness and spiritual servitude. His moral bondage to Dalila was, as he perceives, a more ignoble, more essential servitude than his present slavery:

> . . . servil mind
> Rewarded well with servil punishment!
> The base degree to which I now am fall'n,
> These rags, this grinding, is not yet so base
> As was my former servitude, ignoble,
> Unmanly, ignominious, infamous,
> True slavery, and that blindness worse then this,
> That saw not how degenerately I serv'd.

He rejects Dalila's offer to procure his release 'from this loathsom prison-house to abide With [her]', for he recognizes that her 'nursing diligence' would prove a 'perfect thraldom', a servitude more complete and abject than his present confinement:

> This Gaol I count the house of Liberty
> To thine whose doors my feet shall never enter.

Samson has learned the distinction between inner and outer bondage. Just as his inward illumination contrasts both with his physical blindness and with the 'blindness internal' of the Philistines, his inner freedom of the spirit provides a forceful contrast to his outer servitude. In refusing the Philistine command to perform at Dagon's feast, he meets the threat of outer force by insisting (like the Lady in *Comus*) on the freedom of the mind. In the midst of physical captivity he retains his moral liberty:

> Can they think me so broken, so debas'd
> With corporal servitude, that my mind ever
> Will condescend to such absurd commands?

Outwardly a slave, he retains his inner freedom. Like the saints the Chorus extols for their fortitude, he exhibits a patience which could make him 'his own Deliverer, and Victor over all That tyrannie or fortune can inflict'.

As in *Paradise Lost* and *Paradise Regain'd*, the essential liberty and servitude are inward and spiritual. Their outward counterparts are superficial, accidental, and ultimately contingent on the liberty or bondage of the mind. It is vain to 'seek to free' men who are 'by themselves enslav'd' or to attempt 'of inward slaves [to] make outward free'. Writing in the context of the Restoration and the failure of the Commonwealth-experiment, Milton has gone out of his way to stress spiritual liberty as a precondition of political freedom. Christ's censure of the Romans under Tiberius' tyranny and Samson's condemnation of the governors and heads of Israel have a wider application than to pre-Davidic Palestine and imperial Rome. Embodying principles universal in their scope, but especially pertinent to post-Cromwellian England, they represent Milton's reaction to the political and ecclesiastical failures of his countrymen.

Public leader, saviour, deliverer—these are all facets of the traditional epic ideal of the leader, but they are also theological commonplaces. Milton's innovation consists in introducing both secular and theological aspects of these ideals into a single poetic framework. Christ's headship of the church, his salvation of man, his deliverance of humanity from bondage to Sin and Death—these commonplaces of Christian theology acquire freshness and novelty in the context of the heroic poem, a genre almost exclusively devoted to the exploits of the worldly leader, the secular deliverer, the national saviour. The very act of grafting these

Christian norms on the old stock of the epic tradition is an act of moral and poetic judgement which exposes the ideals of the national and secular epic as inadequate or false.

In the moral crisis underlying the principal action of all three poems, the issue at stake is not merely the welfare of an individual, but that of his entire community. Samson's ordeal concerns the whole people of Israel; that of Adam or Christ affects the eternal happiness or misery of the human race. In all three cases the society with which the hero's fate is so closely interwoven is the true church—the Holy Community, the people of God. His chief antagonist—Philistine or demonic Adversary—is their traditional foe. Stressing the contrast between secular and spiritual concepts of dominion, salvation, or deliverance, all three works subordinate human leadership to that of God.

Like the *fortezza* and *sapientia* formulae, the ideal of the *dux* reduces itself to the norm of heroic faith. For all his fortitude and prudence, the 'good governor' is a subject of divine 'government', a servant of God's will and Providence. He is the instrument of a higher power; and it is God Himself who ultimately governs, delivers, and saves.

V

The Critique of *Amor*

THE heroic poem did not confine itself to the battlefield or the hall of state. It was also at home in the boudoir. Venus usurped her paramour's armour to wage her own battles across the page. The epic poet celebrated Eros' bow as well as Aeneas' arms. *Amor vincit omnia*; he too was a conqueror.[1] In Renaissance tradition love had become almost as conventional a theme as martial valour.[2]

Like Janus, the god possessed a double aspect. Facing towards heaven or earth—inspiring lust or charity, sensuality or sacred zeal—he kindled the spirit, or scorched the flesh. Linking all creatures to God, he also bound the *cavaliere servente* to his mistress. The *catena amoris* could be either the 'holy bond of thynges'[3] (nature's 'golden chain' and the 'great chain of being') or the shackles of moral slavery. Like other epic formulae, love could be a heroic virtue or a brutish passion.

[1] Cf. John Livingston Lowes, *Convention and Revolt in Poetry* (London, 1929), pp. 66–67.

[2] Marino's *L'Adone* begins with an invocation to Venus and professes to sing 'del Giovinetto amato / Le venture e le glorie alte e superbe . . .' [Giambattista Marini,] *Adone* (Firenze, 1924), Canto I, Stanza 3. *Amor* had become so common a theme in Renaissance epic that Ercilla finds it necessary to apologize for treating wars rather than love in his *Araucana* (Facsimile Edition, De Vinne Press, 1902, fol. 1⁴):

> No las Damas, amor, no gentilezas
> De cavalleros canto enamorados
> Ni las muestras, regalos, y ternezas
> De amorosos affectos y cuydados,
> Mas el valor, los hechos, las proezas
> De aquellos Españoles esforçados
> Que a la cerviz de Arauco no domada
> Puisieron duro yugo por la espada.

Subsequently, however, the author makes concessions to contemporary taste and introduces the story of Dido as an amorous episode.

[3] Cf. Geoffrey Chaucer, *Troilus and Criseyde*, Book III, line 1261.

Despite its classical antecedents, the real foundations of this motif were medieval. In the Middle Ages it had been a dominant theme of prose and verse romance; in their emphasis on amorous sentiment and adventure, the Renaissance epics of Ariosto, Boiardo, Spenser, and Tasso reflect a continuous tradition from the older cycles of Arthur and Charlemagne. The sixteenth-century romantic epic was often little more than medieval romance masquerading in classical dress. In Greek and Latin epic the *amor*-formula had usually played a subordinate role, yet this had nevertheless served as a model and stimulus to poets of the Cinquecento. *Essentially*, the love-affairs of Rinaldo and Orlando were rooted in medieval literary tradition; *superficially*, however, they showed marked affinities with classical epic and myth.

The fact that Renaissance heroic tradition comprised the romance as well as the epic gave still greater significance to love as a heroic motif. Literary frontiers had yet to be definitively drawn, and the question of their demarcation was provoking acrimonious debate among such theorists as Pigna and Giraldi, Tasso and Scaliger.[1] For its apologists, the romance constituted a separate genre—related to the epic but nevertheless distinct. For its opponents, the issue was primarily one of structure. Unwilling to recognize the romance as a different species, they dismissed it as little more than an irregular epic; ill organized and loosely composed, it violated the canons of unity. According to this view, epic and romance differed not so much in subject as in form—the distinction between 'correct' and 'incorrect' poetry, classical and barbaric modes.

For several theorists, moreover, the allied question of 'Prose or Rime' seemed largely irrelevant. For Scaliger and Sidney alike,[2] verse was no essential feature of poetry. In their eyes, such prose works as Xenophon's *Cyropaedia*, the Greek novels of Longus, Heliodorus, and Achilles Tatius, and Sidney's own *Arcadia* were heroic poems. They belonged as legitimately to the epic tradition as did the poems of

[1] For controversy over the nature of epic and romance, see Spingarn, Crocetti, and Weinberg.
[2] Cf. Smith, i. 160.

Homer and Virgil. Indeed, in Scaliger's opinion, the perfect model of epic structure was to be found in a prose romance—in Heliodorus' *Aethiopica*.[1]

Thus, for many critics, the epic tradition embraced the romance tradition almost in its entirety. It included prose and verse, multiple and single plots. Besides the romances of the 'erotici Graeci', it comprised such diverse works as Boccaccio's *Teseide* and *Filostrato*, the *Amadigi* and *Rinaldo* of the elder and younger Tasso, the *Orlando*'s of Boiardo and Ariosto, Spenser's *Faerie Queene*, and the epic romances of the minor Caroline poets. Thus conceived, the heroic tradition was much more comprehensive than it seems to modern eyes, and the *amor*-formula played a far more prominent role. Along with military fortitude, it was one of the most persistent of epic motifs.

I

Nevertheless, in classical and Renaissance epic alike, this formula was morally ambivalent. In heroic verse, love served alternatively as an incentive to martial exploits or as a stumbling-block to heroic enterprise. In most chivalric epics it spurred warriors on both sides to feats of valour. On occasion, however, it diverted them from military duty to inglorious pleasure.

On the one hand, *amor* was the spur to heroic achievement. On the other, it was the bait of sensual idleness, the fetters of 'bondage with ease'. Confronted by this ethical ambiguity, the poet found it necessary to discriminate between different forms of love—beneficial and destructive, sacred and profane, true and false. To accentuate these antitheses, several Platonic commonplaces came conveniently to hand. Mythographers and theologians had elaborated Diotima's concept of the dual Venus and twin Eros into a contrast between true love and lust, or heavenly and earthly love.[2] Dante and Petrarch, Ruiz's *Libro de Buen Amor* and

---

[1] Cf. Spingarn, *Literary Criticism*, p. 36.

[2] Cf. Plato's *Symposium* and *Phaedrus*; *Marsilio Ficino's Commentary on Plato's 'Symposium'*, ed. and tr. Sears Reynolds Jayne (Columbia, Mo., 1944); Robert Burton, *The Anatomy of Melancholy*, ed. Floyd Dell and Paul Jordan-Smith

Chaucer's *Troilus*, Sidney's *Astrophil* and Spenser's *Fowre Hymnes* had transubstantiated the 'two loves' of Platonic tradition into the antithesis between love of the Creator and love of the creature. Tasso's *Discorsi* retain the dichotomy; *amor* is moral virtue and carnal vice, both charity and lust.

As the epic became increasingly philosophical, these distinctions acquired comparable importance for character and plot. Tasso emphasized his hero's constancy in the face of erotic temptation. Unlike his followers, Godfrey remains unperturbed by Armida's charms; his zeal to liberate the Holy Sepulchre contrasts forcefully with the passion that seduces the other crusaders. The *Faerie Queene* juxtaposes the chaste love of Britomart and Artegall with the lust of philanderers like Paridell and adulteresses like Ellenore. Una's chastity accentuates Fidessa's wantonness. But in *Paradise Lost* this dichotomy between the 'two loves' acquires greater structural significance; the contrast between heavenly and earthly love assumes a central position in the epic fable.

II

The contrast between charity and passion is, for the most part, peculiar to Christian poetry. More common, in classical and Renaissance epic alike, is another variation on the antithesis between true love and lust—the opposition between illicit passion and holy wedlock. As marriage involved the dynastic principle, it was intimately connected with the hero's responsibilities to his state and throne. Hence wedded love rarely appeared in a pejorative light. On the other hand, extramatrimonial passion not only ran counter to the dynastic principle, but could on occasion prove detrimental to interests of state.

Another facet of the contrast between wedded love and illicit lust in epic tradition is the dichotomy between chastity and lawless passion. This is, on the whole, more prominent in Renaissance epic than in classical poetry. It underlies

(New York, 1927), pp. 617–23. Burton professes (p. 617) to 'examine all the kinds of Love, . . . how it is honest or dishonest, a virtue or a vice, a natural passion or a disease . . .'. Cf. Augustine, p. 477.

Spenser's treatment of Artegall and Britomart, Scudamour and Amoret, Marinell and Florimel, Redcrosse and Una.

Paradise Lost emphasizes both of these motifs. The marriage of Adam and Eve, like that of Aeneas and Lavinia or Ulysses and Penelope, involves the dynastic principle and the welfare of their posterity. But it also exemplifies the antithesis between chaste wedlock and lust:

> Hail wedded Love, mysterious Law, true source
> Of human offspring, sole propriety,
> In Paradise of all things common else.
> By thee adulterous lust was driv'n from men
> Among the bestial herds to range, by thee
> Founded in Reason, Loyal, Just, and Pure,
> Relations dear, and all the Charities
> Of Father, Son, and Brother first were known. . . .

Both as virtue and as vice, the *amor*-motif played a principal role in Renaissance epic. Though its prominence as a heroic theme was largely a heritage from medieval romance, it found theoretical support in the widespread belief that the word *heros* had been derived from *eros*. Etymologically the hero was the lover—a concept implicit in both Chaucer's 'loveres maladye of Hereos' and Bruno's 'eroici furori'. Indirectly this etymology links the Renaissance hero with the 'Heroical Love' or *amor nobilis* of medieval science[1] and the *amour courtois* of medieval literature.[2]

Paradise Lost presents a significant variation on epic tradition. Though Milton discards the military subject and sub-

---

[1] Cf. Burton's account (pp. 643–59) of 'Heroical Love', so called 'because Gallants, Noblemen, and the most generous spirits are possessed with it'. Though 'our Divines call [it] burning lust', it is 'named by our Physicians Heroical Love, and a more honourable title put upon it, Noble Love, as Savonarola styles it, because Noble men and women make a common practice of it and are so ordinarily affected with it. Avicenna calleth this passion Ilishi. . . . Arnoldus Villanovanus, in his book of Heroical Love, defines it a continual cogitation of that which he desires', etc. Cf. J. L. Lowes, 'The Loveres Maladye of Hereos', *Modern Philology*, xi (1914), pp. 491–546.

[2] Cf. Friedrich Heer, *The Mediaeval World: Europe 1100–1350*, tr. Janet Sondheimer (New York, 1963), pp. 153–96; J. Huizinga, *The Waning of the Middle Ages*, tr. F. Hopman (New York, 1954), pp. 67–128; C. S. Lewis, *The Allegory of Love: A Study in Mediaeval Tradition* (Oxford, 1936); Alexander J. Denomy, *The Heresy of Courtly Love* (New York, 1947).

stitutes moral for physical combat, he nevertheless continues to emphasize the love-motif. It remains a decisive causal factor in the epic action, and indeed it underlies the three principal heroic crises in the poem. In one form or another it motivates Adam's crucial decision as well as the central actions of Christ and Satan. Adam's rebellion springs from his passion for Eve. Satan's rebellion is allegorically figured in his incestuous dalliance with Sin. Christ's ministry of redemption is prompted by love of mankind. Contrasting modes of *amor* (concupiscence and charity) motivate antithetical actions (disobedience and obedience) and achieve antithetical rewards (damnation and salvation). In Miltonic epic, as in the heroic poems of earlier Renaissance poets, love spurs the hero's principal act. The chief difference is that the warfare is spiritual rather than carnal, ethical rather than physical.

A corollary of the greater prominence of *amor* in Renaissance epic was the increased emphasis on woman in argument and fable alike. Either as a spur to heroic action or as an obstacle to heroic achievement she plays an important role in precipitating the hero's moral crisis and motivating either his exploits on the battlefield or his withdrawal from combat. Both Ariosto and Spenser include 'ladies' along with knights in the statement of their arguments. Beauty supplements Valour as a heroic motif, and the heroine's charms complement the hero's prowess.

III

For Milton, as for other heroic poets, *amor* possessed a dual significance—as a virtue heroic and divine and as the vice contrary to temperance and charity. The crucial event of *Paradise Lost* turns on a standard dilemma of the heroic tradition—the choice between duty and passion. But the poem also incorporates other aspects of *amor* as developed in epic and romance. The moral ambiguities of *eros*—the antithesis between wedded love and lust, the opposition between physical passion and charity, the gradations of love from flesh to spirit and from creature to Creator—these contrasts, long familiar in epic tradition, assume central importance in *Paradise Lost*. Satan's role as tempter and deceiver parallels that of the unscrupulous seducer and the evil enchanter in the romance; he is both Paris and Diomede, Ismeno and Busyrane. Eve's role in the story displays marked analogies with classical or romantic prototypes. Like Dido, she distracts the hero both from his moral duty to himself and from his dynastic obligations to his posterity. Like Circe, she subverts reason to sensual passion. Like Helen and Armida, she is 'the fairest' of women; and, like Helen, she causes universal ruin. Adam's ordeal, in turn, recapitulates the familiar tension between love and honour and the rival claims of private desire and public good.

Like other heroic formulae in *Paradise Lost*, *amor* possesses both its valid image and its deceptive idol; and, as in the case of other epic ideals, Milton accentuates their differences by juxtaposition and contrast, discriminating between the true and false modes of love, between *amor* as heroic virtue and as bestial vice.

This distinction receives clearer definition in *Paradise Lost* than in most previous epics. As Milton's ethical orientation is both stronger and more consistent than that of his predecessors, he brings the issue into sharper focus. From a purely technical standpoint, however, it presented him with greater difficulties than most heroic poets had faced. Though his recognition of the problem was clearer, it was nevertheless harder to overcome in poetic terms, for *amor*'s diverse shades and gradations of meaning must necessarily be expressed through the same two persons. As Adam and Eve are the only representatives of humanity, they must personify various and often contradictory types of human love; they must embody the contrasts between the virtuous and vicious aspects of *eros* and between wedded love and lust.

Paradise Lost idealizes the romantic theme by expressing it in terms of wedded love. The lust that Adam and Eve experience after their fall differs in one important respect from that of Rinaldo and Armida or Ruggiero and Alcina. It takes place *within* the bonds of matrimony. Lust it may be, but it is not adultery. Relegating the more sordid aspects of passion to the infernal trinity, Milton links Satan, Sin, and Death together by the squalid ties of incest.

Wedlock serves as a matrix for a wide variety of related ideas. Within this single motif Milton introduces an extensive range of romantic conventions as well as Biblical concepts. Some of these are paradoxical or mutually exclusive. Like Chaucer before him, he has perceived the essential contradiction between the theological doctrine of marriage and the poetic tradition of courtly love. 'Court Amours' and 'wedded Love' are irreconcilable. The Pauline insistence on the wife's subjection to her husband's command was logically incompatible with the romantic stress on the supremacy of beauty and the mistress's command over her *cavaliere servente*. Adam's relationship with Eve involves both concepts, but Milton accentuates their inherent contradiction by seizing on the essential point of difference—the issue of sovereignty and obedience. In the first representation of the bridal pair, Eve acknowledges Adam's superiority:

> O thou for whom
> And from whom I was formd flesh of thy flesh,
> And without whom am to no end, my Guide
> And Head . . . [,]
> My Author and Disposer, what thou bidd'st
> Unargu'd I obey; so God ordains,
> God is thy Law, thou mine: to know no more
> Is womans happiest knowledge and her praise.

After the fall, Eve herself accuses him of shirking his natural responsibilities and failing to exercise his authority in the face of mutual danger:

> Being as I am, why didst not thou the Head
> Command me absolutely not to go,
> Going into such danger as thou said'st? . . .
> Hadst thou been firm and fixt in thy dissent,
> Neither had I transgressed, nor thou with mee.

Finally, Adam himself points the moral, even though he refuses to accept full blame:

> . . . perhaps
> I also err'd in overmuch admiring
> What seemd in thee so perfet. . . . Thus it shall befall

Him who to worth in Women overtrusting
Lets her Will rule; restraint she will not brook,
And left to her self, if evil thence ensue,
Shee first his weak indulgence will accuse.

In building up his idyllic picture of the first and archetypal marriage, the poet consciously represents the ideal of
wedded happiness as contingent on masculine dominance.
As long as Adam and Eve observe this principle, they
remain happy and their marriage prospers. As soon as
they neglect it, they forfeit happiness and love alike, and
their marriage founders on mutual acrimony. By carefully
associating the two ideas, *Paradise Lost* presents the principle
of masculine sovereignty as the foundation of marriage.

Milton has consciously revised poetic tradition to accord
with theological doctrine. Medieval lyric and romance had
exalted the praise of woman into a cult. Superficially it had
become a literary religion, with its own hagiography (witness
the *Legend of Good Women*), its own calendar (witness the
literature of St. Valentine's Day and May morning), its
own hymnology and philosophy (witness the verses of the
Dolce Stil Nuovo), and its own theology. If Milton seriously
intended to reorient the heroic tradition toward the principles of Christian ethics, he must necessarily cope with this
well-established convention. What he achieved, essentially,
was to discredit it by representing it as a major cause of the
fall. Satan tempts Eve in the conventional idiom of the
encomium mulieris ('the praise of woman'). The worship he
accords to her beauty, his insistence on her divinity, his
stress on her right to sovereignty lead naturally and per-
suasively to his more direct appeal based on the Biblical
text—the exhortation to partake of the unique fruit that will
confer the full enjoyment of divinity.

In Adam's case, admiration of his lady's beauty overcomes
rational judgement. In allowing her to expose herself need-
lessly to danger, he exhibits the very weakness he had revealed
earlier in his dialogue with Raphael. In the opening scene
of Book IX wisdom all too clearly 'looses discount'nanc't',
as Adam rashly subordinates his better judgement to his
wife's whim and thus precipitates their mutual disaster.

In his own fall the surrender to her will assumes even more catastrophic proportions. Once again he subordinates his reason to her opinion and thus yields to her his natural sovereignty. In both cases female dominance results in ruin. As the psychological effects of the fall all too painfully demonstrate, woman-sovereignty paradoxically destroys love and disrupts matrimonial harmony.

As Milton depicts them, the principles of *Frauendienst* are self-defeating. Founded on the exaltation of woman into goddess, they lead to moral and racial destruction. But they also result, ironically, in the negation of love. After their lapse, Adam and Eve engaged 'in mutual accusation' and 'vain contest':

> Love was not in thir looks, either to God
> Or to each other, but apparent guilt,
> And shame, and perturbation, and despaire,
> Anger, and obstinacie, and hate, and guile.

The final exposure of its moral pitfalls appears in the divine rebuke which echoes the angel's prior warning:

> Was *shee thy God*, that her thou didst obey
> Before his voice, or *was shee made thy guide*,
> Superior, or but equal, that to her
> Thou did'st resigne thy Manhood, and the Place
> Wherein God set thee above her made of thee,
> And for thee whose perfection farr excell'd
> Hers in all real dignitie.

Like Satan's exhortation to taste and 'be as Gods', this rebuke goes beyond the Biblical text to introduce an allusion to female dominance. Satan's appeal to Eve resembles the Petrarchan praise of the lady as divine—a 'goddess humane'; this 'serenate' belongs to the very type of poetry Milton had linked with 'Court Amours' as antithetical to 'wedded Love'. The poem had already drawn on the conventions of woman sovereignty to portray Adam's emotional dependence on Eve and set the stage for his moral surrender. After this careful build-up, the query 'Was shee thy God [?]' provides the final commentary on the romantic exaltation of woman as goddess. It is a divine refutation of *Frauendienst*.

The reverse side of the coin is the Biblical principle of masculine sovereignty. Theologically, it represented the orthodox view; poetically—or at least for romantic poetry— it was heretical. Though it might find support in classical epic, it ran counter to the main currents of medieval and Renaissance poetic tradition. Romantic love usually dispensed with the benefits of clergy. When it was not adulterous, it was usually pre-nuptial. Marriage might provide the consummation, but rarely the precondition, of romance. Though it might be the goal and 'happy ending' of the lover's ordeal, it was seldom the starting-point of his quest. Romantic love might remain unfulfilled, as in the case of Orlando's passion for Angelica. It might aim at eventual marriage, as with Ruggiero and Bradamante, Artegall and Britomart, or Arcita and Emily. Or it might be adulterous, as with Tristan and Iseult, Lancelot and Guinevere, or Paolo and Francesca. But it was not, as a rule, associated with the married state.[1]

When Milton attempts to reconcile the paradoxical ideas of husband and lover and the concepts of marriage and romantic love, he does so on a very different basis. Unlike Chaucer's Franklin, he resolves the paradox in favour of masculine sovereignty, and thus reintegrates literary convention with theological norms. In stressing the husband's '*maistrye*', he not only represents it as the condition of marital bliss, but also invests it with many of the conventions of romantic epic and lyric. He consciously fits the ideal of romantic love into the context of masculine dominion. Adam's very embraces are attended with consciousness of 'superior Love', and the sensuous details of Eve's beauty are linked with the idea of submission:

> Half her swelling breast
> Naked met his under the flowing Gold
> Of her loose tresses hid: he in delight
> Both of her Beauty and submissive Charms
> Smil'd with superior Love. . . .

---

[1] To the great ladies of France, courtly love seemed incompatible with marriage. In their opinion, the offices of husband and lover were separate, distinct, and irreconcilable, and they indignantly repudiated the thesis that a woman might accept her own husband as her lover. Cf. Heer, p. 172.

With its extended description of Eve's nuptial bower, her physical beauty, her lyricism, and her love-affair with Adam, Book IV is essentially a pastoral idyll devoted to the type of *amor* usually encountered in Arcadian romances. The romantic theme, however, is inextricably interwoven with the motif of Adam's unchallenged sovereignty. Milton's first description of Adam and Eve emphasizes their superlative beauty ('Adam, the goodliest man of men since born His sons, the fairest of her daughters Eve') and evokes the romantic tradition through such conventional terminology as 'gentle pair', 'love's embraces', and 'youthful dalliance'. But the same passage also stresses masculine dominion. The contrast between Adam's 'Absolute rule' and Eve's graceful 'subjection' is manifest in their physical appearance. This portrait of the relationship between Adam and Eve in the Earthly Paradise is the diametric opposite of Tasso's picture of Armida and Rinaldo in the 'paradise of love': 'He proud of bondage, of her empire she.'

Both in their paradisal setting and their sensual detail, these scenes bear a distinct resemblance to the love-scenes of romantic epic. But they are, in fact, a mirror-image, where the ethical values are completely reversed. In Eden, sensuous delight is still innocent; in the false paradises of Armida, Alcina, and Acrasia, it is tainted with vice. In the allegorical gardens of these Renaissance temptresses, the hero is a thrall to his mistress's charms; in Milton's garden, as he first describes it, Adam exercises indisputable sovereignty over his lady.

But Eve herself possesses many of the graces of the Renaissance temptress, and Milton portrays her in terms that could have been applied to Tasso's Armida. Eve is 'the fairest of her daughters'. Armida similarly possesses 'such sacred beauties' that

> . . . never yet did heav'n such grace bestow
> On any daughter born of Adam's line . . .

nor has any 'eye to Cupid's service vow'd Beheld a face of such a lovely pride'. Eve possesses 'Beauty, which whether waking or asleep, Shot forth peculiar Graces':

>   . . . for on her as Queen
> A pomp of winning Graces waited still,
> And from about her shot Darts of desire.

Armida's eye likewise 'keeps his shot where Cupid keeps his fort', and when she sleeps,

> Thrice twenty Cupids unperceived flew
> To gather up this liquor, ere it fall,
> And of each drop an arrow forged new; . . .

Eve's beauty fills Adam with 'admiration' and leaves Satan himself 'overawd'; Armida's beauty leaves the crusaders 'amazed' and fills them with 'wonder'. Both Satan and Adam stress the 'merit' and 'worth' Eve's beauty confers on her; Armida's admirers emphasize their own 'unworthiness' in comparison with her beauty and the 'honors due [her] high estate'. These parallels, conventional in romantic lyric and epic, do not, of course, indicate that Milton has modelled his heroine on Tasso's temptress. They *do* indicate, however, that Eve possesses many of the familiar features of the romantic heroine and that she belongs, in part, to the same tradition as Armida.

For Chaucer's Franklin, *amor* and *maistrye* were incompatible; for Milton, they are inseparable. Happiness is contingent on love (for 'without Love no happiness'), but both are contingent on order. Eve's subjection to Adam is the ground of their marital bliss, just as their spiritual blessedness depends on their subjection to divine authority. Love and obedience are not only closely interrelated; they are, indeed, virtually identical. Raphael explicitly defines love as obedience; 'to love [God] is to obey [Him] and keep His great command'. Whereas the Franklin had argued that sovereignty violates love's inherent freedom, the angel associates it specifically with liberty:

>   . . . freely we serve,
> Because we freely love, as in our will
> To love or not. . . .

In equating these concepts, Milton appeals to natural law. If love and obedience are identical, it is because both are rooted in nature and because nature itself exhibits the principle of hierarchy. The 'ladder of nature' is also the 'ladder of love' and the 'scale of contemplation'. Symbolized poetically by the golden chain that ties the universe to Heaven, it links the various orders of created beings in a common bond of love both with one another and with their Creator. But the 'scale of nature' is not only a ladder of love; it is also an instrument of knowledge and a precondition of service. As an object of contemplation it is the means of intellectual ascent to God. As a hierarchy of beings varying in merit and capacity, it is a precondition of the moral order, for it imposes on all created beings a system of mutual duties and obligations. The structure of society is founded on the structure of the universe itself. The order of nature is not simply a metaphysical order; it is also the basis of the ethical order and the order of love.

It is also the precondition of self-knowledge. To stand or fall depends ultimately on insight into one's own nature. For man and angel alike, happiness depends on observing the principle of nature and acting in accordance with his own essence and degree; conversely, transgression of natural order entails as its chief penalty alienation from his true nature and proper bliss. Since beatitude is contingent on love and obedience to his natural superiors, self-knowledge is essential for love, as for righteousness (*justitia*) and happiness. Satan fell through disregarding the angelic nature; the angels are, by their very essence, 'ministering spirits'. The faithful angels retain their original state because they do not contradict their own nature; significantly, the angel who first challenges Satan's claim to independence is entitled '*Servant* of God'. For Adam likewise, self-knowledge is a prerequisite of true *amor*. His interview with his Creator reveals an insight into his own nature and its basic differences from that of higher and lower orders—God and beast; he knows that, by nature, he requires companionship and must take a mate from his own species. He also knows that Eve is his intellectual inferior. Both in this dialogue and in his subsequent conversation with Raphael, Adam displays his awareness of his own nature, its advantages, and its limitations. When he falls, it is through failure to act upon this insight. For man and angel alike, endowed as they are with reason and free will, the concepts of *amor* and self-knowledge are inseparable.

By placing the motif of romantic love within the context of matrimony,[1] Milton gives it a moral elevation notably lacking in most of his predecessors. Even his treatment of sensual details emphasizes the purity of human desire in the state of original innocence. Ennobling the physical consummation of love by representing it as an essential aspect of holy wedlock, he stresses its inherent sanctity. As a divine institution it is holy; as an expression of unfallen nature it is pure. Nature's ministrations to its fulfilment—the evening star, the nightingale's epithalamion, and the floral architecture of Eve's bower—all accentuate its instinctive holiness, its conformity to natural law. The embraces of Adam and Eve are worlds removed from those of Spenser's Ellenore and her lovers or the passion of Ariosto's Angelica and Medoro. The former are untainted by guilt; the latter are the victims of a fallen *eros*.

The same moral gravity characterizes the description of Eve's physical charms. As Milton develops it, this motif too is emblematic of original purity and the state of innocence. In the romance tradition nakedness is not uncommonly associated with lust or shame. The unclad damsels in the gardens of Armida and Acrasia are symbols of carnal passion; poetically and allegorically, they derive from the classical Sirens. The cupbearers of classical myth are equally suspect. But when Eve 'minister[s] naked' to Adam and Raphael at their rural feast she is, on the contrary, a symbol of innocence:

> . . . no veil
> Shee needed, Virtue-proof, no thought infirm
> Alter'd her cheek.

Her beauty inspires delight without prurience:

---

[1] For conjugal love as the 'form' of marriage, see *De Doctrina*, Book I, Chapter 10; cf. Book II, Chapter 15, on the duties of husband and wife; cf. *Doctrine and Discipline of Divorce* (Columbia Edition, iii. 391), . . . 'in God's intention a meet and happy conversation is the chiefest and noblest end of marriage . . .'.

. . . but in those hearts
Love unlibidinous reign'd, nor jealousy
Was understood, the injur'd Lover's Hell.

Clad in 'native Honour' and righteousness, she needs no
other garment. In his treatment of Adam and Eve before the
fall, Milton reconciles the Renaissance delight in the human
form with Biblical ethos. Their very nudity possesses a moral
significance.

Again, what a striking contrast one finds between the
scene of Eve's exposure to Satan's malice and the ordeal of
other poetic heroines similarly exposed, naked and helpless,
to evil! In the romances such scenes are, for the most part,
deliberately sensational. Eve's situation is roughly analogous
to that of Tasso's Silvia bound by a satyr,[1] Ariosto's Angelica
and Olimpia exposed to the Orc, and Spenser's Pastorella
menaced by savages. These romantic heroines are in mortal
peril from violence, Milton's from fraud. But where the
Aminta, the *Orlando Furioso*, and the *Faerie Queene* treat
nudity as an erotic motif, *Paradise Lost* converts it into a
symbol of innocence.

Taking his cue from Genesis, Milton renders the contrast
between man's fallen and unfallen state more forceful
through vestiary symbolism. The antithesis between 'beauty
bare' and beauty clothed and adorned is roughly analogous
to the symbolism of Titian's painting commonly known as
'Sacred and Profane Love'. In her 'naked beauty' Eve is
'more adorn'd More lovely than *Pandora* . . .'. To this
ideal of native, unsophisticated beauty Milton opposes the
corrupt beauty of adornment. The 'daughters of men' who
seduce the 'Sons of God' are 'A Bevy of fair Women, richly
gay In Gems and wanton dress', and Dalila is 'bedeckt, ornate,
and gay, . . . Like a stately Ship . . . With all her bravery on
. . .'. As in Titian's painting, innocent love is associated with
'naked beauty', and fallen *eros* with concealment and adornment.

After the fall, however, 'naked beauty'—originally a
sign of innocence—becomes an instrument of seduction.

[1] *Teatro di Torquato Tasso*, ed. Angelo Solerti (Bologna, 1895), p. 80; *Aminta*,
Act III.

Emblematically, there is a marked resemblance between the picture of Eve extending the fruit of knowledge to Adam and the portrait of Venus receiving the apple of discord from Paris. Their moral significance is essentially the same, and Milton has laid the foundation for the analogy by expressly comparing Eve's 'undeckt' beauty with that of Venus in the Judgement of Paris:

> . . . but *Eve*
> Undeckt, save with herself more lovely fair
> Than Wood-Nymph, or the fairest Goddess, feign'd
> Of three that in Mount *Ida* naked strove,
> Stood to entertain her guest. . . .

Like Paris, Adam submits his 'better knowledge' to 'femal charm' and precipitates the ruin of mankind, just as Paris causes the destruction of Troy. Like Paris, he prefers the 'voluptuous life' to the ideals of contemplation and valour. In his temptation the motif of naked beauty resumes its conventional association with sensual delight and passion.

IV

In its power to arouse admiration even in its enemies, Eve's beauty serves the essential end of the heroic poetry—to arouse marvel and wonder. Its function is thus analogous to that of heroic virtue, and it is significant that Eve's role parallels, to the point of parody, the role of the epic hero. Satan's first glimpse of the 'gentle pair' fills him with admiration:

> . . . whom my thoughts pursue
> With wonder, and could love, so lively shines
> In them Divine resemblance, and such grace
> The hand that form'd them on thir shape hath pour'd.

The sight of Eve alone in the garden again inspires wonder and awe. For a moment it makes him forget his purposed revenge:

> . . . her Heav'nly form
> Angelic, but more soft, and Feminine,
> And graceful Innocence, her every Air
> Of gesture or least action overaw'd

His Malice, and with rapine sweet bereav'd
His fierceness of the fierce intent it brought:
That space the Evil one abstracted stood
From his own evil, and for the time remain'd
Stupidly good, of enmity disarm'd,
Of guile, of hate, of envy, of revenge. . . .

The deliberate paradoxes in this passage intensify the
element of marvel by stressing the quasi-supernatural
efficacy of Eve's beauty; it produces a near-miracle in the
beholder. Momentarily it 'un-Satans' Satan. The Adversary temporarily discards his hostility; the 'Evil one' forgets
his evil. This metamorphosis borders on the miraculous,
and it is designed to emphasize the power of 'Femal charm'.
In this way it lends additional probability and verisimilitude to Adam's lapse.

In thus stressing both the moral force of beauty and its
power to thwart a 'heroic' enterprise, Milton is adapting
two familiar commonplaces of the romantic tradition. His
originality lies in applying these concepts to the devil himself. Unlike the usual epic action, Satan's enterprise is
categorically and absolutely evil, and the beneficial effects
of Eve's charms are all too temporary. Nevertheless, the
scene makes its point by an argument *a minori*. If beauty can
disarm the most malignant of enemies, how much stronger
must be its power over a lover! If it can momentarily para-
lyse an evil enterprise, how great must be its capacity to
block the difficult and laborious tasks of virtue! If it can lend
goodness to the 'Evil one' himself, how much more powerful must be its effects on an upright character! Limited
though it is, its impact on Satan foreshadows its impact on
Adam and thus prepares the stage for his fall. If 'Femal
charm' can divert Satan from malice, it can also divert
Adam from righteousness.

Eve is not, of course, designed for heroism or for exploits
of public moment. Her sphere is domestic, and decisions
that affect the welfare of society are beyond her capacities
and responsibilities. Yet the actual result of forsaking Adam's
protection is to force her into a public role. Unlike her
husband, she meets the grand foe face to face, she encounters

the whole force of his guile, and she makes the decision crucial for her husband's kingdom and for the welfare of their entire posterity. Without realizing it, she acts as a 'public person' and affects the fate of all mankind. In the spiritual duel with Satan, she becomes unwittingly the champion of the whole race, the warrior on whose skill the empire of the world depends.

The spectacle of Eve departing to brave an encounter with her archfoe is a graceful one, like Venus entering the field of combat or Iole sporting Hercules' lionskin and club. But in the event her pretensions prove as futile as those of the goddess of love, who flees from the Trojan battleground after the first blow. When Eve meets her enemy, she fails to recognize him; she fights and loses the crucial duel without perceiving it for what it is.

There are distinct heroic overtones in her ordeal. In seeking wisdom, she pursues the goal of the contemplative hero. In aiming at godhead, she levels at the reward of such classical heroes as Hercules, Castor and Pollux, and Julius and Augustus Caesar. In risking death for the sake of glory, she displays a superficial resemblance to Achilles and Ruggiero, whose destiny offers them a short life coupled with undying fame.

These analogies, however, are intentionally ironic. Milton has as little sympathy for the woman-warrior—the *donna guerriera* and the *femme forte*—as for female sovereignty. Both violate the order of nature and female decorum. In meeting her enemy face to face, Eve usurps Adam's role, just as Adam, in following his wife's leadership, forsakes his own matrimonial office for hers. The fall is closely interwoven with a reversal in the duties of husband and wife. Like Satan, Eve serves as heroic idol. Her 'heroism' is doubly illusory—first, because she exhibits it in an act of sin; secondly, because it befits her husband's nature rather than her own. The conflict she seeks demands contemplation and valour rather than softness and grace. The roles of Adam and Eve in the fall are as much a violation of decorum as those of Hercules and Iole.

V

Adam's temptation is also a spiritual combat, but it belongs to a different order from Eve's. Unlike his wife, he does not meet his foe directly. He does not exercise his powers of contemplation and valour. Nor does he regard his decision as heroic; from the beginning he acknowledges his defeat ('and me with thee hath ruin'd'). His failure exhibits the classic pattern of moral surrender already established in epic tradition. In the crisis of honour he sacrifices duty to love, public welfare to private passion, and reason to appetite. Neglecting his dynastic obligations for personal desire, he subordinates the claims of kingdom and posterity to those of *eros*. He places *amor* before *pietas*, and his physical bond with Eve before his spiritual allegiance to God. Preferring earthly to heavenly love, he yields to his lady the obedience that by nature he owes to his Creator. As a reward his decision wins him 'his ladyes grace', but forfeits the favour of God.

Love can be either a passion or a virtue, and at the moment of his fall Adam is under no delusions; he recognizes his motive as passion and his action as vice. But the moral ambivalence of *amor* is deceptive; ironically enough, Eve hails his transgression as heroic virtue: 'O glorious trial of *exceeding* love!' (Italics mine.) By definition, *virtù eroica* consists in an excess. But so does vice, and Eve naïvely confuses the two. Misreading the vicious excess of passion as virtuous excellence, she mistakes Adam's intemperance and incontinence for heroic love.

Like Eve's temptation, Adam's ordeal involves the idol of true heroism. It bears a superficial resemblance to heroic virtue. He has made what appears, on the surface, to be a heroic renunciation. Like Mark Antony, he has given 'all for love'. He has sacrificed his own life to serve his lady and given up the whole world for her sake. This looks like heroic constancy—a firmness of devotion in adverse fortune, a love that 'looks on tempests and is never shaken'. But, in reality, it is the opposite. Adam has chosen the lesser love before the greater, and his constancy to Eve is inconstancy in love toward God. He has preferred earthly to heavenly love, love of the creature to *amor Dei*.

VI

In defining human love, Milton brought its essential characteristics into clearer focus by contrasting it with the love of beasts and angels—the two levels immediately below and above man in the scale of being. Even more significant for his critique of *amor*, however, are the contrasts with still further extremes—divine love and infernal desire.

The faithful angels love more intensely and more perfectly than man. The fallen angels do not love at all. Bearing within them the fierce extremes of Hell, they burn with unfulfilled desire. When Satan first beholds Adam and Eve, he is struck by their beauty and can almost 'love' them for their 'grace' and 'Divine resemblance'. But, like the other fallen angels, he is incapable of love, and the spectacle of their embrace arouses envy and jealous rage. As Adam correctly perceives, 'no bliss Enjoy'd by us excites his envy more' than 'Conjugal Love'. Finally, immediately before the temptation-scene, the delight that Satan experiences at the sight of Eve's beauty proves all too short-lived and turns instead to 'Fierce hate', the logical contrary of love:

> But the hot Hell that always in him burnes,
> Though in mid Heav'n, soon ended his delight,
> And tortures him now more, the more he sees
> Of pleasure not for him ordain'd. . . .

To Hell's 'fierce desire' Milton opposes Heaven's charity. The moral opposition between *amor* as passion and as virtue is thus mirrored in the divine machinery. In mankind the two modes of love are mixed; Adam can experience either passion or charity. In Heaven and Hell, on the other hand, they are separate and distinct. Though Satan can feel desire, he is incapable of charity. Conversely, God and the faithful angels feel charity without passion. The antithesis to Satanic concupiscence and Satanic hate is Messiah's love, the divine charity that submits to mortality in order to save mankind.

Charity thus unites with fortitude, and the Son's decision to die for man's salvation becomes the supreme example both of *amor* and of *fortezza*. In the Biblical text (John xv. 13, 'Greater love hath no man than this, that a man should lay down his life for his friends') Milton finds the norm of heroic *caritas*.

The very structure of the poem lends clearer definition to this antithesis between divine *amor* and its demonic opposite. The parallel between the infernal and celestial councils accentuates the contrast between Satan's campaign of hate and Heaven's strategy of love. But the fable also emphasizes the further contrast between human passion and divine love. The 'exceeding love' which prompts Adam to die with Eve finds its celestial counterpart in the 'unexampl'd love'—the 'Love nowhere to be found less than Divine'—which moves the Messiah 'to die for man's offence'. Where Adam is seduced by passion, Christ is inspired by charity. The one is merely the idol of heroic love; the other is its true image.

The Son's heroic charity resolves the conflict between the formulae of love and leadership. Through love of mankind he becomes its head and dies to redeem it. Accepting the dynastic responsibilities which Adam has neglected, he restores to Adam's posterity the sovereignty their progenitor has forfeited and elevates humanity to the throne of Heaven.

As Milton presents it, charity[1]—*verus amor*—is the 'soul'

---

[1] Cf. *PL,* Book XII, lines 583–5. Milton's *De Doctrina* distinguishes several senses of love. 'Love [*Charitas*], or the Worship of God' is one of the two 'divisions' of Christian doctrine and is closely associated with obedience (Book I, Chapter 1). As the 'true worship of God', it 'consists chiefly in the exercise of good works' (Book II, Chapter 1). 'The Love of God [*Amor Dei*] is that by which we prefer him above all other objects of affection, and desire his glory.' This is one of the 'virtues belonging to the worship of God', and its opposite is 'a hatred of God' (Book II, Chapter 3). Love (*Charitas*) or holiness of life (*sanctitas vitae*) is one of the effects of the 'new life' (*vita nova*) of the regenerate. It arises from a 'sense of the divine love shed abroad in the hearts of the regenerate by the Spirit, whereby those who are ingrafted in Christ being influenced, become dead to sin, and alive again unto God, and bring forth good works spontaneously and freely. This is also called Holiness [*sanctitas*]'. This type of love is not 'brotherly love' nor 'even the ordinary affection which we bear to God, but one resulting from a consciousness and lively sense of the love wherewith he has loved us, and which in theology is reckoned the third after faith and hope'. It is the 'offspring' of faith and 'the parent of good works'.

of all the other virtues. In the Son it is coupled with wisdom and fortitude and the responsibilities of the leader; out of love towards humanity and obedience towards God, he risks death to save a 'whole Race lost'. It is associated with magnanimity; for only the Son of God is capable of so great a love ('Love nowhere to be found less than Divine'), and only he can redeem the corrupted world and fallen mankind ('whom thou only canst redeem'). It is linked with zeal for God's glory, for it is to 'glorify' the Father that the Son humbles himself to the 'form' of a servant.

In Satan, on the other hand, charity has become its diametrical opposite—malice; love has turned to hatred of Creator and creation alike. He pursues his enterprise in defiance of reason, and thus violates his responsibilities towards his followers; for the sake of revenge he consciously plunges them into deeper damnation and greater torments. Even though he displays constancy in evil and apparent magnanimity in his concern for his own honour, these are spurious virtues. Setting himself in direct opposition to the divine will, he is, paradoxically, constant only in inconstancy, obedient only in disobedience. His magnanimity is counterfeit because based not on a just recognition of his own nature but on a presumptuous overestimation of his merits. He is zealous not for God's glory, but for his own.

In Adam's 'trial of love' the issues are as clear-cut as in the case of Aeneas and Dido—on the one hand, ties of personal passion; on the other, public duty and obedience to the will of God. Though neither hero hesitates, the two men choose very differently. Aeneas forsakes Dido to obey Jove's decree; Adam transgresses Jehovah's[1] ordinance to

Because of 'this love or sanctity . . . all believers are called Saints' (Book II, Chapter 21).

For love as one of the 'general virtues' pertaining to 'our duties towards men', 'infused into believers by God the Father in Christ through the Spirit', and comprehending 'the whole duty of love which each individual owes to himself and his neighbour', see Book II, Chapters 8 and 11.

[1] For Milton, the name Jehovah belongs properly and primarily to God the Father alone. According to the *De Doctrina* (Book I, Chapter 5) such texts as Jer. xxx. 9, Ps. cx. 1, and Deut. xviii. 15 'expressly' distinguish Christ from 'the one God Jehovah'. When the Scriptures apply this term to the Son or to the angels, they do so only by extension. Thus 'the name of Jehovah is conceded

cling to Eve. In thus placing private love before duty and honour, he resembles Rinaldo in Armida's bower, or Astolfo and Ruggiero on Alcina's isle. Though Eve is no sorceress, the term 'Femal charm' evokes the tradition of the fair enchantress. Ethically, her charms have the same effect as Armida's magic and Alcina's spells. Moreover, like Armida and Angelica—and like Dalila after her—she assumes the role of the beautiful infidel. After partaking of the forbidden fruit she lapses into idolatry and drags Adam with her into sacrilege. In seducing her husband from his religious duty, she exhibits the characteristic features of the 'fair idolatresses' of romantic epic and foreshadows such Biblical examples as Solomon's wives and the 'daughters of men'. In yielding to Eve's charms, Adam is, in effect, a victim of Acrasia.

Paradise Regain'd makes only a limited use of the *amor*-formula. The hero's 'constancy' is to be tried by 'manlier objects' than female beauty. Moreover, since Milton's hero is Christ himself, there would be a distinct danger in showing him tempted by sensual passion. The poet might be vulnerable to the charge of sacrilege, and indeed a French religious epic in the following century was suppressed precisely on these grounds. Nevertheless, the *amor*-motif was so deeply entrenched in the heroic tradition that Milton was obliged to explain its absence. By allowing Belial to propose it and Satan to reject it as unsuitable, he retained the moral value of this theme without introducing it directly into the action.

Belial's exhortation to 'Set women in his eye and in his

even to the angels . . ., when they represent the divine presence and person, and utter the very words of Jehovah'. Indeed, 'the Son himself professes to have received from the Father, not only the name of God and of Jehovah, but all that pertains to his own being,—that is to say, his individuality, his existence itself, his attributes, his works, his divine honors . . .'.

In *Paradise Lost* it is by this name that the angels hail the Creator after His 'Six dayes acts' ('Great are thy works, *Jehovah*') and exalt this exploit above His previous victory over the rebel angels. Significantly both acts have been accomplished *by* the Father, but *through* the agency of the Son (*'per eum'*, in the language of the *De Doctrina*). In Milton's draft for a drama on 'Adam unparadiz'd' (Columbia Edition, xviii. 231), 'Justice cites [Adam] to the place whither Jehova call'd for him'. In the judgement scene of *Paradise Lost*, the Judge is the Son, again acting as the agent of the Father.

walk' echoes many of the familiar motifs of the romantic tradition. Women are 'like to Goddesses' and endowed with 'Virgin majesty'. Such details as these are commonplaces of Renaissance love-poetry, and they are also reminiscent of Satan's addresses to Eve in *Paradise Lost*. Belial supplements them, however, with other commonplaces derived more specifically from the Circe-tradition. Women are 'Expert in amorous Arts'. They possess 'enchanting tongues Persuasive'. They are 'Skill'd to . . . draw Hearts after them tangl'd in Amorous Nets'. They have the 'power' to 'Enerve, and with voluptuous hope dissolve, . . . and lead at will the manliest resolutest breast'. They have the ability to seduce the wisest of men from true faith to idolatry.

In stressing the power of 'the fairest' of women, Belial appeals to a tradition that includes Helen of Troy, Armida and Angelica, and Milton's Eve. In emphasizing 'Virgin majesty' he evokes the idea of female sovereignty. In representing beauty as a temptation to constancy, he follows the precedent established by Boiardo, Ariosto, and Tasso. Love had caused Orlando, Ruggiero, and a host of other worthies to break their feudal vows and neglect their duty.

Satan's retort serves a double function. It refutes Belial's argument, but it also emphasizes the dichotomy between amorous servitude and heroic enterprise, the incompatibility of passion with the pursuit of 'Higher design' and 'the accomplishment of greatest things'. Such terms as 'wonder' and 'admiration'—properly applicable to heroic virtue— recall the effect of Eve's beauty on her tempter in *Paradise Lost*. The contrasting concepts of the 'sitting Queen ador'd on Beauty's Throne' and 'one look from his Majestic brow' emphasize the antithesis between female dominion and male sovereignty. In declaring that

> . . . Beauty stands
> In the admiration only of weak minds
> Led captive; . . . .

Satan evokes the idea of erotic bondage foreshadowed in the Circe-myth and elaborated in romantic epic. But he also echoes Raphael's admonition to Adam.

In this brief dialogue of devils, Milton condenses the essential points of his critique of the *amor*-formula—a critique he had presented in greater detail in *Paradise Lost* and would develop dramatically in *Samson Agonistes*. By restricting the pejorative aspects of love primarily to Belial's abortive suggestion, he leaves himself scope to develop more crucial temptations—secular wisdom and power, the 'kingdoms of the world'—and to emphasize the positive aspects of *amor*—obedience and charity.

In the dialogue between Satan and Belial, Milton points his moral by the example of Solomon, lured into idolatry by pagan concubines. Like Armida, they aid the cause of false religion by enticing their victim from divine obedience and making him serve God's foes. A similar situation prevails in *Samson Agonistes*. Once again, sensual passion seduces the hero from his divinely ordained enterprise and renders him subservient to a beautiful infidel. As her own words indicate, Dalila is an instrument of a rival religion and a rival polity. In her appeal to Samson, she employs many of the conventional lures of the romantic heroine. She offers sensual delight. She employs the conventional language and imagery of courtly love. Like Helen and Angelica, she represents the seductive force of beauty—its '. . . strange power, After offence returning, to regain Love once possest . . .'. But Samson is not Menelaus.

Though she is no sorceress, Milton's imagery places her squarely in the tradition of Circe, Alcina, and Armida, and her moral significance is essentially the same:

> . . . I know thy trains,
> Though dearly to my cost, thy gins, and toils;
> Thy fair enchanted cup, and warbling charms
> No more on me have power, their force is null'd,
> So much of Adder's wisdom I have learn't
> To fence my ear against thy sorceries.

Like Armida, she is schooled in the wiles of seduction:

> . . . these are thy wonted arts,
> And arts of every woman false like thee. . . .
> I thought where all thy circling wiles would end;
> In feign'd Religion, smooth hypocrisy.

Finally, like Alcina and Armida, Dalila has reduced her victim to moral servitude and spiritual blindness. Like Alcina's victims, Samson has been deceived, 'effeminatly vanquish't', ruined, and finally dismissed 'ridiculous' and 'despoil'd'.

Dalila's offer of 'ease' and freedom from 'care and chance' is, as he perceives, a further 'snare'—the same sort of moral servitude he has, at great personal cost, escaped. 'Ignoble ease' and 'peaceful sloth' had traditionally been stumbling-blocks to the heroic enterprise and the pursuit of 'strenuous Liberty'. Her proposal amounts in effect to a negation of heroic virtue, and Samson rejects it as the spiritual bondage it really is.

In his drama, as in his epic, the poet has employed a conventional motif of the heroic tradition—the hero's failure in public duty through amorous bondage. Milton has transferred it from its usual context—adulterous passion for a harlot—and adapted it to the framework of matrimony. This enables him to avoid a direct representation of 'adulterous lust', but it also provides an opportunity for contrasting the romantic convention of female sovereignty with the Biblical ideal of masculine dominion. Dalila has admittedly sought to 'get into my power Thy key of strength and safety' and to hold her husband 'Mine and Love's prisoner'. As an antithesis to this 'regiment of women' the Chorus reaffirms the Scriptural doctrine of marriage, the principle of male sovereignty:

> Therefore God's universal Law
> Gave to the man despotic power
> Over his female in due awe,
> Nor from that right to part an hour,
> Smile she or lour:
> So shall he least confusion draw
> On his whole life, not sway'd
> By female usurpation, nor dismay'd.

Dalila's argument is a *reductio ad absurdum* of the sovereignty-motif so prominent in the tradition of courtly love and romance. The actual result of her avowed attempt to make her lover 'Mine and Loves prisoner, not the *Philistines*' has

been to make him, in the fullest sense of the word, a Philistian slave. The metaphorical captivity of the lover has resulted in literal bondage. Milton has given this rhetorical
figure a literal application.

But if female sovereignty is contrary to the law of nature,
so too is the heroic role in which Dalila casts herself. One of
the most galling ironies of Samson's predicament is the disparity between his own abortive heroism and his wife's
triumph. Her victory is the diametrical opposite of his own
defeat, for she has won in the very points where he has so
signally failed. She has delivered her country and served her
gods; he has failed both Israel and Jehovah. He has sacrificed public duty to private affection; she has placed public
interest above personal love. Where Samson has failed in
obedience and zeal to his God, she has demonstrated her
'zeal . . . To please [her] gods'. Where he suffers the penalties
of failure—public dishonour and disgrace—she enjoys the
full rewards of victory—'public marks of honour and rewards
. . . for the piety Which to my country I was judg'd to have
shown'. He is 'to Ages an example' of amorous folly. She is
the Philistine counterpart of the Hebrew heroines Jael and
Deborah and Judith, the pagan equivalent of the *femme
forte*:

> But in my country where I most desire,
> In *Ekron*, *Gaza*, *Asdod*, and in *Gath*
> I shall be nam'd among the famousest
> Of Women, sung at solemn festivals,
> Living and dead recorded, who to save
> Her country from a fierce destroyer, chose
> Above the faith of wedlock-bands, my tomb
> With odours visited and annual flowers.
> Not less renown'd than in Mount *Ephraim*,
> *Jael*, who with inhospitable guile
> Smote *Sisera* sleeping through the Temples nail'd.

Like Eve, Dalila affects heroic virtue; she plays a role outwardly heroic, but as unnatural as that of the female warrior. Yet, as in Eve's case, her heroic pretensions prove vain
and insubstantial; they are merely idols of heroic virtue.
None of these prophecies of future fame and honour are

fulfilled. Instead of saving her country, she becomes the occasion of its ruin. Instead of exalting her gods, she precipitates their humiliation. In the long run, after his race of glory and shame, the flower-decked tomb and the related emblems of public honour fall to Samson.

For Renaissance conceptions of *amor* see J. C. Nelson, *Renaissance Theory of Love* (New York, 1958), and Maurice Jacques Valency, *In Praise of Love: An Introduction to the Love-Poetry of the Renaissance* (New York, 1958).

VI

The Critique of Magnanimity

OF all the moral virtues, magnanimity bore the closest resemblance to heroic virtue. For Tasso, they were almost indistinguishable; the chief difference was that the former aimed at honour, the latter at glory. This theoretical distinction, however, had little effect on heroic poetry. Renaissance moralists disagreed as to the precise distinctions between glory, honour, and praise; and Renaissance poets rarely attempted to differentiate them. The 'magnificence' of Spenser's Arthur is scarcely distinguishable from heroic virtue.

Ethically and structurally, the leitmotiv of Spenser's epic is the relationship between magnanimity and its proper end—honour or glory. Since this virtue includes all others, Prince Arthur intervenes in books primarily devoted to more specific qualities—holiness, temperance, and the like. His pursuit of Gloriana—i.e. glory—links the arguments of the separate books.

Aristotle's discussion of *megalopsychia* had placed primary emphasis on merit. The 'man is thought to be [magnanimous] who thinks himself worthy of great things, being worthy of them; for he who does so beyond his deserts is a fool' and 'vain'. As the magnanimous man 'deserves and claims great things, and above all the greatest things', he is primarily concerned with honours and dishonours; it is 'honour that [he] chiefly claim[s], but in accordance with [his] deserts'. He must, moreover, 'be good in the highest degree; for the better man always deserves more, and the best man most'. He would not 'be worthy of honour if he were bad; for honour is the prize of virtue, and it is to the good that it is rendered. [Magnanimity], then, seems to be a sort of crown of the virtues; for it makes them greater, and it is not found without them'.[1]

Milton's definition likewise stresses merit. Magnanimity consists in 'a regard to our own dignity, rightly understood', when 'seeking or avoiding, . . . accept[ing] or refus[ing] . . . riches, advantages, or honours'. Its opposites include ambition and pride ('when a man values himself without merit, or more highly than his merits deserve . . .').[2]

In the light of such definitions it is hardly surprising that poets should have associated magnanimity ('greatness of mind or soul') with heroic virtue. Both included fortitude, temperance, and the complex of related virtues. Both pursued the 'greatest things'. Both involved the question of merit and its rewards. In Tasso's epic, in Spenser's, and to a still greater extent in Milton's, they became all but identical.

I

Though Renaissance criticism of the epic hero usually concerned more specialized virtues—fortitude, prudence, temperance, and the like—magnanimity remained an essential facet of the heroic ethos. In Homeric epic[3] and its classical

---

[1] Aristotle, pp. 991–5. The *megalopsychos* is concerned with 'honour on the grand scale'. But 'not even toward honour does he bear himself as if it were a very great thing', for 'there can be no honour that is worthy of perfect virtue'. He will be 'moderately pleased' by honours that are 'great and conferred by good men', but he will despise 'honour from casual people and on trifling grounds . . ., since it is not this that he deserves'. He will 'bear himself with moderation towards wealth and power and all good or evil fortune, . . . and will be neither over-joyed by good fortune nor over-pained by evil'. He 'does not run into trifling dangers . . .; but he will face great dangers' and be 'unsparing of his life'. He does not 'aim at the things commonly held in honour, or the things in which others excel'; it is characteristic of him 'to be sluggish and to hold back except where great honour or a great work is at stake, and to be a man of few deeds, but of great and notable ones'.

[2] *De Doctrina*, Book II, Chapter 9. Milton cites the example 'of Christ in rejecting the empire of the world' (Matt. iv. 9, Luke iv. 6, John vi. 15), 'in despising riches', and 'in accepting honours'. This is 'the spirit by which every true Christian is guided in his estimate of himself'. Cf. *Of Reformation* on 'true wisdom and vertue' as the source of 'magnanimity' and 'likenes to God' (Yale Prose, i. 571).

[3] Cf. the adjective *megathymus* in the *Iliad* (i. 123, 135, etc.) and the term *megalētora thymon* (ix. 255, 629, etc.).

and Renaissance progeny,[1] 'great-souled' was a common
epithet for warriors. In *England's Heroicall Epistles*, Drayton
defined heroism as greatness of mind:[2]

> And though (Heroicall) be properly understood of Demi-gods,
> as of *Hercules* and *Aeneas*, whose parents were said to be, the one
> Cœlestiall, the other Mortall; yet it is also transferred to them, who
> for the[ir] greatnesse of Mind come neere to Gods. For to be
> borne of a cœlestiall *Incubus*, is nothing else, but to have a great
> and mightie Spirit, farre above the Earthly weakenesse of Men;
> in which sense, *Ovid* . . . doth also use Heroicall.

Milton's projected *Arthuriad* would have celebrated the
'great-souled heroes' of the Round Table:[3]

> . . . invictae sociali foedere mensae
> Magnanimos Heroas. . . .

Sensitivity to personal honour and the quest of personal
glory are dominant motives in such warriors as Achilles and
Turnus, Ruggiero and Rinaldo. A true magnanimity characterizes Milton's Christ, just as a false magnanimity marks
his heroic 'idols'. Unlike Messiah, who knows his true worth,
Adam either underestimates or overestimates his own
merits. Satan and Eve both fall through a vain overestimation of their proper deserts.

In the *Iliad* and the epics modelled upon it—the latter
half of Virgil's *Aeneid*, Trissino's *Italia Liberata*, Alamanni's
L'Avarchide, Tasso's *Gerusalemme Liberata*, and Milton's
Paradise Lost—the warrior's sense of injured merit leads to
broken alliances and breaches of fealty. The quarrel between Achilles and Agamemnon provides the model for
Corsamonte's break with Belisarius, Lancelot's breach with
Arthur, Rinaldo's separation from Godfrey, and Satan's
revolt against God. In each of these cases the primary motive
is wounded honour.

[1] Cf. Trissino, *Italia Liberata*, in *Opere*, vol. i (Verona, 1729), p. 142; *La
Avarchide del S. Luigi Alamanni* (Firenze, 1570), pp. 66, 68, etc.; cf. Statius,
Achilleid (London, 1928), p. 508, 'Magnanimum Aeaciden'. The epithet
magnanimus could be interpreted etymologically as derivative either from
animus or from *anima* and translated either as 'great-minded' or 'great-souled'.

[2] *The Works of Michael Drayton*, ed. J. William Hebel (Oxford, 1932), ii. 130.

[3] 'Mansus', lines 82–83, in *The Poetical Works of John Milton*, ed. H. D.
Beeching (London, 1932).

As the *eidolon* of magnanimity, Satan displays many of the superficial characteristics of the *megalopsychos*. Like the magnanimous man, he aims at what appear to be the highest rewards—the honour and glory due the hero, the monarch, and the god. But, unlike the truly magnanimous, he aims above his deserts and thus falls into the contrary vices—ambition, vanity, and pride. As the Son perceives, the 'designs' and 'tumults' of the rebel angels are 'vain'; and their vanity serves, by contrast, merely to acentuate his own merits and heighten his own glory. Unlike Satan, Messiah knows his own merit and grounds his magnanimity solidly on self-knowledge; Satan's vanity, on the contrary, arises from a false conceit of his own nature and worth. The Son's equality with God is real, for it is a divine gift; when Satan affects 'all equality with God' his claim is vain presumption. In contrast to Messiah's superlative merit, Satan exhibits merely the 'semblance of worth, not substance'.

His disdain, and scorn are traits superficially associated with this virtue. Aristotle had remarked that the magnanimous man is popularly regarded as proud and disdainful. In Satan's case, however, these qualities indicate vanity rather than true magnanimity. In the soliloquy on Mount Niphates as in the opening scene of *Paradise Lost* his 'disdain' and fear of shame—though conventional traits of the epic hero—make it impossible for him to repent:

> O then at last relent: is there no place
> Left for Repentance, none for Pardon left?
> None left but by submission; and that word
> *Disdain* forbids me, and my dread of shame
> Among the spirits beneath, whom I seduc'd
> With other promises and other vaunts
> Than to submit, boasting I could subdue
> Th' Omnipotent.

The same false magnanimity characterizes the archangel after his fall and in his enterprise against man. In his 'high disdain, from sense of injur'd merit' he resembles Achilles and Corsamonte, Lancelot and Rinaldo. His hatred of dishonour and shame:

> To bow and sue for grace
> ... that were low indeed,
> That were an ignominy and shame beneath
> This downfall; ...

also suggests the Aristotelian *megalopsychos*. His desire for royal honour:

> ... in my choice
> To reign is worth ambition though in Hell:
> Better to reign in Hell, than serve in Heav'n

shadows the magnanimous man's concern for honours. Significantly, Satan himself first introduces the concept of merit, and the theme receives further stress in the catalogue of devils. Raised 'by merit' to the 'bad eminence' of Pandaemonium's throne, Satan accentuates this motif in his opening address in the diabolical conclave:

> Mee though just right, and the fixt Laws of Heav'n
> Did first create your Leader, next, free choice,
> With what besides, in Counsel or in Fight,
> Hath been achiev'd of merit. ...

Besides the theme of merit, the council-scene invokes other commonplaces of magnanimity. Beëlzebub's penultimate speech exhibits the *megalopsychos*'s concern for 'great things'; the great affairs the infernal peers have resolved are, he argues, evidence of their own greatness. Again, in volunteering to undertake the perilous expedition through space 'In search of this new world', Satan displays the magnanimous man's concern for *merited* honour:

> ... till at last
> *Satan*, whom now transcendent glory rais'd
> Above his fellows, with Monarchal pride
> Conscious of highest worth, unmov'd thus spake.
> Wherefore do I assume
> These Royalties, and not refuse to Reign,
> Refusing to accept as great a share
> Of hazard as of honour, due alike
> To him who Reigns, and so much to him due
> Of hazard more, as he above the rest
> High honourd sits?

In pursuit of public fame, he forestalls any volunteers who might prove

> His Rivals, winning cheap the high repute
> Which he through hazard huge must earn.

Finally, as a reward for his demonstrated merit he receives divine honours and praise:

> Towards him they bend
> With awful reverence prone; and as a God
> Extol him equal to the highest in Heav'n:
> Nor fail'd they to express how much they prais'd
> That for the general safety he despis'd
> His own: . . . .

The scene is modelled on the passage in the *Iliad* where Hector calls for a volunteer to 'spy' on the Greek ships and discover 'whether the swift ships be guarded as of old, or whether by now our foes . . . are planning flight'. As in *Paradise Lost*, 'his hearers receive his request 'hushed in silence', until a single volunteer—'Dolon, the son of Eumedes' —accepts the challenge:[1] 'Hector, my heart and proud spirit [*kradie kai thymos agenor*] urge me to go close to the swift-faring ships and spy out all.' As a reward he is promised a chariot and horses and the less tangible recompense of glory (kudos).[2] The parallel is heightened by the fact that in both cases the mission is one of espionage. Moreover, the literal meaning of Dolon's name—'guile'—coincides with Satan's dominant ethical trait and the tactics he consistently employs in his enterprise against man—subtlety, fraud, and guile.

In braving Death at Hell-gate, in spying on Adam and Eve, in taunting the angelic guard, Satan exhibits towards his adversaries the same high 'disdain', 'scorn', 'pride', and 'contempt' that he had displayed in his rebellion in Heaven:

> Know ye not mee? ye knew me once no mate
> For you, there sitting where ye durst not soar;
> Not to know me argues yourselves unknown,
> The lowest of your throng; . . . .

---

[1] *The Iliad*, tr. A. T. Murray (London, 1924), vol. i. 459–61.

[2] Ibid., p. 459. For other passages involving kudos or *kleos*, cf. pp. 183, 197, 295, etc.

He shows the same concern for glory as before; he is grieved that his 'Glory' has 'departed from' him, but contrives to appear 'undaunted':

> If I must contend, said he,
> Best with the best, the Sender not the sent,
> Or all at once; more glory will be won,
> Or less be lost.

This desire to test himself against a worthy antagonist links him with various heroes in the *Iliad* and the *Avarchide*— Achilles, Hector, Ajax; Segurano, Galealto, Lancelot.

The obverse of his pursuit of glory is his 'dread of shame'. When he conceals himself in the serpent, the proud angel feels dishonoured by so ignoble a disguise:

> O foul descent! that I who erst contended
> With Gods to sit the highest, am now constrain'd
> Into a Beast, and mixt with bestial slime,
> This essence to incarnate and imbrute,
> That to the highth of Deity aspir'd; . . . .

This reluctance to assume a baser nature is the moral antithesis of the Messiah's voluntary humiliation in renouncing divine glory to put on man's nature and form.

For a limited time Satan's pursuit of honour seems successful. After completing his mission, he returns to Hell to receive the public honours—applause, triumph, and monuments—his exploit seems to have merited. Sin and Death construct a triumphal bridge—an infernal archetype of the monuments that the fallen world will subsequently bestow on its own heroes. As Sin herself declares, this 'Monument Of Merit high to all th' infernal Host' is a sign of public honour to glorify Satan's victory, for he has achieved no less than the conquest of the whole world. Conqueror, deliverer, and king, he has regained the honour forfeited by his earlier defeat in Heaven.

Underlying both Satanic enterprises is the ethical disparity between false magnanimity and actual sin, between the apparently heroic action ('the strife of Glory') which seems to merit honour and praise and the vicious reality ('the strife of evil') which merits ignominy and shame. In both enterprises Satan aims at honour. In both, divine justice intervenes to punish him with shame. After their defeat the rebel angels are not only expelled from heaven; even their names are blotted out:

> Satan, so call him now, his former name
> Is heard no more in Heav'n; . . . .

Milton's critique of magnanimity entails, almost inevitably, a critique of glory and a critique of merit. The ideal of the *megalopsychos* is too closely involved with the concepts of honour and worth for him to ignore them. In contrasting magnanimity and its contrary vices—ambition and pride—he must also stress the distinctions between true glory and vainglory and between real and apparent merit. The false values he associates, as usual, with the Satanic *eidolon*. Seeking the praise of his accomplices instead of God's approval and seeking it in and through crime, Satan aims at goods that are themselves illusory and counterfeit, at *vana gloria* rather than *vera gloria*. His enterprises and the proud ambition that prompts them spring from a false conceit of his own worth.

II

For real merit and true glory Milton directs us to Messiah and the faithful angels. Like Aristotle's *megalopsychos*, who finds no value in the honours accorded by persons of little worth, the good angels 'seek not the praise of men'. It is valueless in comparison with God's praise, for He alone honours according to desert. For true praise, there must be merit in the praiser as well as the person praised. Hence the supreme reward of Abdiel and other loyal angels is divine approbation:

> Servant of God, well done, well hast thou fought . . .
> And for the testimony of Truth hast borne
> Universal reproach . . .: for this was all thy care
> To stand approved in sight of God, though Worlds
> Judg'd thee perverse: . . . .

The antithesis between the world's false judgement and God's true verdict is epistemological as well as ethical.

Milton expresses this contrast primarily in terms of the opposition of Hell and Heaven. Their 'right reason' obscured, the rebels can no longer discriminate correctly between right and wrong or form a just estimate of worth. With equal blindness they requite Abdiel's virtue with contumely and Satan's apostasy and manslaughter with praise. The 'Monument of merit' which Sin and Death construct for Satan's triumph is the index of their perverted judgement; they reward with honour an action that merits shame. A fallen humanity will erect similar memorials to its destroyers. In their false conception of merit, these 'hellhounds' foreshadow the fallacious verdicts of a corrupted world. The scorn with which the rebels greet Abdiel's 'testimony to Truth' anticipates the contumely with which the world will reward its prophets. Conversely, the divine praise he receives from the Father foreshadows the heavenly reward the faithful will achieve after their ignominy on earth. In thus contrasting divine and infernal conceptions of merit and its due rewards, Milton is sketching the future conflict between worldly fallacy and divine truth.

Abdiel's ordeal, in a sense, foreshadows the future trials of the isolated 'just man' in the secular *regnum*, just as the battle between good and evil angels partly foreshadows the future conflict between the Church and its enemies and just as Pandaemonium itself foreshadows the future kingdoms of the world. Pandaemonium's scale of merit and demerit and the public honours and dishonours it apportions anticipate the world's distorted opinion of true worth. The different receptions Abdiel receives from Satan's forces and the forces of God epitomize the gulf between carnal and spiritual, worldly and divine standards of value. The same antithesis underlies Milton's painstaking delineation of the contrast between secular and celestial glory.

Consistently in *Paradise Lost* the divine insight is the true criterion of merit, and, just as consistently, the reward is divine praise. When the Son enters the conflict against Satan, he extols the faithful angels for their fight:

> Faithful hath been your Warfare, and of God
> Accepted, fearless in his righteous Cause,

> And as ye have receiv'd, so have ye done
> Invincibly: . . . .

He too, in turn, receives celestial praise. When he offers to die for man, the Father bids the angels 'Adore the Son, and honour him as mee'. Coupling his praise with the Father's ('never shall my Harp thy praise Forget, nor from thy Father's praise disjoin') and hailing him as the Father's likeness ('Divine Similitude') and the 'effulgence of his Glory', the angelic choir celebrates Messiah's 'magnific deeds'—his creation of heaven and the angelic powers, his expulsion of the rebel angels, and his future redemption of man. On his return from victory over the apostates, each order in the celestial hierarchy

> Sung Triumph, and him sung Victorious King,
> Son, Heir, and Lord, to him Dominion giv'n,
> Worthiest to Reign; . . . .

The works of the Filial and the Paternal Deity redound to their mutual glory. The Son seeks the Father's honour, and the Father conversely seeks to honour the Son. This relationship has its infernal parody in the mutual glorification of Satan and his progeny; Sin and Death glorify their parent with their triumphal bridge, while he, in turn, glorifies them with regal honours. But where Satan aims chiefly at his own glory and shows a consistent 'dread of shame', Milton's hero transcends the ideal of the *megalopsychos* by voluntarily renouncing glory and embracing shame:

> I for his sake will leave
> Thy bosom, and this glory next to thee
> Freely put off, and for him lastly die. . . .

Obedience and charity lift him above the common level of magnanimity. Like the *megalopsychos*, however, the Son recognizes his own worth and aims at the greatest objects— no less than the salvation of 'the whole Race lost'. Though the Father's reply emphasizes Messiah's 'Merit', it also presents a higher ideal than the conventional conception of magnanimity. The most signal proof of Messiah's highest worth is his voluntary renunciation of glory. Love is more

truly magnanimous than the pursuit of honour; goodness
has more intrinsic merit than greatness and high station.
Magnanimity thus passes into its seeming opposite, humility:

> because in thee
> Love hath abounded more than Glory abounds,
> Therefore thy Humiliation shall exalt
> With thee thy Manhood also to this Throne;
> Here shalt thou sit incarnate, here shalt Reign
> Both God and Man, Son both of God and Man,
> Anointed universal King: all Power
> I give thee, reign for ever, and assume
> Thy Merits; . . . .

The norm of the magnanimous man is transcended by a
higher magnanimity, which—though conscious of its own
merits—does not shun humiliation and which paradoxically
renounces glory. The Son does not seek his own glory, but
aims at that of the Father.

In the Messiah Milton has depicted a norm of magnanimity that is specifically Christian. In his theological treatise,
Christ's humiliation and exaltation provide the pattern
to which all believers must conform; in his poem, they
provide the divine archetype both of Christian heroic virtue
and of its reward. The Son's humiliation displays the image
of true magnanimity, just as Satan's vainglory embodies its
idol.

The same commonplaces of magnanimity underlie
Milton's presentation of humanity before and after the fall.
In unfallen man, invested with 'native Honour', merit
hinges on the integrity of the divine image.[1] 'Magnanimous
to correspond with Heav'n', he bases this virtue firmly on
self-knowledge, and—'by degrees of merit rais'd'—he is
capable of winning Heaven itself as the reward of obedience.
After the fall, however—deprived of virtue and righteousness—he can no longer earn a celestial recompense by

---

[1] Cf. *De Doctrina*, Book I, Chapter 7: 'Man being formed after the image of
God, it followed as a necessary consequence that he should be endued with
natural wisdom, holiness, and righteousness.' Cf. *PL*, iv. 291–4: 'And worthy
seem'd for in thir looks Divine / The image of thir glorious Maker shone, /
Truth, Wisdom, Sanctitude severe and pure, / Severe, but in true filial freedom
plac't. . . .'

his own works; he can attain it only through the merits of Christ.

Michael's survey of human history stresses man's inability to save himself, the necessity of relying on faith instead of his own deserts. Granted to men in order 'to evince Thir natural pravity' and show them that 'Law can discover sin, but not remove', the Law prompts them to look for Christ's atonement and the 'righteousness To them by Faith imputed'. The condition of eternal life is Messiah's merit, not their own performance:

> . . . to all who shall believe
> In his redemption, and that his obedience
> Imputed becomes theirs by Faith, his merits
> To save them, not thir own, though legal works.

Adam's sin radically alters man's inherent dignity and potential magnanimity. Relying on his own deserts, he can, at best, achieve only a temporary and earthly reward. Tainted as they are by sin, his noblest exploits must ultimately incur eternal death and shame instead of everlasting life and glory. On the other hand, by trusting in the imputed righteousness of Christ, he can attain the imperishable honours of Heaven. In either case he falls short of the conventional conception of magnanimity; either he merits shame and the mere shadow of glory, or else he achieves a true glory he has not deserved.

Milton's strongest indictment of the 'vanity of human merits'[1] appears in his 'Paradise of Fools'. Founded on the

---

[1] For Milton's views on human merits, see *De Doctrina*, Book I, Chapters 16, 22; Book II, Chapter 1: 'So far . . . as regards the satisfaction of Christ, and our conformity to his humiliation, the restoration of man is of merit; in which sense those texts are to be understood which convey a notion of recompense and reward. . . . Nor need we fear, lest in maintaining this belief we should lend any support to the doctrine of human merits. For our conformity to the image of Christ is as far from adding anything to the full and perfect satisfaction made by him, as our works are from adding to faith: it is faith that justifies, but a faith not destitute of works: and in like manner, if we deserve anything, if there be any worthiness in us on any ground whatever, it is God that hath made us worthy in Christ.' 'We are justified . . . by a living, not a dead faith. . . . Hence we are justified by faith without the works of the laws, but not without the works of faith; inasmuch as a living and true faith cannot consist without works. . . . This interpretation, however, affords no countenance to the doctrine of human merit, inasmuch as both faith itself and its

Protestant doctrine of justification by faith rather than by works, this satiric vignette stresses man's inability to earn eternal glory by his own deeds:

> . . . all things transitory and vain, when Sin
> With vanity had fill'd the works of men:
> Both all things vain, and all who in vain things
> Built their fond hopes of Glory or lasting fame,
> Or happiness in this or th' other life;
> All who have thir reward on Earth, the fruits
> Of painful Superstition and blind Zeal,
> Naught seeking but the praise of men, here find
> Fit retribution, empty as thir deeds; . . . .

In the light of the Protestant conception of merit, the epic tradition—dedicated as it was to celebrating the exploits of mortal heroes—required reassessment. Whatever merits such 'worthies' possessed were inadequate for a celestial reward and fell short of Heaven itself. Milton expresses the secular nature both of their acts and their rewards by restricting them to the confines of the physical world. The comparison with 'Aerial vapors', in turn, emphasizes their emptiness and vanity. Significantly, the first inhabitants of this 'Limbo of Vanity' are the secular prototypes of heroic virtue, the Biblical 'mighty men' and 'men of renown' whose strength and fame made them the idols of true fortitude:

> Hither of ill-join'd Sons and Daughters born
> First from the ancient World those Giants came
> With many a vain exploit, though then renown'd: . . . .

Their ascent to the 'Paradise of Fools' consciously travesties the Christian's 'exaltation' to the true Paradise. The elect achieve heaven through faith in Christ's merits. The 'fools' rely on their own merits, but their flight terminates at the edge of the world itself. They cannot pass beyond time to an eternal reward. Their recompense, like their virtues

works are the works of the Spirit, not our own.' The 'works of faith' do 'not admit of boasting', as St. Paul realizes in Romans iii. 27, 28: 'Hence may be easily discerned the vanity of human merits; seeing that, in the first place, our good actions are not our own, but of God working in us; secondly, that, were they our own, they would still be equally due; and, thirdly, that, in any point of view, there can be no proportion between our duty and the proposed reward.'

and their exploits, is earth-bound. Paradoxically the exaltation that first seems to be a reward of merit ultimately
demonstrates their want of true desert. They rise towards
heaven not because they have earned a celestial reward, but
merely because their merits are as light and empty as air.
As with the scales-image at the conclusion of Book IV,
Milton has adapted the imagery of weight and lightness to
stress the distinction between true merit and vanity. The
ascent of the giants and the Greek philosophers belongs to
the same order as Eve's imaginary flight towards heaven in
her diabolically inspired dream. Both are symbols of vainglory.

In relegating 'Cowles, Hoods and Habits with thir
wearers, . . . then Reliques, Beads, Indulgences, Dispenses,
Pardons, Bulls' to be 'the sport of Winds', Milton is not
only ridiculing ecclesiastical practices he regards as superstitious; he is also satirizing the Roman Catholic doctrines
of the treasury of merits and justification by works.

III

The commonplaces of magnanimity—the pursuit of 'great
things', the consciousness of merit, the concern with honour
and shame—also underlie the intellectual dialectic of
Paradise Regain'd. As Satan himself recognizes, the hero is
the true *megalopsychos*, endowed with 'amplitude of mind to
greatest Deeds'. Rejecting a secular kingdom, Christ bases
his argument on magnanimity:

> Besides to give a Kingdom hath been thought
> Greater and nobler done, and to lay down
> Far more magnanimous, then to assume.

The debate centres consistently on the dual aspects of
worth—the hero's own merits and the relative value of the
ends and means his antagonist proposes to him. John the
Baptist bears witness to him 'As to his *worthier*'. The Father
extols him as a 'perfect Man, by *merit* call'd my Son' and
exposes him to temptation in order 'To shew him *worthy* of
his birth divine and high prediction', just as Satan had

tempted Job to 'prove him, and illustrate his high *worth*' (italics mine).

In urging Christ to accept a worldly kingdom, Satan argues that it is 'Happiest both to thy self and all the world, That thou who *worthiest* art should'st be thir King'.

In his penultimate speech he appeals to the same commonplace. Hearing Christ 'pronounc'd the Son of God belov'd',

> . . . I thought thee *worthy* my nearer view
> And narrower Scrutiny, that I might learn
> In what degree or meaning thou art call'd
> The Son of God. . . .

Having failed to resolve the question, the tempter concludes his assay with the final test on the tower:

> Therefore to know what more thou art then man,
> *Worth* naming Son of God by voice from Heav'n,
> Another method I must now begin.

Demonstrating Messiah's merits by contrast with the emptiness of Satan's offers, Milton brings into sharper focus these dual aspects of worth. The dialectic process that progressively reveals the Son's true merit also exposes the worthlessness of Satan's highest claims.

In the *Christian Doctrine* Milton had extolled Christ's rejection of the kingdoms of the world as the supreme example of magnanimity; and recent criticism has, with justification, interpreted *Paradise Regain'd* in this light. The hero's systematic rejection of the means and ends sought by worldly heroes establishes his superiority, but it also differentiates Christian heroism from its secular counterpart. Messiah's worth is measured, negatively, by the values he rejects as *un*worthy.[1]

The chief condition Satan attaches to his offer of a secular empire—that Christ accept it from him as a fief and do

---

[1] Rejection of bribes and rewards had long been an index of magnanimity in heroic tradition. The scene in which Achilles rejects the gifts of the Greek ambassadors acquires greater complexity in later epics like the *Italia Liberata* and the *Avarchide,* and its ethical import becomes equally complicated. Milton carries this tradition to an extreme; in *Paradise Regain'd* the pattern of rejection and its moral significance dominate the plot.

homage to its infernal suzerain—is patently incompatible with this virtue. As God's only Son and Heir, Messiah has been anointed universal king over both fallen and unfallen angels and over heaven, earth, and hell alike. Satan is his subject, albeit a rebellious one, and the 'prince of the world' can give him nothing that is not already his own by right:

> Wert thou so void of fear or shame
> As offer them to me the Son of God,
> To me my own, on such abhorred pact,
> That I fall down and worship thee as God?

Since the kingdoms of the world already belong to Christ by right, it would be false humility—the antithesis of magnanimity—to accept them from his own thrall. Furthermore, Christ's own kingdom is 'not of this world'. He is a spiritual king, and these secular means and ends are both irrelevant and worthless for the kingdom of heaven. They are obstacles rather than aids to spiritual dominion. Though 'Honours, Riches, Kingdoms, Glory' have been conventional rewards of the magnanimous man, they are unworthy objects for the Son of God, whose kingdom is spiritual, whose glory and treasure are heavenly, and whose chief merit lies in the voluntary renunciation of honours. For the founder of the Church, to seek worldly ends—or even to employ worldly means towards spiritual ends—would violate both magnanimity and decorum.

Christ's ordeal in the desert tests a variety of virtues, but it primarily demonstrates his magnanimity. The spurious goods Satan offers form an ascending scale; each successive renunciation on the hero's part manifests still further his 'amplitude of mind' and places him a step higher on the ladder of merit. Particularly significant, however, is the fact that all three of the major categories Satan offers—the goods of the voluptuous life and the active and contemplative lives[1]—contain the bait of honour, a lure particularly appropriate for the magnanimous man.

In proposing the goods of 'life contemplative, Or active', Satan presents those aspects most characterized by 'glory,

[1] Cf. Schultz, p. 225.

or fame'—'wealth', 'honour', 'arms', 'arts', 'Kingdom', and 'Empire'. Since they all involve honour and glory, they might logically appeal to the *megalopsychos*; in rejecting them, Christ demonstrates a higher order of magnanimity. Their glory belongs exclusively to this world; the glory he must win for mankind is heavenly. Moreover, the means to this ultimate exaltation is humiliation; the path to heavenly honour leads through earthly shame. As the Messiah has voluntarily renounced divine glory and laid aside the 'form of God' to assume the 'form of a servant', it would be meaningless to pursue the inferior, earthly glory.

Christ's condemnation of the Gentile philosophers likewise hinges on the fallacy of human merit and the vanity of human glory.[1] Ignorant of their own nature, and foolishly arrogating glory 'to themselves', they fall short of true magnanimity and into the contrary vices—vanity and vainglory.

By destroying man's natural dignity, the fall has virtually eliminated his potentialities for magnanimity. In the state of innocence, he had been clad in 'native Honour'. In the state of the fall, he has lost his original worth; whatever dignity still remains belongs to him not by nature but by grace.

As in *Paradise Lost*, Milton's critique of magnanimity centres on the Christian paradox of glory in shame, and honour in lowliness.[2] Founded as it is on the norm of Christ's humiliation and exaltation,[3] this pattern represents a radical departure from the classical conception of

---

[1] 'But why should man seek glory? who of his own / Hath nothing, and to whom nothing belongs / But condemnation, ignominy, and shame.'

[2] In the *De Doctrina*, Book II, Chapter 9, 'lowliness of mind' (*modestia*) is associated with magnanimity as a virtue 'more peculiarly appropriate to a high station'. It 'consists in thinking humbly of ourselves, and in abstaining from self-commendation, except where occasion requires it'. Its opposites are 'arrogance', 'desire of vain glory', 'boasting', 'a crafty or hypocritical extenuation of our own merits, for the purpose of extorting greater praises', and 'a glorying in iniquity and misdeeds'. Closely allied with this virtue is 'love of an unspotted reputation, and of the praises of good men, with a proportionate contempt for those of the wicked'. To this is opposed 'an excessive and indiscriminate passion for esteem and praise, from whatever quarter'. Humility, in turn, 'is that whereby we acknowledge our unworthiness in the sight of God'. Its opposites include 'pride towards God' (Book II, Chapter 3). The Satan of *Paradise Lost* embodies the contraries of all three of these virtues.

[3] Cf. *De Doctrina*, Book I, Chapter 16.

magnanimity, with its conventional emphasis on honour. As Christ himself recognizes, he must first

> Be try'd in humble state, and things adverse,
> By tribulations, injuries, insults,
> Contempts, and scorns, and snares, and violence,

before he 'merit[s] [His] exaltation without change or end'.

IV

In *Samson Agonistes* the critique of magnanimity focuses principally on the relationship between greatness of mind and of deed. Though designed for heroic exploits, Samson has not shown true magnitude of mind; his wisdom has not matched his physical strength, and he has fallen through folly. He has lacked a true conception of his own merit. Over-valuing his might in comparison with wisdom, he has become 'swoll'n with pride' and borne himself like 'a petty god'. This disproportion between sapience and fortitude is characteristic of the Achilles-type hero, and it usually manifests itself in a lack of self-control. Achilles himself acknowledges that his skill in council does not match his valour in combat, and Lancelot's friends exhort him to display wisdom proportional to his martial prowess. The *thymos* ('spirit') of Plato's warrior class easily becomes vicious unless governed and moderated by the wisdom of the philosopher-king. Samson suffers from the conventional disease of most epic heroes. On the other hand, he has *under*prized his worth in comparison with Dalila; 'for a word, a tear', he has 'divulg'd the secret gift of God to a deceitful Woman'.

Yet through his sufferings he achieves a true comprehension both of his merits and his demerits. Just in apportioning the blame for his own situation and for Israel's plight, he assigns the guilt to himself, his treacherous wife, and Israel's governors. His intellectual ordeal demonstrates the self-knowledge essential for true magnanimity. Only after his spiritual struggle does he accomplish the physical exploit for which he had been destined. For the greater part of the drama the hero's magnanimity appears in contemplation, debate, and suffering; in the final section it manifests itself in action.

At the beginning of the play Samson is perplexed by the disparity between his present condition and the high destiny foretold for him,

> As of a person separate to God,
> Design'd for great exploits; . . . .

He avoids blaming divine Providence ('But peace, I must not quarrel with the will of highest dispensation') and acknowledges his 'own default', his own responsibility for his plight:

> Whom have I to complain of but my self?
> Who this high gift of strength committed to me, . . .
> Under the Seal of silence could not keep,
> But weakly to a woman must reveal it
> O'recome with importunity and tears.
> O impotence of mind, in body strong!

Displaying the self-knowledge essential for true magnanimity, he knows the true value of his strength—its merit as well as its limitations. In his earlier lapse, on the other hand, he had both overestimated and underestimated it.

Yet in his awareness of his own worth—his demerits and merits alike—he is also conscious of the limitations of his 'default'. The blame for his country's present servitude rests not with himself but with others. Like Samson, Israel's leaders have undervalued the gifts of God. Just as he has bartered his divine secret for 'importunity and tears', they have slighted the great acts God had accomplished through him. They have despised and envied their divinely appointed deliverer and heaped 'ingratitude on worthiest deeds'. In both cases, there has been a characteristically human misunderstanding of true worth.

Manoa's speech raises the question of human merit in relation to divine justice:

> Alas methinks whom God hath chosen once
> To worthiest deeds, if he through frailty err,
> He should not so o'rewhelm, and as a thrall
> Subject him to so foul indignities
> Be it but for honours sake of former deeds.

As in his first soliloquy, Samson's reply again clears 'heavenly disposition' and accepts the blame for his present evil; his equal awareness of his worth and his default demonstrates his self-knowledge:

> . . . I my self have brought them on,
> Sole Author I, sole cause: . . . .

The interview with Dalila likewise shows how well he understands his own merits. Exonerating neither his own transgression nor hers, he repudiates an uxorious bondage incompatible with his dignity. To live in idleness as her thrall would do violence to his character, his mission, and his vows as a Nazarite. But the debate also involves the theme of honour and dishonour, the double aspect of fame and infamy. As in *Paradise Lost* and *Paradise Regain'd*, the judgement of God's kingdom contradicts that of His enemies; the world and the Holy Community stand in direct opposition. The standards of the elect are diametrically contrary to those of the reprobate. As Dalila herself perceives, her treason holds opposite meanings for the Hebrew community and the Philistine:

> Fame if not double-fac't is double-mouth'd,
> And with contrary blast proclaims most deeds;
> On both his wings, one black, th' other white,
> Bears greatest names in his wild aery flight.

Though she may stand 'defam'd' by the Hebrews, she has, by Philistian standards, merited well both of her country and its gods. She has served Dagon faithfully, and in the inverted perspective of her idolatry she merits praise.

Like the infernal standards in *Paradise Lost* and *Paradise Regain'd*, the Philistian criterion of worth is the obverse—the reversed mirror-image—of the divine standard. The antithesis between the true God and idols has its ethical and epistemological corollary in the opposition between true paradigms of merit and glory and their false resemblances. For the Hebrews Dalila is an impious traitress; for the Philistines she is a heroine—the pious deliverer of her people and the zealous champion of her god. For the Philistines, Samson is a murderous rebel and a robber; for the Israelites, he is a heroic liberator. In all three poems the action involves a moral dialectic—the progressive discrimination between truth and appearance, good and evil.

In all three works divine judgement intervenes decisively to affirm the true values and refute the false. The final books of *Paradise Lost* develop the implications of the verdict pronounced in the garden. Satan's humiliation at the moment of supreme triumph and Michael's prophecy of Messiah's future victories elucidate the sentences pronounced on serpent and man. In *Paradise Regain'd* the final miracle on the temple-tower demonstrates Christ's Sonship. In *Samson Agonistes* Jehovah bears 'witness gloriously' to his champion by still another miracle. In all three cases divine testimony provides the true standard of value.

The dialogue with Harapha brings into focus the contrast between true magnanimity and its contrary—vainglory— but it also emphasizes the relative worth of human and divine strength. Harapha's boasts and professed concern for honour and glory link him with other poetic heroes—Hector and Achilles, Lancelot and Segurano:

> So had the glory of Prowess been recover'd
> To *Palestine*, won by a *Philistine*
> From the unforeskinn'd race, of whom thou bear'st
> The highest name, for valiant Acts, that honour
> Certain to have won by mortal duel from thee, ...

As in the *Iliad* and the *Avarchide*, this pursuit of 'the glory of Prowess' hinges on the idea of a worthy antagonist, whose accumulated honours accrue to the victor who defeats him. Blind and disgraced, Samson no longer seems a 'worthy' opponent, and the Philistine giant refuses a combat where victory could bring him no honour:

> To combat with a blind man I disdain,
> And thou hast need much washing to be toucht.

Harapha's high disdain is merely vainglorious pride rather than magnanimity. He overestimates his own prowess, boasting his merit where he cannot prove it, and taunting an enemy whom he dares not fight. His proven cowardice discredits his vaunts; when he fears to avenge the 'dishonours' with which Samson requites him, his zeal for honour seems false pretence.

In answering the insults and 'indignities' his adversary heaps upon him, Samson shows his progress in self-knowledge. As in the earlier interview with the Chorus, he recognizes how far he himself has sinned and how far the responsibility lies with Israel ('Th' unworthier they; whence to this day they serve'). He knows the source and dignity of his miraculous strength as well as the worth of his divine mission as deliverer. Harapha undervalues the Nazarite's strength by ascribing it to 'some Magician's Art'; Samson acknowledges it as the miraculous gift of God. Harapha berates him as 'A Murtherer, a Revolter, and a Robber'; Samson upholds his dignity as

> . . . a person rais'd
> With strength sufficient and command from Heav'n
> To free my Countrey; . . . .

Besides emphasizing the commonplace of magnanimity—self-knowledge and the antithesis of glory and dishonour—this debate over the nature of Samson's might heightens the disparity between his own worth and his adversary's. Harapha's force is merely human, depends largely on human weapons, and serves no higher end than personal and national glory. Samson's strength is of divine origin, relies on God alone, and serves a heavenly end—Jehovah's will and praise.

Like Samson's interview with Manoa, the scene with Harapha shifts the emphasis from personal glory or shame to divine honour; it probes beyond the problem of Samson's humiliation to the more fundamental issue of God's glory. The 'dishonours' and 'indignities' exchanged by Samson and Harapha are less significant than the greater—though unseen—rivalry between Jehovah and Dagon, a conflict that will achieve its climax in the ironic paradox of the Dagonalia. For, as Manoa points out to his son, Samson has dishonoured God by subjecting Him to idolatrous scorn. The whole purpose of the Dagonalia is to glorify the heathen god for delivering Samson into Philistine hands.

In reply, Samson confesses that he has brought 'this honour' and 'this pomp'

> To *Dagon*, and advanc'd his praises high
> Among the Heathen round; to God have brought
> Dishonour, obloquie, and op't the mouths
> Of Idolists, and Atheists; . . . .

Nevertheless, he recognizes the issues as primarily a struggle for honour between the true God and the false idol. The vital question now is not the shame done to Samson or even the shame Samson has brought on his nation and his God; it is the dishonour Dagon and his worshippers have inflicted on Jehovah and the shame they must inevitably incur in retribution. Though honour and dishonour remain the grounds of 'the contest', they have been transferred from the human plane to the divine. The crucial point now is whether the glory shall be Jehovah's or Dagon's. Underlying the struggle of Hebrew and Philistine is the war of rival gods.

This theomachy also manifests itself in the conflict between Samson and Dalila, each the instrument of a rival deity. In betraying her husband, Dalila was serving her god; it would be a 'meritorious' act to ensnare 'an irreligious Dishonourer of *Dagon*'. She has been Dagon's instrument for delivering his people, just as Samson had been Jehovah's tool for Israel's deliverance. The spiritual warfare between the true and false gods also rages in the domestic sphere, in the hostilities of husband and wife.

Similarly, in the quarrel between Samson and Harapha the emphasis soon shifts from the comparative worth of the two warriors to that of their gods. Asserting his strength to 'be the power of *Israel*'s God', Samson 'challenge[s] *Dagon* to the test' in a duel between himself as God's champion and the Philistine giant as Dagon's 'Champion bold'. The issue now is not his own strength or glory, but Jehovah's:

> . . . if *Dagon* be thy god,
> . . . spread before him
> How highly it concerns his glory now
> To frustrate and dissolve these Magic spells, . . .
> Then thou shalt see . . . whose God is strongest, thine or mine.

The issue of honour and merit thus recurs on several levels in Milton's tragedy—not only in terms of particular individuals (Samson, Dalila, Harapha) but also in terms of the entire Israelite and Philistine nations and their respective gods.

V

Milton's critique of magnanimity places greater emphasis on the moral and psychological preconditions of great actions than on the actions themselves. Despite the artistry he bestows on the structure of his fable, his primary concern remains ethical. His drama is largely a drama of the mind; his story a narrative of spiritual crisis. In describing the exploits of 'great-souled heroes', he stresses the inner conquests that precede heroic action. In depicting the essence of magnanimity—'greatness of mind'—he represents it *in* the mind itself before tracing its effects in heroic action. *Paradise Regain'd*, his epic of 'deeds above Heroic', focuses less on the external *events* of Christ's ministry than on the *moral* preparation for them. Though it celebrates heroic 'deeds', these are not physical actions, but spiritual triumphs—the judgements and decisions essential for the ministry of redemption. Messiah's spiritual ordeal bears the same crucial relation to his future achievements that Hercules' Choice had borne to his twelve labours, or Scipio's Dream to his victory over Carthage. Christ's greatness of mind appears in contemplation and moral choice. Similarly, in *Samson Agonistes*, Milton emphasizes the spiritual struggle that leads to the hero's physical triumph, the labours of the mind that precede the final *agon* in the Philistine theatre. Samson displays his 'Heroic magnitude of mind' in moral judgement before he gives more visible and tangible proof in action. Milton portrays his hero's virtue not simply in deed but, first and foremost, in analysis and choice.

For Renaissance ideas of magnanimity, see Maurice B. McNamee, S.J., *Honor and the Epic Hero* (New York, 1960); Robert Martin Adams, *Milton and the Modern Critics* (Ithaca, 1966), pp. 212–24; Hughes, *Ten Perspectives on Milton* (New Haven, 1965), pp. 12–62; Tillyard, *Studies in Milton* (London, 1951), pp. 100–6; H. S. V. Jones, 'Magnanimity in Spenser's Legend of Holiness', *Studies in Philology*, xxix (1932), pp. 200–6.

VII

Heroic 'Archetype' and 'Prototype'

WISDOM, fortitude, leadership, love, magnanimity—none of the formulae we have examined exists in isolation. As philosophers pointed out, the virtues were interrelated; one presupposed the others. For classical ethics, all of them depended on right reason; for Christian ethics, on charity. No habit could be truly virtuous (theologians insisted) unless it aimed at the glory of God.

Milton's heroic images reflect this interrelationship. Fortitude, as he depicts it, entails other qualities—wisdom and prudence, piety and temperance, charity and justice. His Christian leader needs all of these virtues. Magnanimity demands self-knowledge. Love requires not only temperance and piety, but patience; it 'suffers long'. Piety, in turn, embraces the theological virtues—faith, hope, and charity.

The compound formula was well established in epic poetry; a single hero might often illustrate a whole complex of virtues. The *Iliad* praises Diomedes for combining valour on the battlefield with skill in council.[1] The opening lines of the *Odyssey* link the hero's wisdom and patience with his responsibilities as leader; his wanderings bring him knowledge, but they also entail suffering; not the least of his woes is his unsuccessful attempt to save his companions:[2]

> πολλῶν δ' ἀνθρώπων ἴδεν ἄστεα καὶ νόον ἔγνω,
> πολλὰ δ' ὅ γ' ἐν πόντῳ πάθεν ἄλγεα ὃν κατὰ θυμόν,
> ἀρνύμενος ἥν τε ψυχὴν καὶ νόστον ἑταίρων.

Fulgentius interpreted the proposition of the *Aeneid* (*Arma*

---

[1] *Iliad*, i. 387.
[2] Homer, *The Odyssey*, tr. A. T. Murray (London, 1930), i. 3–5: 'Many were the men whose cities he saw and whose mind he learned, aye, and many the woes he suffered in his heart upon the sea, seeking to win his own life and the return of his comrades.'

M

virumque) in terms of the *fortitudo et sapientia* formula,[1] while
the fable of the poem strongly emphasized the hero's piety.
In Virgilian epic and many of the poems consciously modelled
upon it, the opening lines combine the motifs of action
and contemplation, patience and leadership. Virgil stresses
Aeneas' sufferings on sea and land alike in his effort to
establish a second Troy.[2]

The proposition of Tasso's *Gerusalemme Liberata* unites
action with contemplation, suffering with piety:[3]

> Canto l'arme pietose e 'l capitano
> che 'l gran sepolcro liberò di Cristo:
> molto egli oprò co 'l senno e con la mano,
> molto soffrí nel glorioso acquisto: . . . .

Like the *Aeneid*, the *Lusiads* fuses the Odyssean motif of the
perilous voyage with the themes of land-battles and piety:[4]

> *Armes, and the Men* above the vulgar File, . . .
> Who (brave in *action*, patient in long *Toyle*,
> Beyond what strength of *humane* nature bore)
> 'Mongst *Nations*, under *other Stars*, acquir'd
> A *modern Scepter* which to *Heaven* aspir'd.

The proposition of Cowley's *Davideis* stresses patience as well
as action, piety as well as valour, and the cares of the
sovereign along with the labours of the warrior:[5]

> I sing the *Man* who *Judahs Scepter* bore. . . .
> Much danger first, much toil did he sustain,

[1] See Fulgentius, *Liber de expositione Virgilianae continentiae*; Ernst Robert
Curtius, *European Literature and the Latin Middle Ages*, tr. Willard R. Trask
(New York, 1953), pp. 173–9; Kurth, p. 27.

[2] *Virgil*, i. 240: '. . . much buffeted on sea and land by violence from above,
through cruel Juno's unforgiving wrath, and much enduring in war also, till
he should build a city and bring his gods to Latium; whence came the Latin
race, the lords of Alba, and the walls of lofty Rome.'

[3] Torquato Tasso, *Gerusalemme Liberata*, ed. Luigi Bonfigli (Bari, 1930),
p. 1. Cf. Fairfax's translation: 'The sacred armies and the godly knight/That
the great sepulchre of Christ did free/I sing; much wrought his valour and
foresight,/And in that glorious war much suffer'd he. . . . His soldiers wild, to
brawls and mutines prest,/Reduced he to peace; so heaven him blest.' Beni
(p. 473) contrasts Godfrey's success in saving his companions with Ulysses'
failure.

[4] Cf. Camoens, *The Lusiad*, tr. Fanshawe, p. 29.

[5] Abraham Cowley, *Poems*, ed. A. R. Waller (Cambridge, 1905), p. 242.
Cf. the similarity between David and Samson in their reliance on God, and
between Saul and Harapha in carnal reliance.

Whilst *Saul* and *Hell* crost his strong fate in vain.
Nor did his *Crown* less painful work afford;
Less exercise his *Patience*, or his *Sword*;
So long her *Conqueror Fortunes* spight pursu'd;
Till with unwearied *Virtue* he subdu'd
All homebred Malice, and all forreign boasts;
Their strength was *Armies*, his the *Lord of Hosts*.

Ancient and modern epic alike involved more than one
mode of action and more than one heroic formula. Despite
the Renaissance tendency to interpret the *Iliad* and the
Odyssey as separate but parallel portraits of the active and the
contemplative hero, both poems resist so rigid a distinction.
The characters of the *Iliad* usually excel in council as well
as in warfare, and for all his contemplative qualities the
Odyssey's hero concludes his extended quest with an out-
burst of violent action. Whatever its allegorical significance,
on the literal level the slaughter of the suitors is not the act
of a purely contemplative hero. Structurally and ethically,
it is analogous to Samson's massacre of the Philistines—or
to the final executing of personal revenge, domestic and
national purification in Shakespeare's *Hamlet*.

The fusion of thought and valour is even more marked
in post-Homeric epic. In the *Aeneid* and the *Gerusalemme
Liberata*, interpreters recognized a fusion of active and contemplative ideals. Spenser devoted separate books to particular virtues, with 'magnificence' (i.e. magnanimity) as
a leitmotiv linking the separate formulae—holiness, temperance, chastity, friendship, justice, courtesy, constancy.
The third and fourth of these are aspects of the *amor*-formula.
The second involves one of the most familiar commonplaces
of epic allegory—the conflict between reason and appetite.
The first embodies the formula of heroic piety—the sanctity that, for Christian doctrine, excelled the heroic virtue of
the ancients.

Milton usually subsumes the conventional epic formulae
under more comprehensive concepts—notably obedience[1]

---

[1] The *De Doctrina* (Book II, Chapter 3) includes obedience among the
'virtues belonging to the worship of God'. It is 'that virtue whereby we propose
to ourselves the will of God as the paramount rule of our conduct, and serve

and sanctity.[1] As the Christian equivalent of heroic virtue—
and a primary characteristic of the divine image lost by
Adam and restored by Christ—the latter held, potentially,
a unique significance for the epic poet. It was, however, a
virtue peculiar to the regenerate and largely contingent on
faith.[2]

Obedience occupies a central position in both epics. In
Paradise Lost the 'forbidden Tree' serves primarily as a test of
'obedience'. 'Obedience' is the condition of man's winning
heaven by 'degrees of merit'. Raphael's recital of the angelic
war contains an *exemplum* of 'disobedience'. Filial 'obedience'
is the dominant virtue Christ exhibits in the celestial council
of Book III and in his earthly ministry. *Paradise Regain'd*
displays his 'obedience tri'd through all temptation'.

Nevertheless, this is not an isolated virtue. Milton explicitly links it with love and service. It is a precondition of
righteousness (*justitia*),[3] the universal justice that Aristotle
regarded as 'virtue itself'. Man's first disobedience destroys
his original righteousness—the state of inner justice, in which
the lower faculties obey the higher; only faith in another's
'justice'—the righteousness of Christ—can restore him. In
the final books of *Paradise Lost* the recurrent motif of the
'one just man' foreshadows the perfect righteousness of the
future redeemer.

---

him alone'. The 'love of God' (1 John ii. 3) is to 'keep his commandments'.
Its opposite is 'disobedience', for 'rebellion is as the sin of witchcraft [1 Sam.
xv. 23], and stubbornness is as iniquity and idolatry'.

[1] See *De Doctrina*, Book I, Chapter 18, for Milton's account of regeneration;
cf. Chapter 21 on the relationship between regeneration and comprehension of
spiritual things and Chapter 7 on *sanctitas* as a principal characteristic of the
divine image. Holiness is sometimes synonymous with charity (Chapter 21)
just as sanctification is often synonymous with regeneration.

[2] 'Saving faith' is (like repentance) an effect of regeneration, but it is also a
cause; see *De Doctrina*, Book I, Chapters 18–20.

[3] The *De Doctrina* (Book II, Chapter 3) associated *justitia* with *charitas* as
one of 'the general virtues' belonging to 'our duties towards men'. As a 'general
virtue belonging to the regenerate', righteousness is the virtue 'whereby we
render to each his due, whether to ourselves, or to our neighbor'. Its opposites
are 'unrighteousness [*iniustitia*], which excludes from the kingdom of heaven',
and 'a pharisaical righteousness'. In *Of Reformation* (Columbia Edition, iii.
49), Milton observes that 'the throne of a King, as the wise K. *Salomon* often
remembers us, *is establisht in Justice*, which is the universall *Justice* that *Aristotle* so
much praises, containing in it all other *vertues* . . .'.

I

Obedience possessed a peculiar value as epic formula[1] through its similarity to constancy. As Justus Lipsius defines it,[2] 'CONSTANCIE *is a right and immoveable strength of the mind, neither lifted up, nor pressed downe with external or casuall accidentes.*' Based on reason rather than opinion, it is diametrically opposed to obstinacy or obduracy:

By STRENGTH, I understande a stedfastnesse not from opinion, but from iudgement and sound reason. For I would in any case exclude OBSTINACIE . . . *Which is a certaine hardnesse of a stubberne mind, proceeding from pride or vaine glorie.*

The 'lighthardiness' of the obstinate springs 'of pride and too much estimation of themselves, and therefore from OPINION. But the true mother of Constancie is PATIENCE, and lowlinesse of mind, . . . regulated by the rule of *Right Reason.* . . .'

Paradise Lost usually couples this virtue[3] with obedience and loyalty. God permits man's temptation[4] in order to test his firm obedience and 'constant Faith or Love'. Abdiel refuses 'to swerve from truth, or change his constant mind'. Conversely, Satan's rebellion serves as an *exemplum* of inconstancy and disobedience:

> . . . firm they might have stood,
> Yet fell. . . .

For Adam and Eve the trial of obedience is also a test of

---

[1] The *Iliad* and many of the 'literary' or 'secondary' epics based on it (cf. C. M. Bowra, *From Virgil to Milton*, London, 1948, p. v and *passim*; C. S. Lewis, *A Preface to Paradise Lost*, London, 1943, pp. 32–50) often emphasized the hero's disobedience or breach of fealty and his subsequent return to his natural obligations and 'military obedience'. In Milton's epic, Adam's disobedience and subsequent repentance conform to this pattern.

[2] Justus Lipsius, *Two Bookes of Constancie*, tr. Sir John Stradling, ed. Rudolf Kirk (New Brunswick, 1939), p. 79. Cf. Jason Lewis Saunders, Justus Lipsius, *The Philosophy of Renaissance Stoicism* (New York, 1955).

[3] According to the *De Doctrina* (Book II, Chapter 2), 'Constancy is that virtue whereby we persevere in a determination to do right, from which nothing can divert us'—not the 'derision' of the proud nor the 'snare' of the wicked. Its opposites are 'inconstancy' and 'obstinacy in error, or in a wrong purpose'.

[4] For Milton's doctrine of permissive evil and 'good' or 'evil' temptations, see *De Doctrina*, Book I, Chapter 8.

constancy. She resents the implication that she may prove
inconstant under temptation:

> But that thou shouldst my firmness therfore doubt
> To God or thee, because we have a foe
> May tempt it, I expected not to hear.

Adam warns her against inconstancy ('Firm we subsist, yet
possible to swerve') and explicitly associates 'constancie'
with 'obedience'. After the fall, he protests that he had
thought her 'wise, Constant, mature, proof against all
assaults', but 'understood not all was but a shew Rather
than solid vertu . . .'. Man's first disobedience is also a
breach of constancy.

In *Paradise Regain'd* likewise, constancy and obedience
are practically indistinguishable. Milton professes to sing
'Recover'd Paradise. . . . By one mans *firm* obedience fully
tri'd Through all temptation. . . .' The hero resembles Job
in 'constant perseverance', and Satan attempts to 'try his
constancy' with 'manlier objects'.

In both epics this motif derives peculiar force from the
etymological affinities of 'constancy' and 'stand'. Christ's
ability to 'stand'—on 'the highest Pinnacle' not only attests
his true Sonship. It also confirms his constancy. Throughout
his ordeal the hero has 'stood' firm against his adversary's
lures and threats, demonstrating perfect obedience to the
divine will. This moral constancy receives further emphasis
through the symbolism of the temple-tower. Both ethically
and physically, he has 'stood' where no other man could
stand. The miracle is emblematic, suggesting both his own
constancy and the restoration of mankind. Because Christ
has remained constant under temptation, with him fallen
humanity also 'stands' again.

In *Paradise Lost* also, the antithesis of *stand* and *fall* holds
moral as well as metaphysical significance. When God declares of man,

> . . . I made him just and right
> Sufficient to have stood, though free to fall.
> Such I created all th' Ethereal Powers
> And Spirits, both them who stood & them who faild;
> Freely they stood who stood, and fell who fell[,]

the terms are applicable not only to the general condition of
men and angels, but also to the moral virtue and vice of the
individual. The same dual reference characterizes similar
passages in this epic:

> Upheld by me, yet once more he shall stand
> On even ground against his mortal foe, . . .
>   . . . and do they onely stand
> By Ignorance, is that thir happie state,
> The proof of thir obedience and thir faith?

In contrast to the true constancy that characterizes
Christ and Abdiel and the 'just men' of Biblical history,
Satan and Adam exemplify its idol. Though both are inconstant in their love and obedience to God, both display
the superficial attributes of heroic 'stedfastness'. Satan
seems constant in his pursuit of liberty, his fortitude in adverse
fortune, his quest for honour and glory, his 'fixt mind' un-
changed 'by Place or Time'. Adam *appears* constant in his
love for Eve. They exhibit the external traits of the constant
warrior or the constant lover.

Yet in actuality both portraits illustrate conventional patterns of inconstancy—the ambitious rebel and apostate and
the hero ruined through sensual passion. In depicting this
vice, the epic tradition had usually emphasized two motives
—love and glory. Milton retains this conventional motiva-
tion. Satan disobeys through lust for glory; Adam, through
the power of 'Femal charm'.

The theme of rebellion in *Paradise Lost* gives additional
clarity to the related pairs of antitheses—obedience and
disobedience, constancy and inconstancy, faith and apostasy. Though the poem is unusual in grounding its argument and structure on the hero's vice, rebellion had long
been a conventional epic argument, and England's recent
civil wars must have heightened its impact. In the conflicts
of Caesar and Pompey, Lucan finds a theme for the *Pharsalia*
—'wars worse than civil . . . and . . . legality conferred on
crime'.[1] Statius' *Thebaid* recounts the 'strife of brethren, and the
battle of the alternate reign fought out with impious hatred'.[2]

---

[1] Lucan, *The Civil War*, tr. J. D. Duff (London, 1928), pp. 2–3.
[2] *Statius*, i. 340–1.

Daniel's *Civil Wars* relates the Wars of the Roses, 'with a purpose, to shewe the deformities of Civile Dissension, and the miserable events of Rebellions, Conspiracies, and bloudy Revengements, which followed (as in a circle) upon that breach of the due course of Succession . . .':[1]

> I sing the civill Warres, tumultuous Broyles,
> And Bloody factions of a mightie Land: . . . .

In *The Barons Warres*, Drayton offers to sing 'Of a farre worse, then Civill Warre'—the rebellion against Edward II and the rise and fall of Roger Mortimer:[2]

> The bloudie Factions and Rebellious pride
> Of a strong Nation, whose ill-manag'd might
> The Prince and Peeres did many a day divide;
> With whom, wrong was no wrong, nor right no right,
> Whose strife, their Swords knew only to decide,
> Spur'd to their high speed, by their equall spight; . . . .

Other poets had elevated this theme to the supernatural plane. Hesiod's *Theogony* had related the rebellion of the Titans against Zeus. Valvasone's *Angeleida*, Valmarana's *Daemonomachia*, and other epics based on the hexaemeral tradition (the six days' labour of creation)[3] had imitated the revolt of the angels and Michael's victory over the rebel hosts.

Milton himself had already given quasi-epic treatment to the treason-motif in his poem on the Gunpowder Plot, 'In Quintum Novembris',[4] and in his prose works he had 'heroically celebrated'[5] the role of the Parliamentary forces

---

[1] Samuel Daniel, *The Civil Wars*, ed. Laurence Michel (New Haven, 1958), pp. 67, 71.

[2] Drayton, ii. 9.

[3] For surveys of the hexaemerel tradition, see Maury Thibaut de Maisières, *Les poèmes inspirées du début de la Genèse à l'époque de la renaissance* (Louvain, 1931); Frank Eggleston Robbins, *The Hexaemeral Literature, A Study of the Greek and Latin Commentaries on Genesis* (Chicago, 1912); George Coffin Taylor, *Milton and Du Bartas* (Cambridge, Mass., 1934); Sister Mary Irma Corcoran, *Miltons' 'Paradise Lost' with Reference to the Hexaemeral Background* (Washington, 1945); Watson Kirkconnell, *The Celestial Cycle* (Toronto, 1952); Grant McColley, *'Paradise Lost', An Account of Its Growth and Major Origins* (Chicago, 1940).

[4] See Philip Macon Cheek, 'Milton's *In Quintum Novembris*: An Epic Foreshadowing', *Studies in Philology*, liv (1957), pp. 172–84.

[5] Langdon, pp. 254–5.

in the English civil war. In basing the argument of *Paradise Lost* on man's revolt and in devoting one of the major episodes to the angelic rebellion, he was treating a type of subject-matter well-established, though by no means central, in the heroic tradition.

II

In examining Milton's critique of particular heroic formulae, we have stressed his juxtaposition of secular and divine, apparent and real, conceptions of heroic virtue and the heroic enterprise. We have also emphasized his conscious adaptation and reassessment of the principal ethical traits of classical and Renaissance heroes and his consequent revaluation of the epic tradition. We have noted his exploitation of epic machinery as a device for embodying Christian and pagan patterns of heroism and, in particular, the roles of Christ and Satan as the *eikon* and *eidolon* (the image and idol) of heroic virtue.

One further point requires attention—the relationship between the heroic exemplars (both true and false) of *Paradise Lost* and *Paradise Regain'd* and those of earlier epics. Unlike the conventional heroes, Milton's Christ and Satan represent spiritual and theological ultimates. Instead of being *comparatively* good or evil, they embody *absolute* good and evil—the divine and diabolical extremes of virtue and vice. As supernatural 'archetypes' of heroic virtue and brutishness, they antedate both the world and man. They are both logically and historically prior to the heroes of Virgil and Homer, Tasso and Spenser.

Temporally, however, they stand in a paradoxical relationship to these heroes. Chronologically, the persons and events of Milton's epic precede those of classical poetry; the fall of the angels and the fall of man antedate by millenia the exploits of the Trojan War. As *historical* figures, Christ and Satan are anterior to Achilles and Aeneas. As *literary* figures, however, the *personae* of classical epic are prior. Just as Homer and Virgil provided literary models for *Paradise Lost*, so their heroes served at time as models for Milton's heroes.

Thus, on the one hand, Achilles, Odysseus, Agamemnon, and Aeneas are literary 'prototypes' of Milton's Satan (and, to a lesser extent, of his Christ); but, on the other hand, Christ and Satan, as Milton portrays them, are the ethical and spiritual 'archetypes' to which, in varying degrees, the Homeric and Virgilian heroes—and, indeed, all the worthies of Biblical and Gentile tradition—must conform. This reciprocal relationship serves an important function in Milton's critique of heroic virtue, for it permits him to employ his divine and infernal 'archetypes' as standards for criticizing their literary models. Thus the closer Satan resembles Achilles and Odysseus, the more forceful is Milton's condemnation of these Homeric heroes. The comparison works both ways; if it invests Satan with traditional heroic attributes, it also exposes the heroic pretences of these traditional heroes as essentially diabolical.

The so-called 'problem of Satan'[1] tends to disappear, once one recognizes Milton's portrait for what it is—a conscious and consistent attempt to refute the conventional secular opinion of heroic virtue by assigning its principal attributes to the devil himself. By investing Satan with characteristic traits of Homeric heroes and Biblical 'mighty men', Milton exposes their pretensions to 'godlikeness' as spurious and implicitly condemns them as Satanic. Satan's final metamorphosis into a serpent does not simply punish him for his crime 'in the shape he sinn'd'. It also condemns his particular mode of heroism as an extraordinary 'excess of vice'. By stripping away the 'godlike appearance' to expose the essential deformity of sin, the transformation-scene convicts Satan himself—as well as the classical and Biblical prototypes on which he is modelled—of brutishness.

Satan has been often—and wrongly—called the 'hero'[2] of *Paradise Lost*; this is a fallacy, but, in terms of the structure of the plot, it contains an element of truth. He has also been

---

[1] See B. Rajan, *Paradise Lost and the Seventeenth Century Reader* (London, 1947), pp. 93–107.

[2] Cf. Dryden, *Prose Works*, ed. Malone, iii. 442; G. R. Hamilton, *Hero or Fool? A Study of Milton's Satan* (London, 1944); Calvin Huckaby, 'The Satanist Controversy of the Nineteenth Century', in *Studies in English Renaissance Literature*, ed. Waldo F. McNeir (Baton Rouge, 1962).

labelled the 'anti-hero',[1] and to a limited extent this appella-
tion too is just. Like the 'anti-hero' of the modern novel,
he represents a rejection of the conventional concept of the
hero. Yet here the resemblance ends. Unlike many modern
novelists, Milton does not reject the heroic ideal *per se*; he
denies only to affirm, and refutes Satan's heroism merely to
establish the perfect standard set by the Messiah. As a foil
to Milton's heroic Christ, Satan is really the 'counter-hero'
of *Paradise Lost*.

If one *must* attach a label to him, the most appropriate
category is simply the 'false-heroic'. Satan is the pseudo-
hero, the *eidolon* of heroic virtue, just as he is also the 'Idol of
Majestie Divine'.

In Milton's presentation of the 'heroic' Archfiend, there
are significant affinities with the mock-heroic.[2] But one must
not overestimate them. The element of heroic pretence is
common to both; both deliberately parody epic convention;
and both involve a conscious disparity between style and
content. The chief difference is that in *Paradise Lost* the
essential disproportion is ethical—it results from the contrast
between moral evil and superficial heroism; in the mock-
heroic tradition, on the other hand, it results, for the most
part, from magnifying the insignificant. The one is qualitative, the other usually quantitative. The Homeric *Bat-
rachomyomachia*, Virgil's *Culex*, Spenser's *Muiopotmos*, Chaucer's
'Nun's Priest's Tale', Tassoni's *La Secchia Rapita*, Boileau's
Lutrin, and similar works present trivial matters as though
they were great. They apply the grand style to subjects of
little weight. They deliberately exaggerate the disparity between level of style and level of argument.

In *Paradise Lost*, on the contrary, there is little disproportion in the comparative magnitude of argument and
style; Milton explicitly extols his own subject as 'more
heroic' than those of classical epic; the effects of man's first
disobedience are far more disastrous than the results of
Achilles' wrath or Turnus' rage or the anger of Juno and

---

[1] See Merritt Y. Hughes, in *Essays . . . Presented to A. S. P. Woodhouse*,
pp. 125 ff.

[2] See Richmond P. Bond, *English Burlesque Poetry* (Cambridge, Mass., 1932).

Neptune. The relation of style to content is usually the reverse of that in heroicomic epic. The objects Milton is imitating *exceed* the capacities of style; his problem is not one of expressing small things by great, but of expressing 'great things by small'. His picture of Satanic power and craft rests on the solid foundations of contemporary theology as well as popular belief. The basic inconsistency underlying this portrait is not so much the disparity between grandiose style and real insignificance (though this does at times become an element in the picture) as the disproportion between heroic pretence and essential vice.

For Satan *is* powerful, he *is* crafty—even though his power and craft are ultimately subject to the overruling power and wisdom of God. When a mock-heroic poet ranks the 'imbodied force' of the hero's army (or that of his enemies) above the combined might of Trojan and Greek, Christian and infidel, he is usually speaking with tongue in cheek. The point of such a comparison is to ridicule the relative impotence of the troops he is describing, to call attention to their smallness and weakness. In *Paradise Lost*, on the other hand, such a comparison is, if anything, an understatement. It emphasizes the magnitude of Satanic power.

The might and craft of Hell—like the weapons of the Philistine armies—eventually prove ridiculous. But, even so, Satan surpasses in strength and subtlety the conventional epic hero. Here again Milton's use of the false-heroic differs from the practice of most heroicomic poets. In comparison with earthly glory—the grandeur of Babylon or Memphis or Rome—the magnificence of Pandaemonium is real, and the magnificent style is eminently justified. But in comparison with the glories of Heaven, this is a false glory, a specious magnificence, and in this context the magnificent style itself becomes ironic—vainglorious pretence.

But, if the false-heroic in *Paradise Lost* differs markedly from that of mock-heroic epic, it also differs from the pseudo-heroic of *Don Quixote*. Don Quixote is the victim of a romantic fallacy, Satan of a theological fallacy. In Cervantes's novel, as in the mock-heroic tradition, there is a conscious disproportion between trivial incident and elevated manner, between commonplace reality and heroic appearance. The Spanish knight sees the ordinary as extraordinary, the humble as exalted, the plebeian as aristocratic, the insignificant as fraught with momentous import. He regards the commonplace through the lens of chivalric illusion. As in *Paradise Lost*, there is a fundamental disparity between truth and appearance, reality and phantasy; and in Cervantes and Milton alike, it is rooted largely in the delusions of the character himself.

This disparity is almost as significant in Milton's portrait of Satan as in Cervantes's picture of Don Quixote. Nevertheless the psychological basis differs notably in the two cases. Don Quixote's delusions spring from over-absorption in chivalric romances; Satan's from ambition and from the corruption of the angelic intelligence through sin. Don Quixote's heroic pretensions are innocuous; Satan's are altogether vicious. The false-heroic in *Don Quixote* consists in magnifying the trivial; in *Paradise Lost*, it consists in glorifying evil. Cervantes's hero elevates chance encounters with humble peasants and artisans into adventures with high-born ladies, giants, and enchanters; there is, as in the mock-heroic, a conscious violation of decorum and the social and stylistic levels so rigidly defined in the 'wheel of Virgil' and its successors. Milton's counterhero, on the other hand, invests evil with heroic attributes, and crime with the superficial characteristics of an epic enterprise.[1] Hence the false-heroic of *Paradise Lost* seems, in some respects, fairly close to the false-heroic of Fielding's *Jonathan Wild the Great*. By ironically treating the criminal as a hero, both writers actually pass moral judgement on the heroes of epic and historical tradition.

Milton's exploitation of the pseudo-heroic is essentially a *reductio ad absurdum* of the conventional heroism celebrated by poets and historiographers. As the archetype of the worldly hero, Satan excels his literary and historical prototypes. If physical strength is a measure of heroism, if guile is a heroic norm, if conquest and destruction are heroic exploits, if

[1] Cf. Calvin Huckaby, 'Satan and the Narrative Structure of *Paradise Lost*; Some Observations', *Studia Neophilologica*, xxxiii (1960), pp. 96–102.

Achilles and Alexander, Caesar and Borgia are heroes, then the devil himself must be the perfect hero. In the context of human history and poetry Satan and his achievements are incomparable; no mere man, however heroic, can hope to equal them. Even the heroes of Homer and Tasso strove only to overthrow a single city; Satan, alone and unaided, conquers a whole world.

But these conventional standards are false, and Milton demonstrates their falsity by associating them with the author and supreme exemplar of evil. To represent Satan in heroic terms is, by implication, to condemn the whole series of 'Destroyers' and 'Conquerors' who follow him—the Biblical giants, Nimrod, the military heroes of Greece and Rome, the valiant pagans of medieval and Renaissance epic and romance. The Spanish conquests in the New World and the Portuguese empires in the Orient are, like Satan's victory over Adam, achievements of 'close ambition varnisht o'er with zeal'. Milton's 'heroic' archfiend turns out to be an ingenious literary device for reassessing the heroic tradition. The paradox of a 'godlike' devil enables him to arraign epic and history alike for mistaking brutishness for heroic virtue, and thus celebrating the counterfeit idol of heroism.

III

The comic element in Milton's presentation of the false-heroic results partly from the contrast between pretence and reality, partly from a convention of Renaissance literary theory—that vice is ultimately ludicrous and that the function of comedy and satire alike is to expose it to ridicule. Satan's ambitions, founded as they are on a denial of his proper station and capabilities, arouse divine laughter, just as do man's pretensions to astronomical knowledge and the designs of the builders of Babel. The contrast between what he is and what he pretends to be makes him ridiculous in the eyes of God. Instead of inspiring wonder and admiration—the proper effects of heroic virtue and action—he provokes scorn and ridicule. This heroicomic paradox reaches its climax in his ignominious metamorphosis at the moment of his triumph.

The comic element in Milton's false-heroic is, however, considerably more complex than in the heroicomic tradition. As 'God's ape', Satan and his antics appear ludicrous in the eyes of God, but for man they are too fraught with peril to seem other than tragic. For Adam and Eve and their posterity, the superhuman strength and wiles of the devil are too menacing to be laughed off as merely comic. Satan, as Milton represents him and as theology and popular belief regarded him, is far more dangerous a foe than Achilles or Turnus. He inspires—and is meant to inspire—wonder and marvel. Milton demanded, therefore, a multiple response from his audience. The Satanic idol should not only arouse the fear appropriate to tragedy and the wonder appropriate to epic, but also the ridicule appropriate to comedy and satire. The reader might fear Satan's power and craft, marvel at his exploits, yet share the divine laughter at the incongruity between heroic pretence and moral depravity and at the ultimate frustration of all his schemes. Unlike the mock-heroic, the false-heroic of *Paradise Lost* aims beyond laughter and comprehends heroic wonder and tragic fear.

Satan's role as pseudo-hero is both antithetical and complementary to that of the Son as the true heroic archetype. The two portraits serve, like logical contraries, to define heroic virtue and distinguish it from its opposite. But the Satanic idol performs additional mimetic functions. As the infinite and perfect are essentially inimitable, Milton must necessarily delineate them by approximation and suggestion. Through its resemblance to the conventional heroic pattern, the diabolical exemplar provides a point of departure for suggesting the infinite and perfect virtues of the Messiah. The fact that Milton's true heroic archetype— the Son of God—fails to move the reader as powerfully as the Satanic idol is natural and inevitable, but the poet counters this difficulty by a series of logical comparisons. If Satan's exploits and character—finite and essentially evil as they are—arouse wonder, how much more admirable, how much more worthy of marvel, are those of the Son! Satan conquers

and destroys a world; the Son conquers and destroys Satan
and his host. Yet creation and peace are nobler and greater
than ruin and war. By creating the visible universe the Son
counters the destruction wrought by the angelic war; by
creating anew the divine image in the human soul, he overcomes the effects of sin and death, Satan's vicegerents in
fallen microcosm and macrocosm alike. Through comparison
and suggestion Milton demonstrates the superior merit of
actions that defy literary imitation and consequently cannot
readily inspire the full admiration they deserve. Where
mimesis fails, he relies on suggestion; where the resources of
poetry fall short, he depends on logical comparison and in-
ference. The Satanic idol provides a point of reference for
estimating dimensions infinitely greater and norms immeasurably higher than itself, for approximating a heroic exemplar
which—being spiritual—cannot be truly imitated; being
infinite—can never be measured; being perfect—defies
comprehension.

VIII

The Revaluation of Epic Tradition

MILTON found the heroic poem brick and left it marble. For the praise of men he substituted the glory of God. Instead of human strength, he depicted mortal frailty— accentuating this contrast by juxtaposing divine and human virtues. Instead of the physical warfare of secular polities, he described the moral conflict of spiritual societies. Instead of celebrating heroic exploits, he stressed their imperfections,[1] weighing man's sins against the truly 'magnific' works of God. By this radical reorientation of epic tradition, he based the heroic poem on the cornerstone of Protestant ethics, the 'vanity of human merits'.

A doctrinal system in which the hero must voluntarily 'renounce His own both righteous and unrighteous deeds' demands a drastic revaluation of the epic enterprise. If he can achieve a valid reward not through his own acts, but only through those of another, his exploits lose their traditional significance. Unlike Hercules or Aeneas or Julius Caesar, the hero cannot merit deification by his own 'god-like' deeds. If he does trust in his own deserts, he lives in a 'fool's paradise' of false hope, a Limbo of Vanity. As his 'good works' are 'effects' of the Spirit itself, whatever glory

---

[1] Milton's conception of the value of works is less extreme than Luther's and Calvin's and closer to that of Arminus. Man is justified by faith (Milton maintains)—but not without the *works* of faith. Yet, as these are the works of the Spirit, man has no occasion for boasting. For Arminius's views, see A. W. Harrison, *The Beginnings of Arminianism to the Synod of Dort* (London, 1926). Arminius's opponent, Plancius, accused him of declaring that 'we cannot commend good works enough, provided we abstain from ascribing merit to them'. Arminius admitted the truth of this statement, but declared that 'justification is still by faith and not by works' (p. 29). According to the *Remonstrance* (p. 151), 'God's grace through Christ . . . was the cause of the beginning, progress and completion of man's salvation; insomuch that none could believe nor persevere in faith without this co-operating grace, and consequently that all good works must be ascribed to the grace of God in Christ'. Cf. *PL*, iii. 446–7, 'when Sin with vanity had filld the works of men'.

accrues to them belongs properly to God rather than to man. Whatever traces he shows of the divine image—the 'form' or essence of heroic virtue—he owes to supernal grace. Whatever merit he possesses, he has acquired only by 'imputation' through faith in Christ—a faith which ultimately springs from 'supernatural renovation'.[1]

In founding the heroic poem on internal regeneration and the disparity between divine strength and human weakness, God's wisdom and man's folly, Milton radically altered the conventional character of the epic. The divine machinery dominates and all but dwarfs the human action, reducing the latter either to mere vanity and sin or (at best) to the fruits of faith. As the 'form' of 'good works'[2] and the root of all heroic 'acts of benefit'[3] faith becomes more significant than action itself. Milton placed far greater emphasis than his precursors on the crisis of faith, the act of repentance that precedes it, and the process of spiritual regeneration that underlies both.[4]

Although numerous factors contributed to Milton's 'Copernican revolution', four were of principal importance: (1) his desire to reorient the epic toward the chief end of ethics, politics, and theology—beatitude or the 'highest good';[5] (2) his preference for literal rather than allegorical representation of moral conflict; (3) the equivocal nature of most epic formulae and, in particular, the contrast between their secular and spiritual meanings; and (4) the infinite disproportion between human and divine virtues. These considerations underlay both his choice of subject matter and his development of his theme.

[1] Cf. *De Doctrina*, Book I, Chapters 18, 20.

[2] Ibid., Book II, Chapter 1.

[3] Milton condemns the worldly heroes who through evil deeds—destruction, conquest, injury, slavery—paradoxically seek the titles of 'Great Benefactors of Mankind' and 'Deliverers'; the true right to such titles belongs to the Son. The supreme 'act of benefit' is Messiah's voluntary sacrifice, 'for the benefit of mankind' (cf. Columbia Edition, vol. xv. 311), his deliverance of mankind 'from sin and death' (ibid., p. 251). In Book III of *Paradise Lost* the Father stresses the frailty of fallen man, who is 'upheld' by God alone and owes to Him alone 'All his deliv'rance'.

[4] Cf. *De Doctrina*, Book I, Chapters 18–20.

[5] See my 'Felicity and End in Renaissance Epic and Ethics', *Journal of the History of Ideas*, xxiii (1962), pp. 117–32.

I

If happiness was the ultimate aim of ethics and theology, it was, *a fortiori*, also the final end of poetry, as the handmaiden and instrument of these disciplines. Thus, for Varchi, the goal of poetics was man's 'perfection and beatitude'. It led the reader to true felicity by moving him to pursue the virtues that assist this end and to shun the vices that oppose it.[1] According to Dante's Epistle to Can Grande, the 'end' of his *Commedia* was to lead man 'from a state of misery' (the misery of sin) 'to a state of happiness' (both in this life and the next). Literally, its subject was 'the state of souls after death', but allegorically its theme was 'man himself, in so far as his own merits and demerits made him liable to reward or punishment'. The poem belonged, in short, to moral philosophy.[2]

Like the moral philosopher, the poet taught the nature of man's happiness and misery, virtue and vice. Like the orator, he utilized the resources of deliberative and demonstrative rhetoric to exhort to virtue and 'dehort' from vice, to praise the one and excoriate the other. Unlike the philosopher and orator, however, he sought to achieve his ends by imitation. His method was essentially mimetic, and he observed the end of his art by delineating the beauty of virtue and the deformity of vice and by describing their contrary rewards, happiness and misery.

This conception of the end and method of poetry underlies Milton's presentation of moral concepts. Like Dante, he bases his poetic structure on the opposition between man's supreme happiness and deepest misery—fruition of the divine presence and alienation from God.[3] Like Dante, he expresses this contrast through eschatological symbolism—the conventions of the Christian heaven and hell. Like Dante, he stresses the moral causes of beatitude or misery

---

[1] *Opere di Benedetto Varchi*, ed. A. Racheli (Trieste, 1859), ii. 287, 658–86.

[2] *Tutte le opere di Dante Alighieri*, ed. E. Moore (Oxford, 1894), pp. 416–17.

[3] For Milton's relation to Dante, see the publications cited in my 'Milton and Mazzoni: The Genre of the *Divina Commedia*', *Huntington Library Quarterly*, xxiii (1960), pp. 107–22, and 'The God of *Paradise Lost* and the *Divina Commedia*', *Archiv f. d. Studium d. neueren Sprachen u. Literaturen*, cxcv (1959), pp. 274–89.

—the antithetical virtues and vices which merit contrary rewards. In both poems obedience to God is the source of true happiness and disobedience the root of true misery.

Like Dante, Milton embodies the 'forms' or 'ideas' of virtue and vice in particular individuals aiming respectively at true and false goods. Satan wrongly seeks his good in glory and honour; 'insatiable of glory', he has lost all. Moloch finds his supreme good in his own strength, Belial in ignoble ease, Mammon in material wealth. Thus they represent the vices of pride, wrath, lust, avarice as well as a host of related sins. Conversely, the virtues of obedience and love toward God appear primarily in Messiah and the faithful 'servant of God', Abdiel.

The 'technique of degradation',[1] which Waldock has wrongly censured in Milton's treatment of Satan, has its roots in the conventions of poetic justice. Literary theory demanded that the deformities of evil be stripped and punished—that they meet their due reward of misery and shame. Milton would have been neglecting the basic principles of his art if he had left Satan's 'heroic' crimes without exposure or retribution. The devil's soliloquy on Mount Niphates fills a basic requirement of poetic justice—to display the misery of sin:

> . . . Me Miserable! Which way shall I fly
> Infinite wrath or infinite despair?

Satan reveals himself here—as poetic justice demanded he should—'onely supreme in misery'.

Other aspects of the 'technique of degradation' stress the deformity of sin. Though Milton breaks with poetic and iconographical tradition in deferring the conventional metamorphosis of the fallen angels until the 'transformation-scene' of Book X, he nevertheless makes his point earlier through other means. In the angelic battle, the rebels, 'now gross with sinning grown', first experience pain. In extricating themselves from the mountains heaped upon them, they suffer the encumbrances of materiality. On Mount Niphates, Satan is disfigured by ire, envy, and despair.

---

[1] See A. J. A. Waldock, p. 65.

Confronted by the angelic watch, he learns simultaneously 'how awful Goodness is, and Vertue in her shape how lovly' and that his own 'lustre [has been] visibly impair'd' by sin.

These details foreshadow his final transformation into a serpent—a scene which meets the conventional requirements of poetic justice as well as divine retribution. In reality, his metamorphosis represents a partial execution of the sentence already passed on the serpent—yet *essentially* on Satan himself. But the scene serves other functions as well.[1] Like the stripping of Duessa and Alcina, the metamorphoses of Circe's victims, and the brutish transformation of Sin in Book I, it displays the innate deformity of vice. It is an *exemplum* of punitive justice, and, as such, it becomes all the more effective because God, like the Mikado, can 'make the punishment fit the crime'. A 'higher power' compels the demons to re-enact Adam's crime, to gorge themselves on the delusive fruit and chew the ashes of remorse. Despite adverse criticism by Waldock and other scholars, the scene finds its justification in the ethical demands of Renaissance poetic theory, the precedent set by analogous examples of poetic justice in classical, medieval, and Renaissance verse, and the logical expectations of a seventeenth-century audience. The most original feature of this episode is the skilful fusion of two ethical commonplaces. When the fallen angels are turned into serpents and forced to hiss themselves, their metamorphosis exhibits both the intrinsic deformity of evil and its condign punishment of shame. Both are conventional topics of the 'dehortatory' argument.

The same antithesis—the beauty and happiness of virtue and the ugliness and misery of vice—recurs in Satan's first encounter with Adam and Eve and in his first reflections on the sun. When the fallen angel first beholds unfallen man, he is deeply stirred by Adam's 'divine resemblance'—the divine image that Satan himself has lost forever. Eden itself cannot give him joy, and he beholds, 'undelighted, all

---

[1] See my 'Archangel to Devil: The Background of Satan's Metamorphosis', *Modern Language Quarterly*, xxi (1960), pp. 321-35.

delights'. Similarly, the view of the sun from Mount Niphates reminds him of the beatific vision he has forfeited. The sun retains its divine similitude; Satan has lost his. Ironically, it is precisely this analogy between the sun and the Creator that accentuates his loss of divine resemblance. It awakens the torments of remorse and thereby exposes his angelic disguise as 'counterfeit'.

But Milton places even greater stress on the moral analysis of misery. The theme of *Paradise Lost* is the loss of happiness through sin; Adam's transgression is the cause not only of death, but of 'all our Woe'. After describing the 'growing miseries' which afflict the hero 'from without' after his fall, the poem delineates the 'worse [miseries] felt within' as the result of his crime. Adam feels the misery of loss, the alienation from his true good and beatitude:

> O miserable of happie! . . . who now becom
> Accurst of blessed, hide me from the face
> Of God, whom to behold was then my highth
> Of happiness: . . . .

He experiences the terrors of a guilty conscience:

> . . . miserable
> Beyond all past example and future,
> To *Satan* onely like both crime and doom.
> O Conscience into what Abyss of fears
> And horrors hast thou driv'n me; out of which
> I find no way, from deep to deeper plung'd!

And he is aware of other miseries to come. The execration— the 'propagated curse'—of his posterity. The eternity of death—'endless miserie From this day onward, which I feel begun Both in me, and without me . . .'.

Samson Agonistes likewise analyses the nature of misery. As in *Paradise Lost*, this is the just punishment of sin; the deepest sorrow lies in the consciousness of guilt. In his opening soliloquy, the hero's complaint rehearses external and physical 'miseries of life'—blindness, captivity among enemies, shame and disgrace:

> . . . strength is my bane,
> And proves the source of all my miseries, . . .
> Blind among enemies, O worse than chains,

> Dungeon, or beggary, or decrepit age!
> . . . but O yet more miserable!
> Myself my Sepulchre, a moving Grave. . . .

The Chorus echoes this emphasis on external ills:

> Which shall I first bewail,
> Thy Bondage or lost Sight . . .?

Manoa bemoans the 'miserable change' which has reduced 'That invincible *Samson*' to an unequal match 'against a coward arm'd At one spear's length'.

Nevertheless, the further development of the drama shifts the emphasis from physical to spiritual misery. In the course of the dialogue Samson perceives that his moral bondage to Dalila and his spiritual blindness are far more ignominious than external slavery and material blindness. The state of sin, with its corollaries, bondage of will and darkness of understanding, is the deeper misery. The deepest is the consciousness of sin against God. In the interview with Manoa, Sampson finds his primary source of grief in the 'Dishonour' he has brought to Jehovah and the 'honour' he has given to Dagon; this is his

> . . . chief affliction, shame and sorrow,
> The anguish of my Soul, that suffers not
> Mine eie to harbour sleep, or thoughts to rest.

Samson Agonistes thus tends to 'moralize' afflictions. The hero's miseries are the direct result of his sin and thus represent the causal relationship between vice and its punishment. But they also provide the occasion for exercising his virtue and illustrating his inner victory over outward misfortunes. Finally, they also serve as a point of departure for differentiating between the true misery of guilt and the apparent misery of external affliction. In this respect his situation resembles that of Boethius in the *Consolation of Philosophy* and that of Lipsius in *De Constantia*.

II

The greater moral earnestness Milton brought to the heroic poem led to another variation on epic tradition. Basing his argument on spiritual conflict rather than physical warfare, he prefers to present moral ideas immediately through direct imitation rather than mediately through allegory. *Paradise Lost* differs from many of its predecessors not only in its stress on human frailty, but also in poetic method.

For Tasso, heroic poetry was composed of 'imitation' and 'allegory'; the one gave delight, the other bestowed ethical or scientific instruction. The one presented a direct image of human action; the other provided an oblique figure of human life. Imitation (he declared) is concerned with external action and speech; it does not consider the intrinsic operations of the soul except as they are manifested in action or speech. Allegory, on the other hand, concerns the internal rather than the external operations of the spirit.[1] On the level of imitation, therefore, Tasso's *Gerusalemme Liberata* describes the deliverance of Jerusalem under Godfrey of Bouillon. On the allegorical plane, however, it represents the achievement of human felicity through the subordination of the lesser faculties of soul and body to the sovereignty of reason. The crusaders' army, composed of 'various princes and other Christian warriors', signifies man. Jerusalem, located in a 'rough and mountainous region', symbolizes 'political felicity', which is difficult to attain as it is placed 'on the summit of the alpine and toilsome ridge of virtue'. Godfrey signifies the intellect, which commands the other powers of soul and body. Rinaldo, Tancred, and the other leaders symbolize different 'faculties' of the soul, while the common soldier represents the body.

Because of the imperfections of human nature and the deceits of the devil, man can achieve felicity only by overcoming numerous external and internal impediments. The armies of Africa and Asia and the adverse battles which hamper the Crusaders represent external enemies and the accidents of contrary fortune. Among the internal impediments are love and wrath, which rebel against the sovereignty of reason. The demons who hold council to prevent the conquest of Jerusalem represent infernal opposition to man's 'political felicity, so that it cannot become a ladder to

[1] Tasso, i. 301.

Christian beatitude'. The magicians, Ismeno and Armida, who as 'instruments of the devil' attempt to prevent the Christians from waging war, symbolize the two 'diabolical temptations that subvert two powers of the human soul, from which all sins proceed'. Ismeno signifies the temptation which tries to deceive opinion with false beliefs; Armida represents the temptation which attacks the appetite.

In contrast to these obstacles to man's beatitude are the internal and external aids which lead him to his 'desired felicity'. The diamond shield signifies God's special custody. The angels represent divine aid or divine inspiration. The hermit and the sage who purpose Rinaldo's liberation represent 'supernatural cognition received through divine grace' and 'human wisdom'. Thus 'human wisdom, directed by a higher virtue, frees the sensitive soul from vice and introduces moral virtue instead'. As Godfrey symbolizes the intellect and Rinaldo the irascible faculty, the latter's return and reconciliation with his commander signify 'the obedience which the irascible faculty renders to the rational faculty'.

Since the army symbolizes man, its reconciliation with Godfrey signifies man's return to the state of divine obedience and natural justice, when 'the superior powers command and the inferior obey'. Then the wood is disenchanted, the city taken, and the enemy forces subdued—that is, once the external impediments have been overcome, man can pursue his political happiness.[1]

Thus, underlying the events of the poetic fable, there is a parallel progression of ethical states, and these constitute the moral allegory. Like the fable itself, this has an inner logical structure—a structure derived from moral philosophy and transferred in whole or in part to heroic poetry and the critical tradition associated with the epic. The Renaissance audience was trained to recognize this moral pattern in the heroic poem, and a Renaissance author could depend on his readers to follow the ethical sequence as well as the course of events.

In Milton's epic there are comparable patterns, but he prefers to represent them literally rather than allegorically.

[1] Ibid., pp. 302–7.

Where Tasso separates the functions of instruction and delight and assigns the one to allegory and the other to imitation, Milton usually dispenses with allegory and leaves the didactic function to imitation alone. Like Tasso's allegory, both *Paradise Lost* and *Paradise Regain'd* depict man and the various virtues or vices that aid or hinder him in pursuing his felicity. Both stress the ideal of natural justice—the subordination of the inferior to the superior both within the soul and in external nature. Both emphasize divine obedience. Both exploit the machinery of angels and devils as aids or obstacles to the achievement of human felicity. In both, as in Tasso's 'allegoria', happiness depends on the subordination of passion and appetite to reason.[1]

Samson Agonistes likewise depicts in literal terms ethical concepts that Tasso had presented allegorically. In his amorous 'servitude' to Dalila, the hero subjects right reason to sensual appetite, subordinating his 'rational' and 'irascible' faculties to the 'concupiscible'. Like Tasso's heroes, and like Milton's Adam, he is restored to the state of natural justice and divine obedience by grace and right reason. Much of the earlier part of the drama consists in a rational analysis of the nature, extent, and effects of his sin. Reason reveals to him the ignominy of his moral bondage and the consequent distortion of his true nature through vice. This insight leads to decisive repudiation of his 'sorceress'.[2] It is only after he has conquered his internal enemies—his own passions and appetites—and reduced them to rational con-

---

[1] In both, man's chief adversaries attempt to undermine his felicity either by deceiving his intellect with false beliefs or by appealing to his appetite with false goods. In both, as in Tasso, man is restored to the state of natural justice and divine obedience through the operation of divine grace and the exercise of right reason.

[2] Samson's moral bondage to Dalila places him in the same category as Ruggiero and Rinaldo, who have also been 'effeminatly vanquish't'. The bitter shame he feels when he perceives his spiritual servitude is likewise conventional; it is analogous to that which Alcina's and Armida's victims experience when recalled to reason. In decisively rejecting Dalila, he again conforms to type, following a precedent set by classical and romantic heroes—Ulysses, in leaving Calypso and Circe; Aeneas, in abandoning Dido; Ruggiero, in rejecting Alcina; Redcrosse, in rebuffing Duessa; and Rinaldo, in forsaking Armida. The hero's ultimate rejection of his seductress is a commonplace of the heroic tradition, and Milton's Dalila-episode should be read in this light.

trol that he can proceed against his external foes and defeat them.

Even if Dr. Johnson was partly right about the plot of *Samson Agonistes* (and his complaint that nothing happens between the beginning and end of the drama to bring about the denouement surely needs to be qualified)[1] there is an inner logic in the ethos of Milton's tragedy. The hero's internal victory must logically precede his external victory over his pagan adversaries, just as in the *Gerusalemme Liberata*.

Like Tasso, Spenser had represented the operation of divine grace allegorically. Redcrosse is released from Orgoglio's dungeon by Prince Arthur and brought to the House of Holiness for recovery and instruction. Only then can he proceed on his quest to slay the dragon and free Una's parents. Milton, on the other hand, prefers to depict grace and regeneration literally. In Adam and Samson alike, these are primarily evident in their psychological effects.[2] In Adam the operation of grace manifests itself in penitence and a profession of faith in the merits of his future redeemer. In Samson its effects appear in his repentance and his trust in Jehovah. In both cases, moreover, Milton emphasizes the dependence of heroic virtue and heroic achievement on the prior operations of grace. The essence of heroic virtue—the divine image—is restored in the elect only through the process of 'supernatural renovation'.[3] Similarly, heroic actions— 'acts of benefit'—are, like all good works, ultimately contingent on grace.

In all three of his major poems, Milton places his primary emphasis on the moral virtues—the 'proximate causes' and psychological preconditions of good works—rather than on the heroic act itself. In all three he presents the characteristics of the divine image—truth, wisdom, sanctity, liberty, dominion—as the essence of heroic virtue. In all three he stresses faith as the essence and form of good works. The process of Adam's regeneration culminates in a conclusive

---

[1] See my '"Faithful Champion": The Theological Basis of Milton's Hero of Faith', *Anglia*, lxxvii (1959), pp. 12–28.

[2] Cf. *De Doctrina*, Book I, Chapters 18–20.

[3] Cf. ibid., Chapter 18.

act of faith. Samson's regeneration reaches its climax in a decisive victory over his enemies, but the greater part of the drama is devoted to delineating the hero's moral regeneration[1] and exhibiting the magnitude and excellence of his virtues. *Paradise Regain'd* ends with a revelation of the hero's divine Sonship, but for the most part the fable exhibits in detail the ethical attributes of the divine image. Instead of representing Christ's ministry and final victory on the cross, the action of the poem focuses on his heroic virtues, the 'proximate causes' of his exploits and his ultimate triumph.

The most significant feature of *Paradise Regain'd* is the restoration of the divine image in mankind—the perfect and 'godlike' virtue which the Son alone can exhibit in its highest excellence.[2] Each successive phase of the temptation approaches more closely to the final epiphany on the temple-tower, by progressively demonstrating the hero's superiority to other men. The poem thus provides a detailed and 'compendious' anatomy of heroic virtue, emphasizing its three most significant features—its eminence, its 'godlike' quality, and its comprehensiveness.

[1] For further discussion of Samson's regeneration, see Ann Gossman, 'Milton's Samson as the Tragic Hero Purified by Trial', *Journal of English and Germanic Philology*, lxi (1962), pp. 528–41; Marcia K. Landy, 'Of Highest Wisdom: A Study of John Milton's *Samson Agonistes* as a Dramatization of Christian Conversion' (Rochester dissertation, 1963). For the regeneration-motif in Milton's Eve, see Mary Ann Nevins Radzinowicz, 'Eve and Dalila: Renovation and the Hardening of the Heart', in *Reason and the Imagination*, ed. J. A. Mazzeo (New York, 1962), pp. 155–81. For an attack on the 'regeneration theory', see G. R. Wilkes, 'The Interpretation of *Samson Agonistes*', *Huntington Library Quarterly*, xxvi (1963), pp. 363–79. In actuality, however, Samson's repentance and faith are, like Adam's, 'effects' of regeneration.

[2] Cf. *De Doctrina*, Book II, Chapter 2. Since 'regeneration is sometimes termed sanctification, being the literal mode of expressing that for which regeneration is merely a figurative phrase' (Book I, Chapter 18), this definition reinforces the hero-saint equation. The true hero (in whom the divine image is restored) is the regenerate 'saint'. As Milton defines it, regeneration is 'that change operated by the Word and the Spirit, whereby the old man being destroyed, the inward man is regenerated by God after his own image, in all the faculties of his mind, insomuch that he becomes as it were a new creature, and the whole man is sanctified both in body and soul, for the service of God, and the performance of good works'. Cf. Colossians iii. 9–11. The 'old man' (Book I, Chapter 11) or 'the body of sin' is the 'evil concupiscence . . . of which our original parents were first guilty, and which they transmitted to their posterity, as sharers in the primary transgression, in the shape of an innate propensity to sin'.

This literal approach to ethical concepts not only makes *Paradise Lost* a very different poem from the *Gerusalemme Liberata*. It also accentuates the contrast with the *Commedia*. Though Milton and Dante both present the concept of felicity in terms of the dualism of the earthly and celestial paradises, there is a fundamental divergence between the poetic methods of the two writers. In Dante, the significance of both *paradisi* is largely allegorical. The earthly paradise represents the civil felicity attainable in the church militant, under the dual régime of emperor and pope and through the exercise of the four cardinal virtues. The celestial paradise represents the grades and degrees of virtue and felicity, culminating finally in the beatific vision as man's supreme beatitude. They exemplify the two types of happiness that Dante had already outlined in the *De Monarchia* and the *Convivio*—the civil happiness of natural justice and the spiritual beatitude of the vision of God—the one achievable under the civil magistrate through philosophy and the cardinal virtues, the other attainable under spiritual guidance through theology and the theological virtues.[1] The poet's journey to both paradises is an allegory of philosophical contemplation; the visit to hell, purgatory, and heaven represents his reflections on the nature of virtue and vice and their merited rewards and punishments.

Paradise Lost and *Paradise Regain'd*, on the other hand, attempt (as far as possible) to depict the ideals of earthly and celestial happiness literally. Paradise can be taken, as St. Augustine and Dante after him had taken it, as a symbol of the *vita beata*.[2] But it is not essential to do so, and for the most part Milton describes the 'blessed life' in literal terms, depicting the original happiness of Adam and Eve through a detailed account of their surroundings, their activities, and their reactions to the paradisal life. Unlike Dante's, this earthly paradise is an historical fact. Adam and Eve are, for Milton, real persons in a real garden. In Dante's 'paradiso terrestre', however, the activity of Matilda, Virgil,

---

[1] Cf. Etienne Gilson, *Dante and Philosophy*, tr. David Moore (New York, 1963), pp. 83–224; see especially pp. 132, 190, 197, 200.
[2] Augustine, p. 431.

Beatrice, and Dante himself is a fiction, not an historical fact; it is real only in an allegorical sense. Similarly, though one must make allowances for Milton's 'technique of accommodation', he tends to present the beatitude of heaven literally rather than allegorically. Unlike Dante's, his celestial paradise is not an allegorical hierarchy of the virtues, nor is it basically a symbol of happiness. As with other ethical ideas, Milton prefers to present felicity literally rather than allegorically.

The same tendency appears in his treatment of the nature of man—a concept of supreme importance for classical and Christian ethics alike. For Erasmus, the 'chief point of [the] wisdom [of Christ] is simply to know yourself, an injunction which antiquity believed to have originated in heaven and which great authors have found so pleasing that they consider the whole fruit of wisdom compactly enclosed in it'. The 'only way to virtue [is,] first, that you know yourself; second, that you act, not according to the passions, but the dictates of reason'.[1] According to Thomas à Kempis, 'he that well knoweth himself is vile and abject in his own sight, and hath no delight in the vain praisings of man. . . . The most high and the most profitable cunning is this, that a man have a soothfast knowledge and a full despising of himself.'[2]

The heroic tradition had given particular prominence to man as epic subject. Both Homer and Virgil had included 'man' in the propositions of their heroic poems (*'Andra . . . polytropon'*.[3] *'Arma virumque'*).[4] That Hebrew epic,[5] the Book of Job, similarly began with an explicit reference to 'man': 'There was a man in the land of Uz, . . . and that was perfect and upright. . . .' The *vir* of the Vulgate version

---

[1] *The Enchiridion of Erasmus*, tr. and ed. Raymond Himelick (Bloomington, 1963), pp. 62, 71.

[2] Thomas à Kempis, *The Imitation of Christ*, tr. Richard Whitford (New York, 1961), pp. 4–6.

[3] Cf. *Odyssey*, vol. i. 2.   [4] *Virgil*, vol. i. 240.

[5] See Charles W. Jones, 'Milton's 'Brief Epic', *Studies in Philology*, xliv (1947), pp. 209–27. In her recent study, *Milton's Brief Epic: The Genre, Meaning, and Art of 'Paradise Regained'* (Providence, 1966), Barbara Kiefer Lewalski explores in detail the medieval and Renaissance conception of the book of Job as a heroic poem and relates this tradition to Milton's poetry.

(as commentators hastened to point out) meant 'hero', and the fact that he was described as 'perfect' made him all the fitter subject for a heroic poem. Allegorically, the subject of Dante's *Commedia* and Tasso's *Gerusalemme Liberata* was man ('l'uomo'). In including 'Man' in the proposition of his epics, Milton followed an established poetic tradition. His opening lines not only reflect the classical and Christian emphasis on man's nature as a starting point for moral philosophy; they also conform to an epic precedent established by Homer, Virgil, Tasso, and the Holy Spirit itself.

Nevertheless, in retaining this conventional emphasis on man as epic subject, he introduced a significant variant by basing his proposition on the Pauline distinction between *two* men, two Adams—the 'earthy' and the heavenly—whose disobedience and obedience had brought condemnation and salvation to mankind. Despite their formal resemblance to the propositions of the *Iliad* and the *Aeneid*, the opening lines of both epics exhibit the antithesis St. Paul had developed in Romans and 1 Corinthians.[1]

In basing the propositions of both epics on the Pauline formulation of the parallel between Adam and Christ, Milton gives greater stress to the problem of merit and to the most significant aspects of human nature—its subjection to original sin through Adam and its regeneration through the merits of Christ. This, for Milton, was the essential fact about the nature of man which the Gentile philosophers had missed and which the Biblical revelation alone had clearly recognized and assessed:

> Alas what can they teach, and not mislead;
> Ignorant of themselves, of God much more,
> And how the world began, and how man fell
> Degraded by himself, on grace depending?
> Much of the Soul they talk, but all awrie,
> And in themselves seek vertue, and to themselves
> All glory arrogate, to God give none, ...

With their emphasis on man's central position in the universe, his intermediate position between God and beast,

---

[1] Romans v. 12–20; 1 Corinthians xv. 21–22, 45–49.

and the power of rational choice, the argument and fable of *Paradise Lost* reflect the primary values of Renaissance humanism. Though its standards are theocentric, its universe and action are anthropocentric. Despite the exceptional prominence Milton gives his supernatural machinery, both divine and infernal strategies are directed specifically towards man. Earth occupies the central position in Milton's cosmos, and the central figures are neither God nor Satan, but Adam and Eve. The basic ethical concerns of the poem are the nature, duties, and end of man.

Milton's choice of subject gave him scope to develop the essential paradoxes of man's nature—his dignity and his depravity, his grandeur and his misery, his strength and his frailty, his original worth and his sole dependence on the merits of Christ. It permitted him to portray three states or conditions of man—his original innocence, the state of sin, and the state of grace; the action of *Paradise Lost* comprehends man unfallen, man fallen, and man regenerate.

The *Gerusalemme*, the *Commedia*, the *Faerie Queene*, and many other epics had depicted moral crises and ethical decisions allegorically. Milton's preference for literal presentation is directly responsible for the prominence of the 'temptation-motif', as Greenlaw and Hanford have termed it, in all three of his heroic poems. In *Paradise Lost*, *Paradise Regain'd*, and *Samson Agonistes* alike, he constructs his plot around the ordeal of moral trial; spiritual temptation takes the central place which physical combat had usually held in the heroic poem. As a 'test' or trial of virtue, this served to demonstrate the hero's moral excellence, as in the case of Christ and Samson, or his weakness, as in Adam's case. Though this is a prominent feature of the saint's legend and the morality play, it also had precedents in classical and Biblical epic. In the *Punica* of Silius Italicus, Scipio's dream (like its model, the Choice of Hercules) involves a clear-cut choice between Virtue and Pleasure or Vice. In the Book of Job, God Himself ordains the hero's ordeal in order to test his patience in adversity and his faith in divine justice and providence. In his preference for a literal representation of moral trial, Milton follows the example set by the 'epic' of

Job. Nevertheless, the ethical choices that confront his heroes are not very different from those that had challenged Hercules, Scipio, and Paris. Like these classical figures, Milton's Samson and Adam have to make a positive decision between virtue and vice. Milton's 'temptation-motif' is more firmly rooted in heroic tradition than most of his critics have realized.

III

A third objective of Milton's 'Copernican Revolution' was to spiritualize the heroic poem. In retaining such conventional motifs as kingship and warfare, deliverance and salvation, he altered their traditional character by stressing their internal rather than external significance. The familiar epic themes have been 'transubstantiated'. They are 'more spiritous and pure' than in Homer or Virgil or Tasso. The theological significance of salvation replaces the secular sense, the political preservation and 'public safety' celebrated by conventional epic. The soul's deliverance through inward regeneration supersedes physical liberation by the sword. Moral rebellion against God's law displaces the theme of armed revolt against a secular lord.

In reorienting the epic towards Christian ethical standards, Milton came to grips with one of the principal tensions within the heroic tradition—the conflict between philosophical and poetic conceptions of heroic virtue. Parnassus was at odds with Sion, as Athens with Jerusalem; in imposing a classical and pagan form on a Biblical content and adapting both to Christian ends, he faced the problem of reconciling two different types of imitation and two disparate standards of authority. Poetically he must imitate the ancients, following the 'rules' of Aristotle and Horace and the example of Homer, Hesiod, and Virgil. Ethically he must imitate the moral and theological ideas of the Christian faith, following the precepts of Scripture and the example of Christ. In effect, he must serve up the 'new wine' of the Spirit in the classical amphora bequeathed by ancient Greece. Yet, as he well knew, a literary form designed for pagan worthies might not fit the Christian hero.

The 'matter of Palestine' was informed with a different spirit from that of the matter of Troy. Aeneas' armament would only be cumbersome luggage for the spiritual warrior. Achilles' armour would chafe the Christian saint.

At the outset, then, Milton had to take account of the cleavage between divine and secular, carnal and spiritual conceptions of heroism. The sacred and the profane hero seemed as far apart as the 'heavenly man' and the 'earthy man' of the Pauline epistles. To celebrate the former in a genre largely consecrated to the latter was a labour fraught with ambiguities. A given idea—'deliverance', for example, or 'peace', or 'patria'—meant one thing to the spirit and another to the flesh. In clarifying these equivoques, Milton consciously integrated them into his poetic structure, playing off one meaning of the same term against another. This quest for essentials inevitably led him to look beyond the secular aspects of heroism for their 'spiritual referent'. Where the traditional epic had stressed physical warfare, Milton emphasizes spiritual conflict. Where the conventional heroic poem had celebrated material deliverance, he extols the liberation of the soul. Where the usual epic had concerned worldly kings and captains, he shifts his attention to spiritual sovereigns. For the foundation of cities and nations, he substitutes the creation of the world and the establishment of the church, the kingdom of God. For external government he stresses the rule of Providence and the priority of the 'inward law'. For deliverance from external dangers and worldly foes, he substitutes the inner liberation from sin and death.

Thus, in *Paradise Lost* and *Paradise Regain'd* alike, the physical is usually contingent on the spiritual. Adam forfeits his sovereignty over the world after losing his inner sovereignty over himself. The state of natural obedience and natural justice, in which the passions obey reason, is the foundation of both internal and external liberty.[1] Outward tyranny is the corollary and 'objective correlative' of inward bondage. As Michael points out to Adam, the victims of Nimrod's tyranny are themselves self-enslaved. Similarly, the

[1] Cf. *De Doctrina*, Book I, Chapter 27, on Christian liberty.

Christ of *Paradise Regain'd* refuses to seek external liberty for
the lost tribes of Israel, inwardly enslaved through idolatry,
or to free from Tiberius' yoke a Rome already in bondage
to vice.

Inner sovereignty is the essence of true government, and
external dominion is merely an empty show without it. The
precondition of the good governor is the good man.

> Yet he who reigns within himself, and rules
> Passions, Desires, and Fears, is more a King:
> Which every wise and vertuous man attains:
> And who attains not, ill aspires to rule
> Cities of men, or head-strong Multitudes,
> Subject himself to Anarchy within,
> Or lawless passions in him which he serves.

Spiritual leadership is more excellent than political sovereignty. The Christ of *Paradise Regain'd* aims at the essential
liberty, the essential sovereignty, the essential 'safety'; the
world aims merely at their superficial qualities and 'accidents'.

The same emphasis on inward essence rather than external accident, the same orientation towards the spiritual,
recurs in *Samson Agonistes*. The hero attains a progressive insight into the true nature of liberty and servitude, blindness
and vision. His moral bondage to Dalila was, he perceives,
ignobler than his external slavery, and his spiritual blindness
worse than the physical want of sight. Israel's external
servitude, in turn, is rooted in a baser and more essential
inner slavery to vice:

> But what more oft in Nations grown corrupt,
> And by thir vices brought to servitude,
> Then to love Bondage more then Liberty,
> Bondage with ease then strenuous liberty . . .?

Undeniably this emphasis on the contrasting idioms of
flesh and spirit presented formidable aesthetic difficulties.
Though the contradiction between secular and divine meanings is fundamental to the poem, Milton had to present them
through the same poetic medium—to depict the human and
the divine alike in anthropomorphic terms, to portray the

sensuous and the ideal through the language of the senses. Aesthetically, therefore, it was hard to avoid blurring the distinction between flesh and spirit.

To meet this difficulty, Milton relied largely on the sharp theological contrasts his epic machinery afforded him. The cleavage between divine and diabolical agencies enabled him to preserve the clearcut distinction between spiritual and carnal significance. His exaggerated reliance on supernatural 'machines' served an epistemological function. It allowed him to contrast true and apparent meanings in terms of the dichotomy of God and devil, heaven and hell. The antithesis between infernal and celestial agents gives concrete expression to the opposition between worldly and heavenly values, fleshly and spiritual ideas—an opposition ultimately resolved by a decisive intrusion of divine judgement. In all three poems, divine judgement intervenes at a critical moment to clarify these equivoques and resolve their ambiguities.

IV

An emphasis on the infinite disproportion between divine and human merits appears not only in Milton's choice of argument, but also in his treatment of other epic conventions—prophecies of the future, summaries of the past, and supernatural 'machines'. His transformation of these traditional features of the heroic poem is representative of the changes he makes in the genre as a whole.

Whatever praise the epic poet might incidentally bestow on the gods, his primary object was to praise men by recounting their laudable achievements. Thus he invested the epic fable with moral significance, a causal structure based largely on poetic justice: heroic virtue→heroic action →merit→reward.

Paradise Lost alters this pattern. Adam's fall has destroyed it. It is to God's glory rather than man's honour that Milton dedicates his heroic poems.

In his epics the conventional praise of country and ruling dynasty is conspicuous by its absence. Though this feature results partly from his subject matter, it is primarily due to personal conviction. The defender of the regicides has no desire to laud the ancestors of the royal martyr.[1] Virgil's praise of Rome and Camoens's exaltation of Portugal find no parallel in *Paradise Lost* or *Paradise Regain'd*. Also absent is the eulogistic invocation to actual or potential patrons, so characteristic a feature of many national epics.[2] Milton reserves his praise for God, his invocations for the heavenly muse, the Spirit of God, and divine light; he does not misapply them to man or to secular commonwealths.

Traditionally, the epic prophecy had celebrated the praise of men. Milton adapts it, instead, to the themes of human depravity and divine glory. Delineating the disastrous effects of Adam's transgressions on his descendants, Michael's survey of world history consistently stresses the interplay of divine grace and human sin, 'supernal Grace contending With sinfulness of Men'. Its function is not to exalt the hero and his 'Ofspring' but to humble them, not to praise them but to shame them, not to emphasize their greatness but to stress their misery. The few individuals it singles out for praise are conspicuous by their rarity; they are 'The onely righteous in a World perverse'. Milton has radically altered the conventional nature and function of the epic prophecy. Instead of glorifying the hero's posterity, it provides a detailed survey of their depravity. Instead of praising men, it celebrates the grace of God and the merits of the Messiah.

A similar reorientation characterizes his treatment of another epic convention—the survey of events prior to the main action. As with Michael's prophecy, Milton has converted Raphael's history into an *exemplum* of obedience and disobedience. Ethically, both episodes are far closer to the moral pattern of the fable itself than in most other epics. To a degree unparalleled by the majority of heroic poets, Milton has tightened the narrative, as well as the ethical, structure of his poem by adapting the 'moral' of the episodes to that of the fable proper. Not only does he make the motif of

---

[1] Cf. Roberta F. Brinkley, *Milton and the Arthurian Story* (Baltimore, 1932); Tillyard, *Miltonic Setting*, pp. 174 ff., 198 ff.

[2] Cf. *Pharsalia*, *Lusiads*, *Gerusalemme Liberata* and *Gerusalemme Conquistata*, *Faerie Queene*, Daniel's *Civil Wars*, Ronsard's *Franciade*, and others.

obedience and disobedience central to fable and episodes
alike; he does the same with other dichotomies—faith and
apostasy, righteousness and unrighteousness, truth and
falsehood, peace and confusion. Like the fable itself, the
episodes exhibit the larger rhythms of destruction and
creation, either physical or spiritual. Like the fable, they
juxtapose the kingdoms of heaven and the world. Like the
fable, they contrast the relative merits of creature and
Creator. In Raphael's account, the glory of destruction
and creation belongs solely to Messiah and his Father. Though
the faithful angels receive a reward of praise for their service,
it is the Messiah who singlehandedly expels the rebel angels
and fashions the visible universe. Michael's prophecy likewise bestows praise on the few 'just men' in a fallen world,
but reserves the supreme praise for the acts of God; again,
the glory belongs primarily to the Father and his Messiah.

The imbalance between human and divine virtues and
between man's works and God's is especially pronounced in
Milton's transformation of the conventional epic machinery.
Dryden's observation that 'his heavenly machines are many'[1]
is just, so far as it goes. But it fails to go far enough. This
exaggerated role of divine and infernal agents in fable and
episodes alike serves a valid purpose. It compensates for one
of the inevitable drawbacks of Milton's subject—the paucity
of human actors. But its primary advantage is moral and
religious, rather than strictly literary.

Christianity had long represented the human soul as a
battlefield where grace and sin, heaven and hell, contended
for possession. This motif had received dramatic treatment in
morality plays like *Everyman* and *The Castle of Perseverance*,
while Bunyan's *Holy War*, describing the battle between
Diabolus and Shaddai for the city of Mansoul, would
develop the military imagery to quasi-epic proportions.[2]
For Christian tradition, man's moral life—and, indeed, the
whole of human and cosmic history—involved the spiritual

---

[1] Dryden, *Prose Works*, ed. Malone, iii. 95: '. . . his heavenly machines are
many, and his human persons but two.' Cf. ibid., pp. 442–3, 'and if there
had not been more machining persons than human in his poem'.

[2] Cf. Tillyard, *English Epic Tradition*.

warfare between good and evil, God and Satan. Milton's machines gave dramatic force to this convention. In *Paradise Lost* and *Paradise Regain'd* the 'holy war' between heaven and hell, waged in the individual soul but also prosecuted over the entire span of space and time, is transferred from the morality-tradition and adapted to the requirements of epic machinery.

Second, these 'machines' give concrete expression to the operations of 'eternal Providence' and thus further the epic's avowed intent. Adapting literary conventions to theological ends, Milton exploits the device of the celestial council as a means of giving explicit statement to the divine decrees. Similarly, he utilizes the device of the celestial messenger to represent their execution. The heavenly machines thus provide a comprehensive picture of the divine economy and the interrelationship between God's intellect and will. But the infernal machines also 'assert eternal Providence' by negative example. Illustrating the doctrine of permissive evil, they plot and execute a strategy diametrically opposed to heaven's intent, but 'thir spite still serves His glory to augment'.

Third, the exaggerated role these machines play in *Paradise Lost* emphasizes the Protestant conception of the relative merits of man and God and the comparative efficacy of human and divine virtue. In drawing his subject from the first chapters of Genesis, Milton combined two distinct literary traditions—'divine'[1] and 'heroic' poetry. These had usually served different ends—the glory of God, or the glory of man. Epics celebrating the six days' labour of creation had inevitably laid primary stress on the works of God; the prevailing tradition of heroic poetry, on the other hand, had chiefly emphasized the deeds of man. The one

---

[1] See Lily Bess Campbell, *Divine Poetry and Drama in Sixteenth-Century England* (Cambridge, 1959), p. 5, on the subject matter of 'divine poetry' and the 'movement to substitute Biblical story for secular story, to substitute a Christian mythology for a pagan mythology, as well as to substitute prayer and praise of the Christian God for poetry addressed to an unkind mistress'. I am using the term in the somewhat narrower sense of Peter Martyr's *Common Places*: '. . . humane Poems doo set foorth the renoume of kings, princes, feelds, cities, regions, castels, women, marriages. . . . But divine Poems doo onlie sing of God, and celebrate him onlie.'

had imitated the *gesta Dei*; the other had extolled the *gesta hominis*. Such epics as Tasso's *Il Mondo Creato* and Du Bartas's *La Sepmaine* might or might not be accepted as heroic poems (critics were divided on this point); in any event they lacked a human hero. Their 'epic person' was God himself rather than a 'godlike man'. They focused on the acts of God[1] rather than on human achievements. In hexaemeral literature, the protagonist is usually the Creator himself; in heroic poetry, the 'epic person' is a man—a demigod perhaps, but still a derivative being.

In fusing the two traditions, Milton employs his machinery contrapuntally; the deeds of God and Satan not only contrast with one another, but also counterpoint those of the human hero. By bringing together within the same epic structure the acts of God, the exploits of the devil, and the works of man, Milton subjects them inevitably to comparison and thus emphasizes their qualitative and quantitative differences. The result is to accentuate the supreme greatness and goodness of God, in comparison with fallen angel and fallen mankind.

In transforming his machines into heroic archetypes— the image and idol of heroic virtue—Milton made what appears to be a unique contribution to the epic tradition. There is no outstanding parallel in heroic poetry before him. Transferring the norm of *virtus heroica* and the conventional structural pattern of a heroic enterprise from the 'epic person' to the 'machines', he radically altered the conventional relationships between the 'principal hero', the epic machinery, the epic enterprise, and heroic virtue.

In this way he pushed to its logical conclusion the central emphasis of the heroic tradition—its stress on superlatives, its quest for excellence and 'highest worth', its definition of heroism in terms of 'godlikeness' and 'excess of virtue'. Finding the true essence of heroic virtue in divine virtue, recognizing in God himself the heroic archetype of man, he tuned the epic lyre an octave higher than most of his predecessors. Instead of the praises of men, it sounds the honour of God.

[1] Cf. the recurrent Biblical emphasis on the 'acts of God', especially in Psalms and the Book of Job.

This transformation represents, in a sense, the death and resurrection of the heroic poem; the epic undergoes a humiliation and exaltation analogous to Christ's. Adam's defeat tolls the knell of heroic poetry; Christ's victory revives it.

Rejecting the purely 'natural' and secular hero as a logical impossibility, Milton replaced him with the supernatural and spiritual hero. For human virtue he substituted the divine, the virtue and example of God himself. In both epics the chief heroic exemplars are divine persons, the principal heroic exploits divine works, and the primary heroic formulae divine virtues. In Milton's hands the heroic poem became, in the fullest sense of the words, a 'divine poem'.

Index

Thymos, 154.
Tillyard, E. M. W., xiii, 160, 197.
Titian, 123.
Tragic person, 82.
Trask, Willard R., 162.
Trissino, G. G., 11, 20, 22, 32, 84, 88, 91, 96, 119, 139, 140, 151.
Truth, xv, 16, 25, 39, 42, 44, 51–54, 66–67, 69, 74–77, 100, 144–5, 147, 187, 196, 198.
Tyrant, xviii, 81–82, 91–92, 97, 99, 194.

Valency, M. J., 136.
Valmarana, Odorico, 22, 168.
Valour, 9, 12–14, 79, 82, 108, 110, 113, 124, 126–7, 162.
Valvasone, Erasmo da, 3, 22, 168.
Vanity, xx, 137, 140, 144, 147–9, 153, 157, 172, 177–8. *See* Merit.
Varchi, Benedetto, 22, 179.
Vengeance, 8, 29, 35, 47, 55–56.
Verisimilitude, 32, 125.
Vermigli, Peter Martyr (Pietro Martire), 199.
Vestiary symbolism, 123.
Vida, Marco Girolamo, 1, 22, 41.
Villanovanus, Arnoldus, 112.
Virgil, xiii, xiv, 4, 6, 9, 11–14, 17–18, 20, 21, 32–33, 41, 52, 85–86, 88, 91, 96, 108, 110, 112, 130, 139, 161–3, 169–71, 173, 175, 177, 186, 190–4.

Waldock, A. J. A., 49, 180–1.

Waller, A. R., 162.
Walther, Rudolph, 84. *See* David.
Warrior, xvii, 1, 2, 5–7, 23, 42, 51, 108, 113, 177, 184, 194.
Watt, F. W., xviii.
Weinberg, Bernard, 2, 109.
Whitford, B., 190.
Wilkes, G. A., xiii, 188.
Williams, Ralph C., 2.
Wilson, Thomas, 9.
Wisdom, xv, xvi, 9, 10, 16, 19, 43–78, 105, 130, 147, 154, 161–2, 181, 185, 187, 190. *See* Divine Image, Truth, Prudence, Contemplative Hero.
Wolfe, Don M., 2.
Woman-warrior, 126.
Wonder (admiration, *maraviglia*), 2, 4, 5, 12, 25, 32, 54, 56–57, 59, 60, 62, 81, 105, 116, 120, 124–5, 132, 174–6. *See* Effect of epic poem, Miracle, Marvellous (Christian).
Works, good, 129, 148, 177–8, 187–8. *See* Faith, Merit, Justification, Reward.
Worldly hero, 15–16, 36, 38, 40, 42, 44–45, 66, 71–72, 76–77, 90, 133, 144, 149–52, 178, 201.
Worth. *See* Merit.
Wrath, xviii, 8, 12–14, 18, 55, 74. *See* Faculties, *Thymos*, Warrior.

Xenophon, 11, 109.

Zeal, xvi, 66, 100, 108, 130.

PRINTED IN GREAT BRITAIN
AT THE UNIVERSITY PRESS, OXFORD
BY VIVIAN RIDLER
PRINTER TO THE UNIVERSITY